D0455656

PRICKLY HEAT ■ SIMON DONALD

'Four loveless characters – a boxer, his trainer, a runaway country girl and a peculiar landlord (who keeps beers and frocks in the fridge) – jostle for position and squirt milk, oil and water over each other . . . I really enjoyed this one'. (*Financial Times*)

INVENTING A NEW COLOUR ■ PAUL GODFREY

'Surprisingly this is Paul Godfrey's first play. It is hard to categorize him. He's part philosopher, part poet: and, excitingly, very much part dramatist . . . *Inventing a New Colour* echoes to the authentic sound and reverberations of local history.' (*Guardian*)

LOW LEVEL PANIC ■ CLARE McINTYRE

'Set in a dingy shared bathroom, the play is innocently and painfully foul-mouthed and has all the vitriolic truths of youthful self-doubt. McIntyre has a deadly accurate ear, a subtle sense of humour and a deep fund of compassion: she writes with thrilling understanding . . . This is an exciting debut.' (*Sunday Times*)

LEAVE TAKING ■ WINSOME PINNOCK

'Enid is one of those West Indians who came to England in the fifties, determined to become "little Miss English". Abandoned by her husband she has struggled to bring up two daughters to live her dream . . . Winsome Pinnock's play is a beautifully observed, deeply moving account of this alienated limbo.' (*Guardian*)

A HANDFUL OF STARS ■ BILLY ROCHE

'He certainly fulfils the Irish dramatist's traditional role of pumping verbal energy into the anaemic English bloodstream: his dialogue sings . . . The play has the feeling of a fifties, black-and-white American movie; which is itself a comment on the time-warp of present-day small-town Ireland'. (*Guardian*)

In the same series

First Run 2
Selected and introduced by Kate Harwood

Inés de Castro by John Clifford
Back Street Mammy by Trish Cooke
Sleeping Nightie by Victoria Hardie
Una Pooka by Michael Harding
Loose Ends by Stuart Hepburn
Valued Friends by Stephen Jeffreys

First Run 3
Selected and introduced by Matthew Lloyd

Mr Thomas by Kathy Burke
The Awakening by Julian Garner
Sugar Hill Blues by Kevin Hood
Bold Girls by Rona Munro
Infidelities by Richard Zajdlic

FIRST RUN

New Plays by New Writers

PRICKLY HEAT
Simon Donald

INVENTING A NEW COLOUR
Paul Godfrey

LOW LEVEL PANIC
Clare McIntyre

LEAVE TAKING
Winsome Pinnock

A HANDFUL OF STARS
Billy Roche

Selected and Introduced by Kate Harwood

NICK HERN BOOKS
London

A Nick Hern Book

First Run first published in 1989 as an original paperback
by Nick Hern Books.

Reprinted 1996 by Nick Hern Books,
14 Larden Road, London W3 7ST

Typeset in ITC New Baskerville and printed in Great Britain
by Athenaeum Press Ltd, Gateshead, Tyne and Wear.

British Library Cataloguing in Publication Data

First run: new plays by new writers
   1. Drama in English, 1945- – Anthologies
   I. Harwood, Kate   II. Donald, Simon
   822'.914'08
   ISBN 1 85459 010 3

Contents

Introduction

Prickly Heat   1

Inventing a New Colour   39

Low Level Panic   85

Leave Taking   139

A Handful of Stars   191

Introduction

When asked to compile this volume, I was pleased that a few more of the plays that I had admired over the past year would find their way into print. Few enough of the thousand or so scripts that I encounter as Literary Manager of the Royal Court Theatre reach the stage, and the future prospects for those that do can look bleak without some form of publication. With three or four publishers now actively publishing plays, the situation has improved. But despite highly successful first runs, many unpublished plays exist only as dusty prompt copies, and, as memories fade, the chances of future production by other theatres, or indeed by student companies or foreign theatres, fade too. The idea behind this volume, then, was to select for publication five first-rate plays by writers who had established themselves on the scene in the twelvemonth between autumn 1987 and autumn 1988 – which is when the volume went to press. Though the selection is necessarily personal, these five plays do represent the broad diversity of style and subject matter in contemporary new writing, and the writers themselves range widely in terms of cultural background, influences and geographical location.

There are, however, two common factors. All five playwrights have had a long-term practical involvement in theatre – four are actors, one a director – and, secondly, all five have produced work which will, I feel sure, continue to stimulate and challenge well into the future.

Despite all the odds, the explosion of new theatre writing that marked the end of the fifties has managed to sustain itself and continues to fill the dramatic repertoire. More importantly it is clear that writing for the stage is still considered a serious mode of expression for many new or would-be writers. This may have much to do with the apparent accessibility of the medium – it is nearly always possible to get a first play on *somewhere* even if you have to find money and actors yourself. But it is also because of the special challenge of writing for the stage. There is an immediacy and a tangibility – your writing actually takes place in front of you – that makes it peculiarly suited to a young writer.

But sustaining a career as a playwright is much harder. Theatre history is littered with the names of writers whose fame rests on a couple of plays. William Congreve had only four successes; Sheridan only two of any substance. Of the plays of Oscar Wilde only three are regularly performed. In our own time, Alan Ayckbourn is the exception that proves the rule, for where are the later plays of John Osborne, Ann Jellicoe, John Arden or Arnold Wesker? Collaborative by nature, theatre is a demanding medium, and playwrights become frustrated at having to rely so heavily on the uncertain fortunes of an increasingly impoverished theatre. They often feel dependent, too, on particular directors: if those directors move on, the writers may be abandoned; if the directors lose power or position, the writers, like artistic consorts, are fearful of crashing with them.

As their careers develop, therefore, writers begin to want more control over their writing than the theatre can give them. It is not surprising that many are tempted by the study or the novella, or at least by the financial rewards of film or television. If the theatre is not as careful about nurturing the new work of the established writer as it is diligent in encouraging emerging talent, then even fewer writers will be tempted to keep up the struggle.

But are the theatres there to accommodate these writers? In London, with new plays opening every month, it would seem that the situation is healthy. But how many regional theatres can afford to nourish new writing to this degree? In most, new plays are shunted into studios for shorter and shorter runs where they cause less financial damage if they fail. Few theatres expect a première to be the season's big 'earner'. Gradually new writing is acquiring a medicinal flavour – theatres do it because they 'ought' to, or because it is 'good' for their audiences. There are also, of course, the small-scale touring companies that specialise in new work. But two of these, Joint Stock and Foco Novo, had their grants removed in 1988. The rest are forced to dash round the country on a series of one-night stands, with the consequence, at the box office, that there is no time for favourable word of mouth to build audiences. It is clear that the outlets are getting fewer and fewer as well as poorer and poorer.

So, if the enduring playwright is the one that can take on and celebrate the hybrid nature of the art form, then he or she is, of necessity, also going to have to share theatres' accumulating financial burdens. This means small casts in simple sets, performing plays written for small spaces and expecting short runs. Is it any wonder that the new play is in danger of paralleling the short story or the manifesto rather than anything more substantial?

But if we encourage ambition, what can the playwright hope for? Once an apprenticeship has been served with a few plays produced in a studio, most writers will hope for a main stage commission. This is unlikely to be forthcoming unless a good deal of commercial appeal is evident alongside writing talent. It is no wonder that many writers increasingly suspect that things may have been better before the studio theatres were built in the late sixties. Before that the new play could take its chance on the larger stages. One of the few theatres where this still happens is the Royal Exchange in Manchester, which now produces a good deal of new work through the Mobil Award which it administers. The fact that it has no studio, and that therefore the winning play will receive a mainstage production, is an additional prize for the winner.

With all of these limitations it seems miraculous that anyone is still writing plays. But despite the gloom there is much to be excited about in the work produced over the last year. What keeps British theatre vibrant is the delight with which so many of the writers have risen to the challenge of limitation. There has long been an aesthetic of poverty in contemporary British theatre. It informs even quite lavish productions of plays by certain authors. However, it is notable that newer writers are re-engaging with the benefits that this can bring. One can observe several encouraging factors. Writers seem to be wringing as many characters as possible out of six or so actors and making genuine creative use out of the necessity for doubling. There is both an interest in using the set as a dramatic image and a weariness with writing plays that demand the endless carting on and off of furniture. Even the one-set drama is being re-explored in inventive and theatrical ways. Most of all there is a sense of new delight in the dramatic power of language, as young writers investigate poetic or heightened forms of writing. If one can point to any hopeful way forward, it is towards a new rejoicing in the precious specifics of theatre.

It is useful to see the plays chosen for this volume in the context of other new work during the same period. Most of the plays in the survey which follows showed pleasing willingness to embrace these 'precious specifics' and to rise to the challenge of limitation in one sense or another. All of them made an impact, although not all were universally admired.

Nick Ward's work certainly was, however. His plays, *Apart from George* (a National Studio Production toured by the National Theatre's Education Department, seen at the Edinburgh Festival and in the Theatre Upstairs) and *The Strangeness of Others* (Cottesloe Theatre) won him the George Devine Award for most promising playwright and a good deal of attention. *Apart from George* took a Fenland family through crisis as the loss of a job led to family breakdown. This familiar-sounding scenario was given a rare rural setting, and the play was enriched by a tense, poetic style. Its heightened use of language was counterpointed by the taut physical presence of the actors, subtly choreographed by Ward (also the director) to convey through their body language much of the play's sub-textual story. This actual presence of the actor, of course unique to theatre, was also delicately exploited in *The Strangeness of Others*, a layer-cake of London life in which apparently unconnected characters are gradually revealed to be part of the same tale of corruption and family estrangement. Although the leap made by the writer between the two plays seemed not to be fully controlled, it is clear that the theatre has found a new and powerful voice.

Some of the critics chose, falsely I think, to compare Gregory Motton's new play, *Downfall* to *The Strangeness of Others*. *Downfall* was staged, like his previous play, *Ambulance*, in 1987 in the Theatre Upstairs. Superficially the plays are set in similar territory – the underbelly of urban life – but Motton is a fierce original. Highly imaginative, his brashly theatrical pieces present unsentimental, bleak images that slowly fill with tenderness. *Ambulance*, set in a far corner of a night-time world, seemed to be about love and the search for it to give meaning to an empty life. The characters demand endlessly of one another: dance, kiss, or fight. *Ambulance* received some acclaim but *Downfall*, a play of totally different rhythm, found fewer friends. It was a kind of danse-macabre in which a huge mass of characters whirled through a darkened city in the throes of revolution. Bitterly funny, chillingly surreal, *Downfall* confirmed Motton as a challenging modern.

Both Nick Dear and Timberlake Wertenbaker wrote plays on the kind of historical subject more usually covered by books, indeed Wertenbaker's play was an adaptation of a novel which was itself based on fact. But both playwrights successfully drove their stories through on a focused theatrical idea.

In *The Art of Success* (The Other Place, Stratford, then The Pit, London) Dear looked at the role of the artist in society, taking Hogarth as his biographical subject. The bulk of the play is set on one (brilliantly sustained) farcical night as Hogarth attempts to return chastely to his marriage bed. He loses his clothes to an erstwhile mistress while being pursued by an escaped murderess whose image he has 'stolen'. It manages to make pithy points about patronage and the role of the artist in a romp of scatological hilarity. Wertenbaker's *Our Country's Good* (Royal Court) was taken from Thomas Keneally's novel *The Playmaker*. The idea for the project came from the Royal Court's director, Max Stafford-Clark, who wanted to enact the novel's story of how convicts newly arrived in Australia came to put on a play, and then himself revive that play,

(*The Recruiting Officer*), alongside the story of its Antipodean premiere. Because the subject of *Our Country's Good* is theatre itself, its theatricality might seem assured. But it had in addition an epic twist and a directness which made the style of the piece completely alive to its subject.

Iain Heggie followed his previous year's success – *A Wholly Healthy Glasgow* – with the even better *American Bagpipes* (Royal Exchange, Manchester). Heggie owes much to the American playwright David Mamet and shares his delight in classic theatre convention. The play is a frenetic farce in which a warring Scottish couple is visited by their children – a daughter from America who trumpets all things American, and a son with a grip on family secrets. The play's heightened, machine-gun Glaswegian effortlessly filled the space of the Exchange. His plays may have few characters and single sets, but there is something in the level of his language that would sit ill in any other medium.

Two plays that were very successful regionally jumped off from biographical subjects in a theatrically inventive way. *Self Portrait* by Sheila Yeger explored the painter Gwen John while *Every Black Day* by Don Hale took the Black American thriller writer, Chester Hines as its subject. *Self Portrait* took a brave look at the way talented young women bury themselves in powerful older men, paralleling the story of a modern young writer with Gwen John's destructive relationship with Rodin. *Every Black Day* took a fragmented line, interspersing the story of Hines's life with one of his detective thrillers.

Between them the high-funded companies, who could do so much more for putting some scale and cash into new writing, managed only one main-stage premiere. But that was David Hare's passionately moral *The Secret Rapture*. They did, however, present in addition to the Nick Ward and Nick Dear plays already mentioned, two superb smaller stage plays, Robert Holman's *Across Oka* at The Other Place in Stratford and Nicholas Wright's *Mrs Klein* at the Cottesloe. On the surface both plays seem simple pieces of realism, but in fact they are driven by powerful metaphors. Holman's compelling linear narrative tells the story of two boys' journey into the wild to replace a Siberian Crane's egg. Gradually, a powerful image of the hopes for peace between two cultures is released and the play's conclusion is profoundly affecting. This is Holman's unique and very special talent and it is good to see that public awareness of him as a writer appears to be growing. *Mrs Klein* is an invigorating, polished play that almost bounds through family tensions. It is based on the relationship of Melanie Klein and her daughter, both child psycho-analysts. The story concerns the events following the apparent accidental death of Mrs Klein's son. Despite the intimate and personal details of the subject the play is set in an almost Noël Coward world of drinks cabinets, hidden letters, mornings-after and ostentatiously lit cigarettes.

Howard Barker's theatrical ambition is already legendary, but the past year saw no fewer than twelve premieres from him (if one is to count all ten short plays that made up *The Possibilities*) culminating in *The Bite of the Night* (The Pit), a monster-epic exploring the various ages of Troy over nearly five hours. One longed for more control of rhythm, but one also longs for more writers with his daring. Their number might be increased if more theatres were like the Royals (Exchange, Court and Stratford East) and put new plays on main stages. Stratford even put on a first play by an immensely promising new writer, Harwant Bains. *The Fighting Kite* was the story of a would-be intellectual caught up in racial violence in Southall, and it had a quirky, idiosyncratic humour. His second play *Blood* (given a staged reading at the Royal Court) adds to that a powerful epic imagination.

There were other first plays that are worth mentioning here: *Sanctuary* won the Samuel Beckett Award for Ralph Brown and was produced by Joint Stock. Its lively, hip-hop style brought the company great success with young audiences. Martin Crimp's *Definitely the Bahamas* at the Orange Tree in Richmond introduced to the stage a writer with a deft control of sinister subtext. Out of a couple of the Young Writers' Festivals came two new comic talents: *Dead Dad Dog*, from the Edinburgh Traverse Festival, 'Scottish Accents', was an extremely inventive story of how the 'big day' in the life of a Glaswegian would-be yuppie is ruined by the untimely re-appearance of the ghost of his dead father; while Hannah Vincent's play, *The Burrow* (Royal Court Young Writers' Festival), was an adaptation of a Kafka short story, in which the small rabbit of Kafka's story becomes a catalogue-style housewife who is driven to neurotic mania as she tries to make perfect her house and family.

There was nothing in the West End that gave great cause for cheer in the way of new writing, although the arrival of Michael Attenborough and Howard Panter with Turnstile, an innovative management intending to produce new work in the commercial sector, may change all that. As for new plays, only Tom Stoppard's *Hapgood* (Aldwych Theatre), a beguiling, if reactionary theatrical thriller, stays in the memory, though the continued success of Steven Berkoff's plays with the revival of *Greek* indicates that there is an audience out there for up-front new writing.

The Mobil Playwriting Competition, which is open to everyone and judged without knowledge of the writers' identities, brought forward another crop of award winners, with the main prize going to Michael Wall's play, *Amongst Barbarians* (due to be staged at the Royal Exchange, Manchester, in February 1989). I hope as many find productions this year as before.

The plays in this volume were spread throughout the year. I saw *Leave Taking* at Liverpool Playhouse in November 1987 and *Inventing a New Colour* opened almost exactly a year later. Looking at them together they all retain a feeling of freshness and originality that initially commended them.

Simon Donald has long been known as an actor at the Traverse Theatre, Edinburgh. Clearly all the work he has done in new plays has taught him well because *Prickly Heat* is, above all, a delight for performers. There is economy in the language and a feeling of charged roominess in which there is terrific freedom. The piece plays surrealistic theatrical games with the audience, who feel confined in the same hot, sticky room as the characters. A sensual use of sub-text and a languid obliqueness in the language make this a powerfully sexy play. Although other work of his has been seen at the Traverse, this was his first full-scale, full-length play. A powerful debut.

Paul Godfrey also has a background in Scottish theatre where he worked as a director for some years. *Inventing a New Colour* was his first play and, although apparently miniature in world, the beauty of the writing and the sharpness with which he explores the imaginations of his characters suggest a writer of great presence. At times the play's luminous use of language reveals a surprising pain, the characters seem hyper-intense, as if searched by spotlight. I first read the play as an unsolicited script, reaching it through readers' reports of babbling enthusiasm. I am delighted its premiere is a co-production between the Royal Court and a West Country theatre because that is where the play is set.

Winsome Pinnock is now so heavily commissioned as a writer that the delivery dates she can offer any theatre belong in the world of science fiction. *Leave Taking* was simply moving and revealing about the difficulties of bringing up children in a country that they understand so much better than their mother does. Seeing it made me realise how little has been expressed on our stages of the world of black women in this country. Another play by Pinnock, *Picture Palace*, was toured by the Women's Theatre Group during 1988, and the Women's Playhouse Trust will produce *A Hero's Welcome* early in 1989.

Clare McIntyre's play, *Low Level Panic*, was also produced by the Women's Playhouse Trust (surely it is about time that this adventurous company got some permanent funding) in association with the Royal Court. The simplicity of the play, which is set in a bathroom with only three characters, is matched by the ambition of the ideas. Despite the lightness of the tone, the play debates a powerful contemporary issue in a determined way. What effect, McIntyre asks, does pornography have on the daily lives of three very ordinary young women sharing a London flat? The answers are more complex than we might first expect, and the fact that the Theatre Upstairs was packed with a young female audience for most of the run showed clearly who was curious about the conclusions. McIntyre is also well known as an actress, and, as with Simon Donald, her writing has an easy clarity that makes it a joy to perform.

Billy Roche has also inadvertently started an acting career. It began when he was forced to take over the role of Stapler for a short period during the run of *A Handful of Stars* at the Bush Theatre. This is another first play, by a writer with a rueful eye for the comedy inherent in the tragedy of everyday life. It presents two boys in a small Irish town trying to make sense of their approaching manhood. The Ireland that is presented is not the one with which we are familiar from most contemporary Irish drama; the Troubles and the history are a world away. What makes most sense are the dreams imported from across the Atlantic, the place where every gilded elder brother went. I look forward to seeing more of his tender, generous charm.

All five writers gave their audiences a good and challenging night in the theatre. I am confident that their work, bred as it is from clear, practical understanding of the nature of theatre, will grow and develop in the coming years. I can only hope that the theatres of tomorrow will be tough and vital enough to accommodate them.

Kate Harwood
November 1988

Simon Donald was born in Lanark in 1959, brought up in Wishaw and studied at Aberdeen University. In 1982 he formed the Abattoire Theatre Company with Michael Duke and wrote and performed in *A Tenant for Edgar Mortez*. In 1984 he wrote *In Descent* for the Traverse Theatre, Edinburgh. Subsequently he has worked as an actor with the Traverse Company in *Losing Venice* by John Clifford and *Elizabeth Gordon Quinn* by Chris Hannan and most recently in *The Conquest of the South Pole* by Manfred Karge and *Prickly Heat* by himself. Most of his performances have been in new plays, at the Traverse, the Tron Theatre in Glasgow and the Crucible Theatre in Sheffield. In 1987 he married Carol Gordon, with whom he now lives in Edinburgh.

To Carol

Prickly Heat was first performed on 11 June 1988 at the Traverse Theatre, Edinburgh, with the following cast:

LENNOX, an old man	Robert McIntosh
BRENDA, a young woman	Hilary Maclean
DANNY, a middleweight boxer	Tom Mannion
DUVALIER, a lay preacher	Simon Donald

Directed by Jenny Killick
Designed by Antonio Lagarto

Scene One

*A big fridge between the windows, a bucket of water on the window-sill and a
fire-escape passing the other window.* LENNOX *the caretaker, old and
scrawny, lies on the floor next to a folded Zed-Bed, his head on some clean
sheets and pillows. Chain smoking, he listens to the news from a radio in the
courtyard below. A song comes on;* LENNOX, *in vest, trousers and braces,
pads barefoot to the window. Leans out to look.*

LENNOX. Look at the arse on that. Come on, son, she's showin' it
tae ye. Ach . . .

*Disappointed, he begins to unfold the Zed-Bed. It is rusty and reluctant.
He lays the folded bedclothes on it and takes a can of beer from a supply in
the fridge and opens it surreptitiously at the side of the window, looking
out and below. A young woman comes in carrying two suitcases.*
LENNOX *shushes her and points to the bed. She lays the cases on it. He
beckons her to the window, still shushing. He aims and lobs the water out.
Two dogs yelp.*

LENNOX. Got ye, ya pair a dirty wee tykes. We'll have nane a that in
ma yard. (*Laughing hard, watching the dogs.*) Ay, shake yer arse now,
he's nae interested. (*He turns his attention to the girl.*) I cannae
allow that sort of thing.

BRENDA. No. I suppose not.

LENNOX. D'ye want me to fling the drops at you?

BRENDA. No, I'm okay just now thanks.

LENNOX. Ye've only got tae ask.

BRENDA. Thanks. Are you Mr Lennox?

LENNOX. That's me. Lennox by name and Lennox by nature.

BRENDA. Pleased to meet you, Mr Lennox, I'm Brenda . . . (*She tries
to shake his hand.*)

LENNOX. I know who you are, hen. I've had this place ready for
days waitin' for ye.

BRENDA. I'm not that late . . .

LENNOX. Days!

BRENDA (*pause*). A matter of hours.

LENNOX (*pause*). I believe you come from a farming background, is that right?

BRENDA. Uhuh.

LENNOX. Have you ever been involved in slaughter?

BRENDA (*laughs*). I suppose I have though I wouldn't look at it like that. I wouldn't say 'Involved in slaughter'. I mean, do you mean wholesale slaughter or retail? (*Laughs.*)

LENNOX. I mean butchery.

BRENDA (*stops laughing*). Why?

LENNOX. What I'm gettin' at Brenda is corruption. See it's my experience that in hot weather things go off a lot faster. They corrupt.

BRENDA. That's right, they do.

LENNOX. So, as far as I'm concerned we're talkin' about days not hours.

BRENDA. Look, Mr Lennox. I said I would be here this morning and I'm sorry I'm late but I didn't know there was any rush. Anyway where I come from we don't let things 'Go off'. We put them in a fridge. We have freezer cabinets just for that very purpose. (*Points.*) You've got a fridge – if you're worried about something going off then you just have to stick it in there.

LENNOX. I was talking about people, Brenda. I was using a metaphor.

BRENDA. Oh you were were you.

LENNOX. To make my point. (*He breathes in deeply through his nose.*) Smell that? Soon I'll have to put cling-film in my armpits. I'll no' even be fit to feed to those dogs.

BRENDA. Uhuh. Yes I get the point. You're not talkin' to a child you know.

LENNOX. No. I'm not, am I. I'm talkin' to a young woman in the full flush of her youth.

BRENDA (*pause*). Yes.

LENNOX. It took me all my life to get to your age, Brenda – then see the next fifty years . . . (*Snaps his fingers.*) like THAT!

I've no' got time to waste sittin' around waitin' on wee lassies.

BRENDA. The rails buckled and the train had to wait. We sat for ages on the cliffs at Stonehaven. We even ran out of water.

LENNOX. Everybody's running out of water.

BRENDA. Two men sat next to me and one of them let me have a sip of his lager. The other one said he used to fly helicopters in Vietnam. He said it was hotter on the train than it is in the jungle.

LENNOX. And you believed him did ye?

BRENDA. His shirt was sticking to him with sweat.

LENNOX. Yanks will always sweat when they're abroad.

BRENDA. I think he said he was from Dundee.

LENNOX. What's in the cases?

BRENDA. My things.

LENNOX. Things eh! Things to put on when the things you've got on get dirty. Things to unbutton and things to unzip. (*Pause.*)

BRENDA. Do you want my rent in advance?

LENNOX. *My rent!*

BRENDA. *Your.* Rent. Then.

LENNOX. This is my building now. I am in sole charge of its vacancy.

BRENDA. I was only wondering if I had to give the rent to you or to the owner.

LENNOX. The owner has died.

BRENDA. Whoever then. To the lawyer.

LENNOX. Suddenly. By her own hand. Leaving it all to me. With her last words.

In a building like this a gunshot echoes off the walls till the day you knock them down.

Especially in a heat like this and then it can escape. My Christ, hen. You talk to me about Vietnam! I was in North Africa for the war. I spent the daytime soakin' in a bath of tea to dye my skin and at night I'd dress up like an Arab and I'd crawl under one of the tanks in Rommel's convoy and drain all the oil out the sump so they'd seize up in the desert and bake.

If you got caught you were up against a wall quick as a flash but I never felt the heat like today and a gunshot was never as loud as that.

When she killed herself it was ME who had to clear up. It was ME who fetched the bucket and the mop.

See how a stain like that soaks into the floorboards, you can never wash it away.

I put the bed over it in case it made you upset.

You know, Brenda, you look a wee bit like her. When she was your age of course. An expression round the eyes. She had that look sometimes if she was unhappy. I throttled a Jerry in Cadiz and kept his luger as a souvenir. She must have found it under my pillow. Let's call it a hundred pounds in cash in advance. Have you got such a thing in your case?

BRENDA. I think I've got a cheque.

LENNOX. S'got to be cash I'm afraid.

BRENDA (*takes an envelope from her case and a cheque from the envelope*). It's for a hundred and fifty pounds.

LENNOX. I know a boy that can look after that for us.

BRENDA. Could I maybe have a rug? For under the bed.

LENNOX. Well, Brenda, I like this place just the way it is now. Nae clutter. It was that full of dusty auld junk you couldnae breathe. I've humped that much garbage down those stairs and into that skip.

What are you runnin' from, Brenda?

BRENDA. I'm on my holidays.

LENNOX. You've certainly brought the weather for it.

BRENDA. I know. It's wild, isn't it. It leaves you breathless.

LENNOX. Sign it on the back. And 'Pay S. Duvalier'.

BRENDA. Who's that?

LENNOX. The invisible man. Next floor up. He looks after Danny.

BRENDA. So who's Danny?

LENNOX. Danny is a one-off. An inspiration to us all. And Duvalier's an inspiration to him. They're a team. Boxer and trainer. Body and soul. I like that, don't you?

BRENDA. Sounds like a perfectly balanced relationship.

LENNOX. So it does. Mind you their personal arrangements are none of my business. I make that a rule. I'll tell you now so's you know. A cast iron rule, Brenda. (*He takes the cheque from her and lifts a blouse from the case.*) Very chic. I'll bet it's lovely on.

BRENDA. I wouldn't know. I've never worn it.

LENNOX. For your holidays.

BRENDA. Uhuh.

LENNOX (*laying five blouses on the bed, one by one*). Monday, Tuesday, Wednesday, Thursday, Friday . . . (*Looking in the case.*) Nothing for the weekend.

BRENDA. Leave them, please.

LENNOX. Funny holidays. What sort of things are you planning for your days off?

BRENDA (*shoves the blouses back in the case*). Stop it.

LENNOX. A blind man could see through those. They're transparent. Tell me what you're trying to hide from.

BRENDA. You've got your rent so I can ask you to leave. I'd like some time to settle on my own.

LENNOX (*takes a pair of old gym shoes out of the freezer box and puts them on*). The fridge is communal. The bed is not.

He leaves.

Scene Two

DANNY *and* DUVALIER *come in.* DUVALIER *looks at his watch. Click.* DANNY *begins sparring on the bag.*

DUVALIER. Sixty seconds Danny.
Keep your hands up.
Stay busy with the jab.
Combinations, Danny.
Don't slap at him. Dig in.
Don't slip. Turn it up. I can't feel it. You're not hurting me.

DANNY. How long?

DUVALIER. 30 seconds.

DANNY. Fuck's sake.

DUVALIER. Drop your hands like that and he'll put your lights out for good. Busy it up for Christ's sake, keep that jab going. Double up, head – body. Upstairs. Take it upstairs. Elbows in.

DANNY. Christ's sake.

BRENDA. Poke him in the bread pan.

DUVALIER. Aye, poke him in the bloody bread pan. Poke him somewhere for God's sake, don't just dance around in front of him.

BRENDA. Kick him in the shins.

DANNY. Shut up.

DUVALIER. Buy a gun and shoot him.

DANNY. Fuck off.

DUVALIER. Five. Four. Three. Two. One. Time!

DANNY. Bastards.

BRENDA. Did he win then?

DUVALIER. His legs are gone. His guard's down and his time's up. You could take him. (*To* DANNY.) You're pathetic.

He flicks DANNY *with the towel – a vicious snap!* DANNY *jerks then looks at* DUVALIER *for a moment, then he jabs him in the stomach.* DUVALIER *goes down on his knees.* DANNY *drops to his hunkers, exhausted. He puts his hand on* DUVALIER'*s head.*

DANNY. I'm warning you, Duvalier. Don't fuck about with this. Don't start, okay. (*He points to the fridge. Speaks to* BRENDA.) You too. Okay. Now. Would you get me a bottle of milk please.

BRENDA. You've hurt him.

DANNY. How could I hurt him? I'm pathetic.

BRENDA. What did you do that for? (*Goes towards* DUVALIER.)

DANNY. Leave him.

BRENDA *stops.*

I'll hurt him alright,

Hey. Duvalier.

DUVALIER *looks up.*

Get a bottle of milk out the fridge.

DUVALIER *obeys.*

Bring it here.

DUVALIER *obeys.* DANNY *shows his gloved hands.*

Open it for me, please

DUVALIER *obeys and holds it for* DANNY *to drink.* DANNY *finishes it.*

Gloves off please.

DUVALIER *unlaces the gloves.* DANNY *begins to shake his limbs out, preparing for a run.*

Okay. Good. Now, you gonnae time me? Docks and back?

DUVALIER *nods.* DANNY *takes the empty bottle from him on the way past and thrusts it at* BRENDA.

BRENDA. Am I supposed to do something with this?

DANNY *is gone.*

What a bloody pig. What are you helping him for?

DUVALIER. There's no one else.

BRENDA. So? You should just let him get on with it.

DUVALIER. He couldn't on his own. He's got to have someone watching him. He's in the area final at the end of the month and if he wins that he'll be able to go professional and earn some money.

BRENDA. Oh I see. Of course. And you get some of the money.

DUVALIER. No. (*Laughs.*) He's not going to win. He's going to get killed.

BRENDA. Christ. You're as bad as each other.

DUVALIER (*crosses to the window and shouts*). Hear me, Danny? You are going to get killed! Your bones pulled and your heart consumed! Your tongue ripped and your jaw smashed! You are going to be dust, Danny. Dead dust! (*Pause. He turns back to* BRENDA.)

He's fighting a Catholic boy called Moody who's so good and smart and vicious and fast that . . . He's going to get killed.

LENNOX *comes in.*

LENNOX. What's all this shoutin' then?

BRENDA. Nothing . . .

LENNOX. Quiet. I'm talkin' to this one here, Brenda. Givin' it bloody sermons out the window. It's not a civilised house you belong in, Duvalier, it's a fuckin' mountain top.

BRENDA. It was my fault as well, I'm sorry.

LENNOX *doesn't look at her. He fixes on* DUVALIER.

LENNOX. Mr Duvalier here is fully aware that shouting out the window is in none of our interests due to certain circumstances. I think he knows exactly what I'm referring to, doesn't he? (*Pause.*) Don't you, you piece of hysterical . . .

DUVALIER. I forgot, Mr Lennox. Danny got a bit wild and . . and he hit me.

LENNOX. You encourage him you mean. Flauntin' yourself at him, all pathetic. Course he hits you. He's a fuckin' boxer isn't he, that's what they dae – hit folk. And you . . . And you're turning into a bloody woman, Duvalier.

DUVALIER. There's no need . . .

LENNOX. No need what? You're a woman. (*To* BRENDA.) You've seen it.

BRENDA. Me?

LENNOX. The way he teases him and flirts. Strokes him and watches him. Like lovers.

DUVALIER. I'm not!

LENNOX. Not for want of trying eh? 'Cept you arenae man enough. You had nae tongue on you when you got here and now you have all you want to do is shove it down his throat.

BRENDA. He's worse than that. He wants to hurt him not kiss him. He wants to see him dead. That's what he told me.

LENNOX. What he told you. Means nothing. I know him. His secret. He can't hide that.

DUVALIER. What?

LENNOX. The smell. The female stink of him. Christ, Duvalier, you smell more like a woman than she does.

BRENDA. What did you say?

DUVALIER. No. That's where you're wrong.

BRENDA. What did he just say just now?

LENNOX. You think.

DUVALIER. If you'd been here. If you'd seen her just now. With Danny.

BRENDA. What?

LENNOX (*pause*). She glowed did she?

DUVALIER. Like Jezebel herself.

LENNOX. Did her eyes light up?

DUVALIER. All of her.

LENNOX. And? . . .

DUVALIER. Her spirit was inflamed.

Pause.

LENNOX. Uhuh . . .

DUVALIER. And was tormented in the heat of the sun. (LENNOX *cackles*.) The red sun of decision and desire.

LENNOX. Ohh. I like that. Could you feel your hackles rising, Brenda when you heard that? 'Tormented'. 'The red sun of decision and desire'. Can you feel the blood rushing around in your skull? Are you hot?

BRENDA. Course I'm hot. We're in a heatwave.

LENNOX. No. It's him. The beads of sweat on your bare shoulder, the nape of your neck, sweat running down to the small of your spine.

BRENDA. Okay.

LENNOX. The moisture on your thighs.

BRENDA (*to* DUVALIER). What is this?

LENNOX. Your hot, sweet breath.

BRENDA. Okay. That's enough!

You pair think you can just come out with stuff like this and it'll scare me or something. Or make me curious, eh? You can fuck off.

Pause.

Because I'm a girl you think you know all about me, well you don't know a thing about me, not a single real thing. Nobody here does. Not one thing.

To tell you the truth Mr Lennox, I couldn't care less about any of this. This is not what I'm here for. Nobody knows what I'm here for so BOTH of you can just stop it. Right now, please.

LENNOX. We're not ganging up on you Brenda.

BRENDA. Bloody Right you're not. The three of you.

LENNOX. Four. Of us. I think the heat is starting to get to you hen. You should talk to someone. You're not giving anything away. What you just said. Get it off your chest. Make a lonely man happy.

BRENDA. You'd like that, wouldn't you?

LENNOX. I'm not talking about me. Him! Tell the invisible man. Tell him a single real thing, and then he will know. I don't care what it is.

BRENDA. Why do you call him the invisible man?

LENNOX. That's what he is.

BRENDA. Not to me he isn't.

LENNOX. You can hear him.

BRENDA. I can see him.

LENNOX. No. That's the problem. You can only see Duvalier when he's speaking. Not like Danny – Danny's solid, he's got a shape, he takes up space, for God's sake you can even smell him through the floor. But not Duvalier. He's odourless. Just a whiff of paraffin after a fire.

DUVALIER. What fire?

LENNOX. You know fine what fire.

BRENDA. He started a fire?

LENNOX. Ashes to ashes.

BRENDA. Did people get hurt?

LENNOX. I didn't say he was a murderer I said he was a pyromaniac. It's a talent. Like invisibility. (*Pause.*BRENDA *is unsure.*)

He set fire to a church and he set fire to a brothel. Both of them were derelict. And he keeps some ashes from the church and some ashes from the brothel in separate shoeboxes in his room.

DUVALIER *giggles.*

BRENDA. Why are you telling me this? It's irresponsible to tell people things like this. People you hardly know. They don't want to hear it.

LENNOX (*laughs*). Oh Brenda. Wee Brenda. (*To* DUVALIER.) Why don't you explain it to her properly Duvalier? So she understands. So she's on your side. (*Pause.*) Yes. It would be good if you two got to know each other. (*Goes out.*)

BRENDA. Your hair's dyed isn't it?

DUVALIER. His idea.

BRENDA. Duvalier's not your real name is it?

DUVALIER. It suits me fine.

BRENDA. I suppose so. I dyed my eyebrows once. They went fluorescent. It was carpet dye. I was only a girl then. I got into a lot of trouble for it.

DUVALIER. Look. When I came here . . .

BRENDA. Before the heatwave.

DUVALIER. Sorry?

BRENDA. Did you move in here before the heatwave started or did your arrival coincide with the beginning of the heatwave?

Pause.

DUVALIER. Why?

BRENDA. Do you not remember?

DUVALIER. No. Why?

BRENDA. It hasn't always been hot like this.

DUVALIER. No.

BRENDA. So when did it start?

DUVALIER. That's what I'm telling you.

BRENDA. On you go then.

DUVALIER. Okay. First Mr Lennox says if we do things properly then nobody gets hurt, just the insurance company and they can afford it. It's a thing called indemnity against an act of God, to do with a particular provision in the estate stipulated by the previous owner.

BRENDA. Who left it to Lennox.

DUVALIER. Yes.

BRENDA. And he told you about her.

DUVALIER. Yes.

BRENDA. About the woman.

DUVALIER. What woman?

BRENDA. Who killed herself.

DUVALIER. Yes. What the fuck do you know about it?

BRENDA. Absolutely nothing. Really. Honestly. Sometimes you can see something in a man. Even Mr Lennox.

DUVALIER. What could you see?. What do you know about him?

BRENDA. I said I was sorry.

DUVALIER. He told me! In this room. Where it happened. Hanging from the roof. And he was the one who found her and the one who had to cut her down and the only one who knew why she did it and he TOLD ME!

BRENDA. I said I was sorry.

DUVALIER. That's not enough! You can't guess things like that. It's wrong. It's not a fucking game, a thing like that, a fucking guessing game that you play at – 'Oh, look at me, everybody, I'm so clever 'cause I guessed.'

BRENDA. I didn't guess. I knew.

DUVALIER (*pause*). How?

BRENDA. Why do you think I'm here eh?

DUVALIER. I don't know.

BRENDA. My mother died. He needs someone whose mother is dead. As a daughter. The insurance.

DUVALIER. I don't believe this.

BRENDA. So what are you for?

DUVALIER. Does he know you know?

BRENDA. Are you going to tell him?

Pause. BRENDA *then* DUVALIER *laugh.*

DUVALIER. I never tell him anything.

DANNY *comes in, red-faced, breathing hard and sweating.*

DANNY. Fuck me, I've had it. What a heat out there. It's deserted. I think those dogs have got rabies. I jumped right over them. They didn't move. They didn't even flinch. (*He feels the heat in his limbs.*) Oh shit that's it. It's too hot. No more running.

DUVALIER. You've got to run.

DANNY. I can't. I'll stand and fight. I'll root myself to the spot. I'll use science and cunning and speed and strength and skill. Fuck running. It's too hot for it.

BRENDA. I've heard he's very good.

DANNY. Who?

BRENDA. Moody.

DANNY. Oh yeah. He's very good. He's young and hard. No hiding place. Oh, my legs. I've burnt my shoulders. Yeah he's good alright. But is he ready for me? Ready to get poked in the bread pan and kicked in the shins, eh Brenda? What I'm saying is, is he hungry, does he want it enough? Is the boy a killer at heart?

BRENDA. Are you?

DANNY. I am. I am a killer at heart. Amn't I, Duvalier?

DUVALIER. You are a killer at heart.

DANNY. What were you shoutin' out the window at me?

DUVALIER. Words of encouragement.

DANNY *takes his vest off.*

DANNY. Aye, that's what I thought. Get the oil?

DUVALIER *gets a bottle of rubbing linament from the fridge.* DANNY *sits down on a boxer's corner stool.* DUVALIER *splashes oil on his hands and kneads* DANNY's *neck and shoulders.*

DANNY. That's brilliant.

DUVALIER. It's not too cold?

DANNY. No it's brilliant. I think I got the sun on my shoulders.

DUVALIER. They're very red.

DANNY. Are they burnt?

DUVALIER. A bit raw.

The rubbing continues. BRENDA *watches for a while then gets herself a beer from the fridge.*

DANNY. Bring that here?

BRENDA *brings him the beer. He takes it from her and rolls the cold can across his forehead then gives it back to her. She holds the can under his chin and snaps the ring-pull so that the spray hits his neck and face.* DANNY *laughs.* BRENDA *drinks.*

DANNY. Fuck me this is heaven.

BRENDA. Is he good at that?

DANNY. The man has the hands of an angel.

DUVALIER. Not like you.

DANNY. No. Not like me. (*He stretches his arms in front of himself.*)

My hands are meat-cleavers. (*He clenches them.*) My fists are bombs.

DUVALIER. Put your head forward.

DANNY *bows his head.*

DANNY. With my eyes shut it's like the most beautiful hands in the world are making love to me. Giving me their strength. Making the muscle supple again.

It's like the most beautiful woman in the world was walking towards me across a desert and with my eyes closed I can see her standing in front of me in the desert like a vision. (*He looks up straight at* BRENDA.) Shimmering in the heat.

BRENDA. You mean a mirage.

DANNY. That's right. (*Stands suddenly.*) You should get yourself a job in a massage parlour, son. Earn yourself a few spare bob on the side.

DUVALIER *turns away.*

Heh! Where you goin' – Heh, don't waste all that good oil, give the young lady a rub.

BRENDA. I'm okay.

DUVALIER. For a few spare bob, eh, Danny.

DANNY. No, for free. For love or kindness or something.

BRENDA. I'm okay.

DANNY. You always say that, don't you? You're so nervous all the time. Nobody's going to hurt you.

BRENDA. I'm not nervous.

DANNY. He's not going to strangle you.

DUVALIER. She's not nervous, are you? It's you that's nervous, Danny.

BRENDA *giggles*.

BRENDA. He's right. It's you. You're scared of Duvalier. (*She sits down*.) Would you do my neck please.

DUVALIER. I don't know about that.

BRENDA. On you go. As hard as you like.

DUVALIER *begins to massage* BRENDA's *neck and shoulders*. DANNY *watches*.

I am poured out like water, and all my bones are out of joint: my heart is like wax; it is melted in the midst of my bowels.

DUVALIER. My strength is dried up like a potsherd; and my tongue cleaveth to my jaws; and thou hast brought me into the dust of death.

DANNY *leaves*.

Scene Three

LENNOX. Why's he not up, eh? He should be running. Pounding the pavements, building up muscle and stamina. This isn't a sweat-box. Is that what he's up to? Curled up in his room with a heap of blankets over his head. Rolled up in a sleepin' bag sweatin' off the excess poundage.

God, if he cannae cope with this how's he gonnae manage in the open air car park in Las Vegas or under the arc lights in front of five thousand heaving fight fans in Madison Square Gardens. Look what happened to McGuigan, eh? If he cannae stand the heat in the kitchen he should keep his face out the fuckin' area.

Is it somethin' fancy you've cooked up, eh, Duvalier. No. You've no' got it in ye, have ye?

Is he startin' to get the hots for young Brenda, eh? Is that it?

Am I conducting this conversation with thin air?

DUVALIER. You can do too much you know.

LENNOX. Oh, right. I see. So it's all in hand, then. This is just part of the regime, that's all. A wee vacation before the final push.

DUVALIER. Why do you ask me. ME. If he's 'Getting the hots for young Brenda' Mr Lennox?

LENNOX. Have you not got eyes?

DUVALIER. Why *him?*

Pause. LENNOX *laughs.*

LENNOX. Listen closely to what I'm gonnae tell you, Duvalier and I'll fill you in on some necessary background details.

Danny is a boxer, a pugilist, a fighting exponent of the fistic arts. It's all he lives for and it always has been and will be till the day his brain's too addled to know any different.

She is an innocent from the far, rural, picturesque countryside, arrived in all her innocence and beauty in the big city. She is a story-book distraction that we have to guard against. This is not Hollywood. She'll put him off.

DUVALIER. He's a fuckin' electrician.

Pause.

LENNOX. What?

DUVALIER. He is an unemployed elec –

LENNOX *grabs and slaps* DUVALIER.

LENNOX. Shut your fuckin' mouth. Shut your fuckin' mouth! You!

They tussle.

DUVALIER. He's gonnae get killed.

LENNOX. Liar. That's a brazen . . . downright lie . . .

DUVALIER. He's no chance.

LENNOX. He has. He has so! What do you know?

DUVALIER. I know!

LENNOX. What? He's a killer. He could snap you.

DUVALIER. Oh, yeah . . .

LENNOX. Yes! Like that! He's a natural talent, a . . . a . . . born fighter.

DUVALIER. He's. Too. Old

LENNOX. Nonsense. Fuckin' nonsense. He can do anything.

Shoves DUVALIER *away.*

Look at you! What do you know about his age? About what he can do. Fighting. Fighting another man in single combat. Fighting him, not touching him.

DUVALIER (*quietly*). Okay stop it.

LENNOX. You and Brenda, don't think I can't see it, don't believe for one minute that I'm as blind as . . . (*Pause.*) You know what you are, Duvalier. You and me both, we both know.

DUVALIER. Okay.

LENNOX. Don't we?

DUVALIER. I hear you.

LENNOX. Don't we!

DUVALIER. Yes!

Pause. They get their breath back.

LENNOX (*calmer*). Yes. Alright. My God Almighty. I could . . . I could . . . I'd teach you a lesson myself if I thought you and her were . . . It sickens me. To think about it.

DUVALIER. It won't happen.

LENNOX. Too true it won't. It would be like something . . . unnatural. Like . . . like . . .

Those dogs. Like two dogs or . . . You're all red, son.

DUVALIER. Am I?

LENNOX. See you've got all worked up about Danny's chances and you're worried – It's a different world for you I know; body blows and concussion and the left jab, stabbin' itself like a piston again and again into your opponent's face till the cartilage gives way and his corner throw in the towel.

DUVALIER. I know.

LENNOX. You stick to what you know best.

DUVALIER. I'm sorry.

Pause.

LENNOX. Ach. You'll do alright. You're a great lad. A thinker. A talker. What an imagination, eh?

'I killed her mother.'

DUVALIER. It's what she told me.

LENNOX. I mean. If that was the case. I'd be her father, wouldn't I?
Does she think I wouldn't recognise my own daughter? Pullin'
your leg like that. She needs a good talkin' to that one. You want a
beer?

DUVALIER. No.

LENNOX. No. Something stronger. Some a' this stuff. (*He gets a
bottle of tequila from the fridge. Gleefully.*) This is the stuff. See that
worm in the bottom? It has aphrodisiacal properties. I once ate a
whole bucketful of them with a man called Lopez in Vera Cruz.
Sick as dogs we were, the pair of us. Rollin' on the ground,
heavin' our guts up and dyin' for a shag. That's some country I'll
tell you. (*He takes the top off the bottle and drinks.*) Yer meant tae take
this with a pinch of salt. And a slice of lemon.

Me and Lopez – he was a gun-runner – or something. And there
was this . . . this . . . Border insurgency. We were caught in the
open and we'd've got killed but this wind blew up – like a
sandstorm – we clung to each other, me and Lopez, and
staggered around till we fell in a ditch, laughing. We laughed in
the face of death. And he had all this tequila. And the wind was
like, like a furnace – with sand screamin' into yer face. 'El
Diabolo'. The wind from Hell.

And when it died away we were by ourselves. In a ditch full of sand
and empty bottles. Pished. South America, North Africa and the
Tropics. The sirocco, the khamsin and the monsoon. I have been
blasted by every hot wind on every continent on God's earth.

See this? (*He touches his face.*)

That's not Age. It's Erosion.

The wind here hasnae even got a name.

DUVALIER. There isn't any wind here.

LENNOX. There isn't any wind here.

DUVALIER. It's still.

LENNOX. Have a drink, Duvalier. (DUVALIER *drinks.*)

See I've only got these three weeks left, you know. In three weeks'
time the thunder and the rain will come. Our boxer will have his
fight.

The demolition men will move in here; strip this place down to
the bare slats and then kick the feet out from under it. The girl
will move on to an even bigger city. You'll go back to where you

came from and what will I do, eh?

Maybe I'll just sit tight.

Drink your drink, Duvalier. Drink it all right down to the last liquid drop. And then maybe you can eat the worm.

Scene Four

BRENDA *is at the window, looking out,* DANNY *is doing sit-ups.*
LENNOX *is sitting on his legs. A Dansette record player without plug is on the floor.* BRENDA *has been wiring the plug but has stopped. She has the screwdriver in her hand.* DANNY *counts aloud – up to fifty.*

BRENDA. Is that the docks?

LENNOX. Past the big cranes?

BRENDA. Yes. There's another one there. I can see the glow. And the smoke.

LENNOX. That's the old bonded warehouses.

BRENDA. Do you think it's him? Every night since he went out. At least one big fire.

LENNOX. I'm sure of it. You want to finish puttin' that plug on?

BRENDA. He's lighting up the sky all round the city. Bit by bit. Night after night. It's beautiful.

LENNOX (*to* DANNY, *underneath him*). She thinks it's beautiful.

Are you gonnae get that thing working?

BRENDA. I see no reason why not. (*She gets back to the plug.*)

LENNOX. 'Cause it's important. Mobility's important. You have to be light on your feet. If you're not gonnae run then you have to dance. All the greats danced. Marciano was a demon in a tango.

BRENDA. Can you tango?

LENNOX. Can I tango. I can waltz, quickstep, foxtrot, jitterbug and charleston. But first and foremost – I tango.

BRENDA. Is he alright down there?

LENNOX. 'Course he's not. He's experiencing great agony.

BRENDA. Looks it.

LENNOX. Great agony – aren't you son? In body and soul. Joints cracking, ligaments popping – the works. Sheer murder.

BRENDA. But we're getting him licked into shape.

LENNOX. Great shape. Great shape demands great agony.

BRENDA. And we've turned him into putty in our hands, haven't we? More of a machine than a man.

LENNOX. A fighting machine.

BRENDA. And while Duvalier's out there, putting the city to the torch, raging like a fiiery angel making his judgements burn, purifying . . . releasing . . .

LENNOX. We're in here.

BRENDA. We're in here, shaping another man, like the Inquisition.

LENNOX. Making him ours.

BRENDA. To do our bidding.

DANNY. Twenty! (*Collapses.*) Get off me.

LENNOX. You can have a minute to catch your breath, then – ON!

He joins BRENDA *with the Dansette.*

Are you done yet?

He picks up the record player and they wander round the walls looking for a socket. They plug it in – it works.

LENNOX. Brilliant. Let's see what we've got.

She looks through some records which were already in the box.

BRENDA. You want something you can tango to.

LENNOX. I know exactly what I want. (*He takes a record from the fridge.*)

I want . . . THIS!

BRENDA. What is it?

LENNOX (*putting on the record*). You'll know it the instant you hear it. It's in your blood. Your mother and I danced to this the first night we were ever together.

BRENDA. My mother could tango?

LENNOX. She taught me.

DANNY *has risen to his feet.*

Mademoiselle? S'il vous plait. (*He grabs* DANNY.) Maestro.

BRENDA *starts the music.*

BRENDA. And you danced with her the night you met?

DANNY. I'm not sure if I see how this helps.

LENNOX. Precision, split-second timing, rhythm and instinct, and above all, Art.

They are dancing.

DANNY. I follow you?

LENNOX. Follow the music! The tempo, follow your heart.

BRENDA. Like you did on the night you met my mother?

LENNOX. YES! Yes.

DANNY. You think I won't be able to do this, don't you?

BRENDA. Did your hearts skip a beat?

DANNY. The pair of you – you think you're going to humiliate me.

LENNOX. Time stood still that night, Brenda.

DANNY. And I have to put up with this drivel, 'cause there's no one else to help me.

LENNOX. Our love was bigger than both of us.

BRENDA. And you were young, footloose and fancy-free.

LENNOX (*stops dancing*). What's that got to do with it?

BRENDA. What?

DANNY. Keep dancing! Come on, don't stop.

He drags LENNOX *a few steps,* LENNOX *pulls free.*

LENNOX. What you just said. The way you said that.

BRENDA. Said what!

DANNY. Brenda! Dance with me. (*He is still dancing, on his own.*)

Don't leave me on my own. He thinks he can make me look ridiculous. Well he fuckin' can't.

He has BRENDA *and they dance.*

LENNOX. You know what – like it happened then and it's gone. I was telling you about now! (*He is almost tearful.*) How I was dancing with your mother and we waltzed and tangoed like you and him and she was soft in my arms and I was strong and . . . and I held her and she melted and we MADE LOVE! (*He is in a tearful rage.*) Do you think that fuckin' changes! Eh! You pair! Do you think that I've forgotten what's beautiful and young and fresh. Do you think I'm a fuckin' corpse! 'Cause I'm not. Do you think I never wanted to dance a tango with a beautiful young woman on the bank of a river with the moon and stuff . . .

He is crying. He kicks the record player, the record stops. BRENDA *and* DANNY *stand together. Shocked and listening.*

BRENDA. Don't, it's okay . . .

LENNOX (*bubbling*). No it's not fuckin' okay! How can it be? How can anything every fuckin' be fuckin' okay for me again. Eh? Eh! Fuckin' look at me.

BRENDA. You're alright. Really.

LENNOX *has gone.*

DANNY. What's all that about?

BRENDA. I don't know. The woman. I wasn't thinking. The woman who killed herself with his gun in my room. She left him this place and he thinks he's my father.

DANNY. And she hung herself in Duvalier's room and she drowned herself in mine.

Lennox is the fuckin' jannie.

BRENDA. How?

DANNY. He's the odd-job man. Nobody left him anything. He's making a few bob out the place before it gets knocked down.

BRENDA. No.

DANNY. On the sly. Your father! And Duvalier's name's not bloody Duvalier for a start either – he's been thrown out by the Sally Army and the DHSS and all the rest and Lennox is just a wee nyaff making a fly bob out the three of us. And what the fuck are you doing here anyway?

BRENDA. I'm going to find a job. My mum and dad didn't want me to leave home. I need to see if I can have a life . . . Danny. I need . . . I feel a bit faint. Could you get me some water or . . . I don't feel well.

DANNY. And Duvalier . . . for God's sake – he's just . . .

BRENDA. I know all that. Do you think I'm stupid!

DANNY. Well . . .

BRENDA. I know he's just a harmless wanker pretending!

DANNY. Maybe he's not so harmless.

BRENDA. 'Course he is. He's just a pathetic . . . benighted . . . creep that Lennox makes up stories for. 'Course he's harmless . . . I just feel sorry for him, that's all. Christ, Danny – Do you think I don't know all that?

DANNY. Then what are you pretending for, eh?

BRENDA. And you!

DANNY. Okay, me! But you. Tell me. Why are you pretending?

DUVALIER's voice, very loud, from out of sight.

DUVALIER. Mr Lennox is all upset!

They turn to look for him.

But I managed to calm him down a bit I think. He took one look at me and a sense of calm returned to him as though he knew everything was being taken care of.

BRENDA. Duvalier?

DANNY. Heh! What're you hiding for?

DUVALIER comes into the room. His face is black with smoke, his hair is singed and his clothing still smoulders. He has a can of petrol in his hand.

DUVALIER. You can run but you can't hide, eh, Dan. I've come home to the ones I love. To the ones who love me. (*He takes the tequila bottle from inside his coat. It is empty except for the worm.*) He said I could have this. (*He drops to his knees.*) He said it has aphrodisiacal properties. (*His voice is a croak.*) I'd like to share it with you both. (*He pitches onto his face.*)

Scene Five

DANNY *and* DUVALIER *sit opposite each other,* BRENDA *on the floor beside the Dansette.* DANNY *wears boxer shorts,* DUVALIER *only a pair of trousers and* BRENDA *a cotton-print dress. It is now oppressively hot.* DUVALIER *is learning how to wind bandages round* DANNY's *hands; it is meticulous work, the loose ends must be tucked away and then the gloves (not new ones) tried on.* BRENDA *is examining and cleaning a collection of old records. All three are by turns languid and feverish.*

DANNY. I should have a cuts-man. he should have a little cotton-wool stick and a little bottle of adrenalin. (*To* BRENDA.) Do you know anything about cuts?

BRENDA. Nothing.

DANNY. No. It doesn't matter. In an amateur bout they stop the contest if there's a bad cut and the referee checks his card to see who's ahead and awards them the fight.

BRENDA. It might be best if you got cut.

DANNY. Maybe you're right. Who knows? We'll see. Anything nice in that pile?

BRENDA. They're too dusty.

DANNY. Oh. I thought you were lookin' for a tune for us. To cheer up greetin' face here.

BRENDA. They're too dusty. (*Pause.*) Do you bleed?

DANNY. Fuck, aye. Like a pig. I've never been cut in the ring, though. Everybody bleeds. Clash of heads is all it takes – the other guy goes in with the nut and (*Makes a noise.*) . . . blood everywhere. (*Pause.*) Listen do we have to talk about blood. I'm not fond of blood – just because I'm a boxer – you still get squeamish like everybody else.

BRENDA. You started it.

DANNY. Aye, okay. Just not so much of the gore. It's my face we're talkin' about here – my good looks Anyway – it's a defensive art.

DUVALIER. Not against the Catholic boy.

DANNY. What do you know?

DUVALIER. You'll have to stop him.

DANNY. How do you know? Just because he's fast and fancy – if I cut him he'll bleed same as anybody else. If I knock him out he'll go down. Christ, if I hit him hard enough he'll die. Same as anybody.

Pause.

BRENDA. Same as you.

DANNY. Look! Are the pair of you tryin' to get me mad or something. God Almighty – cooped up in here with you pair it's like being in the inside of a goldfish bowl.It's a simple, ordinary matter of an amateur boxing contest. Three short rounds of three

minutes each with a qualified referee whose job it is to protect
either of us from serious injury and a . . . and a doctor on hand
lookin' after us if the worst comes to the worst. Which it won't.
Okay. It's not Raging fuckin' Bull. It's not a video nasty.

Pause.

Anyway!

Pause.

BRENDA. Anyway what?

DANNY. Anyway at least I'm gettin' on with something! Keepin' my
head. What about you, eh? I thought you were going to get
yourself all set up to be the big career . . . secretary in the big city
so you didn't have to marry your bloody cousin in Aberdeen.
Where's the job interviews? Eh? Have you been to one? Eh? . . .
Have you fuck. You haven't even been to the job centre – you
haven't even signed on. You haven't even been out this house
since you moved in.

BRENDA. Stop it!

DANNY (*mimicking her*). Stop it!

DUVALIER. Leave her alone.

DANNY. Aye and as for you. Sneakin' about with your can of petrol
settin' yourself on fire.

DUVALIER *looks at him.*

Aye. All that talk about the avenging angel burnin' up the city.
Fuckin' Batman and Robin more like. Do you think we swallowed
any of that shite about pyro-bloody-mania. It's all shite from the
pair of you. You're just a daydream, Duvalier. You're nobody's
nightmare. Not even your own.

DUVALIER. I did things.

DANNY. Stop it will you! Look! (*He forces himself to calm down.*) Look,
I've got to train and I've got to get ready and it's hot enough as it
is. I've got to get ready to get hurt, maybe, and that's no fun – so
just behave yourself and help me. It's all in proportion so just
help me, that's all – to keep it small and simple and nice and
straightforward.

DUVALIER (*pause*). Very well. (*Pause.*) I did things though.

DANNY (*referring to the bandages*). Take them off and start again,
you're making an arse of it.

BRENDA. What things?

DUVALIER. Batman and Robin, pff!

BRENDA. What sort of things, Duvalier? With the petrol?

DUVALIER. No. Not the petrol. Worse.

BRENDA. What?

DANNY. Don't encourage him. He's got to concentrate.

DUVALIER. I am concentrating.

DANNY. You're not. You're useless. Take that off and start again.

DUVALIER. It's true what I did, Danny. Out there, at the fires – Last
night at the fire at the warehouse. I went to all of them – the last
five nights, all over the city – there's fires everywhere and I went
to watch.

DANNY. Just to watch?

DUVALIER. Yes. And there was this gang of thugs. Kids, drug
addicts. They were always there as well. They never saw me
though. Except last night. The fire engines were coming and I
was walking away so no one would notice me and they were
waiting for me. They were pushing me and shouting things at me
and spitting. I thought they were going to do something nasty so I
was shouting back at them but I was really scared so I didn't know
what I was saying – just shouting.

BRENDA. What did you shout at them.

DUVALIER. Nothing. How do I know? They were just kids. I ran
away and they chased me. There was a dead end and I went under
some corrugated fencing. They'd tricked me and I was in the
burning building. They shouted at me to come out but I went
into the fire and came out the other side. And I was in a different
place, in an alley-way and there was no one there. At the end of
the alley I could see a glow from the front of the building and
little bits of charred wood were floating past and my clothes were
smoking and burning. I stood there and got my breath back and
let my sweat soak into my clothes. And then one of them
appeared. He came walking down the alley backwards towards me
and I stepped out of the shadows and let him walk right into my
arms. He turned round and looked at me and I held his arms and
he was so light and I made him walk backwards until his back was
pressed against the hot bricks. I squeezed my thumbs between his
muscles and his bones and he was so thin and frightened and I

looked into his eyes and I said 'Don't be afraid,' and I put my head against his head, gently, (*He holds* DANNY's *head.*) then I took it away and did it again, harder. (*He butts* DANNY. *They fall together.*) I pinned him against the wall and did it again and again, harder and harder like a piston into his face till the cartilage gave way then I left him alone. So now I know what it's like and I'm as good at it as you. And nobody can say any different.

Silence. BRENDA *laughs.*

BRENDA (*to* DANNY). See what you've done. You're contagious. Like a fever.

DANNY. It's not funny.

BRENDA. Maybe I'll catch it too.

DANNY. I said it wasn't funny!

BRENDA. And maybe we'll all go down with it. You're worse than Lennox.

DANNY. What about the petrol? What was that for, eh? Did you use it on him, Eh! Did you . . . You stupid little get! (*He stops. He puts his face in his hands and laughs.*) Oh God. Brenda. Put on a record.

She does so. DUVALIER *starts to laugh.*

Oh God. I'll tell you what's really funny . . . (*He takes his hands away from his face.*) I stopped boxing for a while, see – a while ago. In the last fight I had. I was eighteen and . . . and I was gettin' a real maulin' – against the ropes and . . . and I couldn't see – this boy kept his hands low and they came in from all over angles.

The record starts. It is Peggy Lee singing 'You're My Thrill'.

In over the top, upper-cuts, right hooks – I couldn't do anything about it. Blasting away at my head, firing everything he had at me. It was half way through the second and I thought – I'm gettin' gubbed here. I'm gettin' a right pasting. This is no use. What am I gonna do about this? So I bounced off the ropes into a clinch, hanging on him . . .

LENNOX *comes in behind* DANNY. BRENDA *and* DUVALIER *both look at him. He is wearing a dress and a fox-fur and lipstick.* DUVALIER *smiles at him,* BRENDA *is astonished.* DANNY *looks from one to the other around the three.*

DANNY. Ignore him.

Pause. Then, to LENNOX.

Get out, you! (*Trying to continue his story.*) Listen to me. I was only eighteen. I bounced . . . off the ropes – right? (*He laughs over his own story.*) Oh God – he was all over me that boy. Don't look at him – please – listen to this, it's a scream. So I grabbed him and we lurched about for a bit – then the referee . . . the referee pulled us apart and he said – 'Step back boys. Break. Come on, step back.' And I put everything I had into a big right – a bloody haymaker – every ounce of my strength . . . (*He is still laughing weakly.*) And I . . . and I hit the referee on the chin and over he went. (*He topples backwards to illustrate.*) Stretched his length. (*He spreads out on the floor.*) Like Richard fuckin' Dunn. Out like a light, with his foot shakin'. (*He makes his foot shake.*) And his eyes rolled back. (*He rolls his eyes.*) And he . . . And he . . .

He twitches and laughs, quietly, hysterically, then twitches more but stops laughing. The twitching becomes convulsive and DANNY *is having a fit. The record sticks after the second verse on Peggy Lee singing 'Oooh . . . oooh . . . oooh . . . ooh . . . ooh . . .'*

LENNOX (*to* DUVALIER, *indicating the record player*). Get that would you, son. (DUVALIER *turns it off.*)

LENNOX *goes to* DANNY *and tenderly cradles his head, stroking and soothing him.*

LENNOX. My wee boy. My ain wee boy. What's the matter now then, eh? Lie still my poor wee boy. Poor wee soul . . . there then are you not well then, my poor wee soul.

BRENDA *kneels down next to* LENNOX *to help.*

BRENDA. What's happened to him?

LENNOX (*to* BRENDA). Well dear . . . I would have thought you'd be the one to know that.

BRENDA. Me?

LENNOX (*forgivingly*). I know. Don't blame yourself. (*To* DUVALIER.) Something . . . cooling, maybe? . . . Yes?

DUVALIER *gets champagne and three glasses from the fridge. He brings them over, pops the cork and pours.* DANNY *has stopped shaking and is now curled up. All three stand over him, glass in hand.*

DUVALIER (*suggesting a toast*). Danny's health?

LENNOX. To Danny. Wherever he's gone, may he return to us soon. Sound in mind and body . . . and fit and strong to triumph in adversity.

ALL. To Danny!

They clink glasses and drink.

Scene Six

BRENDA, *wearing a slip, sits on a stool facing* LENNOX, *still in his dress, who holds a full-length mirror so that she can see herself. The five blouses and the suitcase are on the floor between them.* DANNY *is in the bed – eyes open – motionless.* DUVALIER *is on the edge of the bed holding* DANNY's *hand. Every so often* DUVALIER *leans over as though to catch some words from* DANNY, *who says nothing.*

BRENDA *picks up and puts on the first blouse.*

LENNOX. O, yes. That's very pretty.

BRENDA. You like it?

LENNOX. Put your hair up.

She holds her hair up and regards herself.

LENNOX. Very pretty.

BRENDA. It's Monday. It's Monday morning.

LENNOX. Breakfast time.

BRENDA. My mum and dad had a row last night so he's sulking. He said that I don't do enough around the house and my mum stuck up for me so they had a fight. But she'd never stick up for me if I was there. And I think. I'll bloody show him. I'm not his skivvy. I'm not going to end up like my mother. Fuck you mate.

LENNOX. Language, language.

BRENDA. I don't care. I said it to his face. (*She takes off the blouse and chucks it in the suitcase then tries on the second one.*) This would be nice with grey, don't you think?

LENNOX. Something icy. Severe.

BRENDA. Yes. (*Pause.*) Tuesday. (*Pause.*) I was suffocated. Even in the winter, we'd get snowed in and they'd all come in blue and huffing and panting and stamping. But I was stifled – I couldn't breathe.

LENNOX. You'd have to open a window.

BRENDA. Yes.

LENNOX. Step outside.

BRENDA. What do other girls do? I thought. At my age.Do they get away, make a bid for freedom? Find a job, a little flat, share? How do you do that? At least that's what they do on the telly, the career girls. (*She discards the second blouse and tries on the third one.*)

LENNOX. A girl has to find herself a handsome beau – with his own chateau and a private income. She needs a ball-gown.

BRENDA. Wednesday.

The young farmers' dance every summer. My god. I was so excited the first time. All that beer they drunk. Their breath! My brothers took me. Douglas and Malcolm and Colin. But I still got my dress torn. And there was a fight in the car park. And my dad was waiting up when I got home and it was me that got into trouble as though it was my fault for leading them on.

LENNOX. That one's very nice. Very chic and sensual. Perhaps with a single string of pearls?

BRENDA *discards the blouse and tries on the fourth one.*

BRENDA. Thursday. Interestingly enough . . . Are you interested?

LENNOX. Agog.

BRENDA. I'd always thought one day my dad would throw me out. I think he knew I wasn't going to marry my cousin Peter – Christ, who'd want to marry that . . . Blob. He was a second cousin.

I was supposed to be meeting him to go to the pictures but I stood him up again and he must have phoned and when I got home my dad had gone out to look for me and my mum was in the kitchen. She was drunk. My mum. Drunk. She had two glasses of sherry at the most every Christmas and there was a half-empty bottle of my dad's whisky on the kitchen table. I don't think she'd even bothered with a glass, just gulped it back in a oner out of sheer desperation.

LENNOX. Your poor old mother.

BRENDA. Driven to that.

LENNOX. A mother understands.

BRENDA. Yes. She needed to be drunk for what she was going to tell me. About my dad and her. I just stood there in the kitchen crying. It was the saddest thing I'd ever seen. My mummy.

Slavering at me and swearing and swearing and swearing . . . and . . . saying terrible things to me. I'd always loved her, only loved HER, and I would have leapt between her and my dad if he'd gone to hit her. And she told me how much she hated me. (*She takes the blouse off and picks up the fifth one.*) So she gave me a cheque in an envelope and went with me to Marks and Spencer's the next day to buy me these.

There's your independence. She said. Get yourself a job in a shop or an office and marry the boss and don't ever come near us again. (*She rips the blouse in two and stuffs it, with the rest, into the suitcase.*)

LENNOX. Quite right, hen. If I've seen one blouse like that I've seen a million. Put them on and straight away you feel like you're snowed in. See, in this heat you've got to have something cool. Something with a bit of breath in it. (*He goes to the fridge and takes a cocktail-dress from the freezer box and holds it out for* BRENDA. *She puts it on.*)

BRENDA. My father and my brothers and my cousin; when I grew up amongst them it was like it was my fault. All those bloody men, accusing me of turning into a woman. And then even my mother joined in. And I was innocent. (*She goes and sits on the bed opposite* DUVALIER. *She looks at* DANNY.)

(*To* DUVALIER.) Do you think he can hear me?

DUVALIER. No.

BRENDA. Do you think he knows we're here?

DUVALIER. No.

BRENDA. Do you think he's in love with me?

DUVALIER (*pause*). No.

BRENDA. This is my room and my bed and I've paid my rent so I'd like you to leave me alone now please.

DUVALIER. Alone?

BRENDA. With the invisible man.

DUVALIER *joins* LENNOX. BRENDA *gets into the bed with* DANNY.

DUVALIER. I had a bite of that worm thing you gave me.

LENNOX. It did the trick?

DUVALIER. It made me feel sick to my stomach.

LENNOX. Maybe it didn't agree with you.

DUVALIER. No that's right. It didn't. (*He goes to the fridge.*)

LENNOX. There's none left. We've drunk it all.

DUVALIER *takes two cardboard shoeboxes from the fridge.*

DUVALIER. What's in these again?

LENNOX (*pause*). Ashes of desire.

DUVALIER. Uhuh. (*He empties them both onto the blouses in the suitcase.*) They just look like ashes to me. Or dust. Like you'd find in a hoover-bag. (*Indicating the suitcase.*) What a bloody mess that is. That lot needs to go out on the skip. (*He closes the suitcase.*)

LENNOX. Are you going to take it, Duvalier?

DUVALIER. Uhuh. I'm going to chuck it all out.

LENNOX. Then what?

DUVALIER. How do you mean?

LENNOX. Are you coming back to me?

DUVALIER. To this place?

LENNOX. Yes.

DUVALIER. And you.

LENNOX. And me.

DUVALIER. Do you have any idea what you look like?

LENNOX. Tell me.

DUVALIER. A Jezebel. (*Laughs.*) In a fuckin' pantomime. They're going to drop the roof on your head, Lennox. Do you want me to sit and hold your hand? Pray with you.

LENNOX. There's something I haven't told you.

DUVALIER. Don't. Don't start. (*Silence.*) Does your head hurt?

LENNOX. Yes.

DUVALIER. So does mine. Do you know what that is?

LENNOX. What?

DUVALIER. It means the thunder's coming. Tonight or tomorrow night.

LENNOX. Danny's got his fight tomorrow night.

DUVALIER. Then that's when it'll be. When the bell goes for round one. When the crowd get to their feet to roar him on.

LENNOX. You think he'll fight?

DUVALIER. 'Course he will. Fuck knows. Maybe. If there's anything left of him now you've finished.

LENNOX. What do you say you and me go down to the pub and have a quiet pint. I know a nice wee place down the road. Blow the rent money. Get ourselves tanked up, play some darts. Then a curry.

DUVALIER. I don't think so. I don't think you'd make it. I think if you stepped outside you'd frazzle up and blow away. You're a husk you know, Lennox. A wee ghost. Anyway I've got things to do.

LENNOX. O well then.

DUVALIER. Before it rains and puts the fires out.

LENNOX. Uhuh. I see. O well then. It was just a thought. What sort of things is it that you've got to do?

DUVALIER leaves.

Secrets, eh? There's never any good came of that.
Everything should be kept out in the open where you can keep your eye on things.
You hear me.
You're an ungrateful wee bastard.

LENNOX *exits.*

Scene Seven

BRENDA *is in the bed.* DANNY, *dressing, is crouched on the bottom of the bed facing her. He holds a cigarette in one hand and a lighter in the other.*

DANNY. This'll be my first fag in three months. I could almost have given up, you know.

BRENDA. I've heard it's dead hard.

DANNY. Ay, you're right there. The price of them too!

He lights, inhales and coughs.

Fuck me. God that's good. Feel that reaching into my lungs.
Killin' me. Lovely. Do you want one?

BRENDA. I never really got the taste for them. On you go though. I like the smell.

DANNY. Aye, I know, it's good . . . You gettin up?

BRENDA. No, I'm fine thanks.

DANNY. Okay. (*He smokes.*) Bet yon boy Moody's dyin' for a fag.

BRENDA *smiles.*

I used to work next to a man smoked a hundred and twenty a day. Players untipped, full-strength. And he used to blow down them before he sucked like this . . . (*He demonstrates.*) To get the end really burny . . . (*He shows her.*) Then suck like fuck . . . (*He sucks.*) To fill himself up. (*He coughs.*) It's true. A hundred and twenty a day, sixty-five years old, fit as a fiddle, runnin' marathons! (*They smile.*) It's true – Glasgow marathon, came two hundred and eleventh last year. (*He laughs.*) No, I'm lyin' – he had emphysema, coughed his lungs up and died.

BRENDA *laughs.*

DANNY. I was an electrical engineer you know. Still am I suppose but I got made redundant in 1976. Plessey in Bathgate. Shut the whole fuckin' place down, everybody ... (*Snaps his fingers.*) Like that. Out on your ear.

Then I set up with another boy. But we went bust as well. Then . . . you know . . . here and there, bits and bobs, sign on . . . re-wire somebody's house for them, then . . . sign on. My wife says to me: Don't go gettin' any smart ideas about this boxing lark or I'm offski! So I told her I was going down to the Midlands to look for work and I'd be in touch. Send the money. She took the kid to my mother's – they get on great. Her and me though . . . You know, married too young, had a wean . . . didnae really get on all that well. She's alright though . . . it's me I suppose. I couldnae handle the dole all that time. Years. So I thought I'd give the boxing another shot. I was very good at it once you know.

BRENDA. Why'd you stop?

DANNY. Medical advice. Might be hereditary – Never know when it might happen, might never happen again, you know – so it seemed stupid to risk it. Still. Desperate times and all that. (*Pause.*) And I loved it. I love the training – self-denial. You turn yourself back into a virgin.

BRENDA. Like Duvalier.

DANNY (*laughs*). No. I wasn't thinkin' of him. More like you.

BRENDA. Uhuh.

DANNY (*pause*). Still. All for the best I suppose. I could have taken Moody once upon a time but now . . . who knows. I mean the money's crap at the sort of bouts I'd get but . . . beats signing on any day.

DANNY *has moved to the punchbag and now lands some desultory punches on it as he talks.* BRENDA *has taken her second suitcase from under the bed and laid it on her lap. She stares at it.*

See, so much of it is in your attitude. Take McGuigan. Before Barney Eastwood took him on he was useless. I mean he could box, but he trained that hard he was always jaded and tense and his attitude was all wrong. That fight with Pedroza! I watched that on my own on the telly and I'll you I could have given the best in the country a run for his money. Except I couldn't. But I felt as if I could. Do you know what I mean?

BRENDA *opens the suitcase and looks inside then she turns it round so* DANNY *can see. He goes to her and lifts a fistful of material, silk boxer's vest and shorts with the word 'Everlast' printed on them. He shuts the suitcase.*

Will you be here when I get back?

BRENDA *shakes her head.* DANNY *smiles.*

. . . If I get back.

BRENDA *smiles too.*

BRENDA. The men are coming tomorrow.

DANNY. What'll you do?

BRENDA. Move out. I don't want to live in a heap of rubble.

DANNY *leaves.* BRENDA *gets out of the bed. She turns on the record player. Peggy Lee sings the same song as before. This time the record doesn't stick but at that same point swells to fill the room. It grows dark.*

DUVALIER *comes in, covered in blood, his hair matted with sticky gunk. His arms clasping his ribs. He ignores* BRENDA *who stands motionless and watching him. He goes, whimpering, to the fridge and opens the door and pulls fridge trays out and throws them around till the fridge is empty. He climbs inside, closing the door on himself.* LENNOX *has changed and comes in. It gets darker.* LENNOX *has a coat over his arm which he holds out to* BRENDA. *She takes it, puts it on and begins to button it up.*

BRENDA (*pointing at the floor beneath the bed*). I managed to get rid of that stain for you.

LENNOX. Very good of you. (*The thunder starts.*) You'd better run or you'll get wet. You look a bit like Barbara Stanwyck in this light. (*He laughs.*) Except nobody here looks like Barbara Stanwyck because that's the sort of shite that you only see at the pictures.

BRENDA *leaves.* LENNOX *goes to the fridge and opens the door. The only light in the room is from the fridge's interior. The thunder cracks and* LENNOX *closes the door leaving* DUVALIER *inside. He goes to the wall and unplugs the fridge. He sits on the bed.*

End of play

Paul Godfrey was born in Devon, trained and worked as a director in Scotland 1982-7 and is at present in London. His first play *Inventing a New Colour* was produced by the Royal Court Theatre and the Bristol Old Vic. His second play *A Bucket of Eels* was commissioned by the Royal Court Theatre. Paul holds a BBC radio script commission and is currently writing a play about Benjamin Britten for the National Theatre Studio entitled *Once in a While the Odd Thing Happens*.

Inventing a New Colour was first performed at the Bristol Old Vic
Theatre on 26 October 1988 and subsequently at the Royal Court
Theatre, London, in November that year. The cast was:

PETER   Simon Gregor
FRANCIS   Nicholas Hewetson
ERIC   Sam Kelly
JUNE   Valerie Lilley

Directed by Phyllida Lloyd
Designed by Anabel Temple
Lighting by Tim Mitchell
Music by Gary Yershon

Characters

JUNE, Eric's wife, working as a librarian, 46
ERIC, June's husband, working as an engineer, 52
FRANCIS, June and Eric's son, 16
PETER, an evacuee, 17

The Scene

Exeter.
The Spring and Summer of 1942.

The text comprises nine scenes: Act One has five and Act Two has four.
These are interspersed with individual speeches by the characters. I have
given locations for the scenes only.

In staging, the scenes should be indicated simply, and all the action set
against a background suggesting landscape, perhaps with bands of colour:
greens, greys, blues and soft browns.

While the play is set in 1942, the period needs also to be shown only
lightly: it is that moment, as if now.

ACT ONE

1

JUNE. I look out from here
and I see the line of hills,
beyond that another
and beyond that
mist.

There is not anywhere
here in this city
that you cannot see the hills
and I know
that is the quality of this place.

A city in the country.

Neither forgets either.

To be here, is to see more.

Even our devastation is hemmed by fields.

2

ERIC. When I was courting your mother,
I used to wear wide turn-ups,
And once
we'd been out
courting in the bracken,
and I noticed
that one of my turn-ups was heavy.

Then when I got back
a green snake fell – bang –
on to the kitchen floor,
and whipped away under the sink.

You can imagine my mother
'How did that get there?' she said

'Been lying down?'

3

FRANCIS. At school
     I was told to paint the view
     from my bedroom window

     and I painted a dull green square
     that filled the paper,

     with a smaller grey rectangle,
     that was the step down.

     Other pictures were different,
     the views you would see looking out.

     I mixed and remixed that paint
     'til it flaked off.

4

JUNE. There is no clock in this house,
     that's the right time.

     Eric sets the alarm a few minutes ahead
     now and then
     so he'll think he's late for work
     and gain time in the morning.

     Sometimes he alters the others
     but I'm not certain which
     neither is Eric, I think.

     We still get to work though.

5

In the kitchen: February. FRANCIS *comes in.* PETER *is waiting. He has his things.*

FRANCIS. Is this you, just arrived then? Peter. The evacuee.

PETER. Me. Yes. Here, here in the country.

FRANCIS. Oh.

PETER. So much green here.
   It's all green, the countryside round here, isn't it?

FRANCIS. Exeter's not exactly like that.

PETER. Ah, but Exeter's so old.

FRANCIS. What's left.

PETER. My father said it was a place to have property, Devon.
   I'd really like to have property round here.

FRANCIS. Why here? When you've come from London.

PETER. I mean to retire to, I'd give anything to be rich enough to
   retire down here.

FRANCIS. It's damp you know, here.
   If you retired here you'd die, of rheumatism.
   Wettest valley in England, brilliant place to retire to this.

PETER. I was told we have to go and work in the fields out of term.

FRANCIS. Yes. We can walk back each day though, or cycle, along
   the canal.

PETER. There's no tram?

FRANCIS. Look, I'd better tell you now. My parents, they're at the
   funeral. My grandmother she died this week.
   You've not come to a happy house.

PETER. Should I do something?
   What should I do?

FRANCIS. Nothing; just don't worry if they act out of the ordinary
   when they get back.

PETER. Oh, dear.

FRANCIS. It's all right, don't expect them to be normal that's all.

PETER. No one's parents are normal:
   My mother she's Italian.

FRANCIS. That must be strange.

PETER. It's difficult sometimes, but I don't mind it.

FRANCIS. Is that all you've brought?

PETER. Yes.

FRANCIS. You've brought quite a lot with you.

PETER. I'm late, I should've registered by five.
   Is that the time?

FRANCIS. It'll do.

PETER. Perhaps I can do it tomorrow.

FRANCIS. Would you like to see the river?

PETER. Why, is it interesting?

FRANCIS. There's a weir.

PETER. Oh I've seen that, from the train.

   Did she die in the bombing then your granny.
   Was it a bomb?

FRANCIS. Not a bomb, old age.
   She wasn't bombed.
   She was very old.
   You shouldn't laugh.

PETER. You are.

FRANCIS. She was my granny.
   I cried earlier.
   She was more than eighty.
   On Monday my dad found her in bed asleep;
   dead.

PETER. Where do I stay?

FRANCIS. My father asked me to clear half of my room and he's
   brought in another bed.

   Yours is going to be the one under the window, and there's a
   desk, but you could use this table for your homework.

PETER. There's going to be a lot of that, isn't there?

FRANCIS. School certificates you mean.
   Are you taking them too?

PETER. That's why they sent me. I missed them last year.

FRANCIS. But you look grown-up. Too old to be an evacuee.

PETER. I'm only seventeen. These exams are important.
   Aren't you a bit young to be taking them?

FRANCIS. I've been sixteen for a long time.
   How many are you taking?

PETER. Six, six is all you'll ever need.

You?

FRANCIS. Eleven: Maths, English, Language and Literature, History, French, Latin, Greek, Chemistry and Physics.

PETER. That's only nine.

FRANCIS. R.I. and Art too.

PETER. You're the smart one.
There's no straw in your hair.

FRANCIS. The only way to face these things is head on.

PETER. What?
Exams.

FRANCIS. Head on and by the throat!

PETER. Don't you know there's a war on?

FRANCIS. Half measures is no good.
To the hilt or not at all.

PETER. But why condemn yourself to all this rubbish then?
Where does it get you?

FRANCIS. You'll see.

PETER. When we get back to work?

FRANCIS. When we get back to school.

PETER. Do you think I'll get on all right?

FRANCIS. You will.

PETER. Now tell me your name.

FRANCIS. Francis.

PETER. Francis: the original Devon pirate.

6

JUNE. A woman came into the library today, she put the books on the counter and ran, she ran away. That's the fines, you see. Perhaps one day, there will be an amnesty.

If I can get this Library Association exam it puts me up a level and I may be able to keep my job if, when, the war ends.

It would mean no more stamping books at the desk too. My hands are black from that ink and the action has been mindless for months long gone.

Take the book, turn the book, take the card, change the card, stamp the card, shut the book. Next book. Hand the pile back, library card on top.

I wish the Anglo-Saxon was not so difficult. We had to go to a once only class in Bristol, and the man looked around the room and said, 'There's someone here who'll know more about this than anyone else.' We were all silent and then he looked at me and said, 'You'. 'The Exeter Book, I expect you know all about it.'

I knew nothing.

That the earliest shreds of our poetry were recorded here, in the cathedral library. I'd never heard mention. A thousand years sitting there, more: and it's been a beer mat, and a cutting board and for lighting candles.

'Exeter people did that,' he said, 'to the earliest poems in the English language.'

Mid-afternoon, I sit in the library annexe and I work on it.

Piecing one word with another, slowly.

Incomprehensible.

7

Kitchen: JUNE *is there,* ERIC *has just arrived.*

ERIC. There's a letter for Peter, come through the door just now, and caught open on the box.

JUNE. Eric, for God's sake don't read the boy's post.

ERIC. I was just interested, that's all.

JUNE. You want to be careful, he'll be here in a minute.

ERIC *puts the letter on the table.*

PETER *comes in and looks.*

PETER. Hello Eric, June.

ERIC. How are you boy?

PETER. I saw a cat roll in a puddle!

JUNE. There's a letter for you, from London.

PETER. At last! (*He goes out with the letter.*)

ERIC. Hah! Look at that. Hidden that boy.

JUNE. Not deep then?

ERIC. How long's he been here? Three weeks and he's like a bullet out of a gun, and he's bright too.

FRANCIS *comes in.*

FRANCIS. Anything happen today?

JUNE. No, just a letter for Peter.

FRANCIS. What's the date?

JUNE. Twelfth of March.

FRANCIS. Wet enough. (*To* ERIC.) Hello.

ERIC. Just a minute, can you walk properly Francis?

Come on now, walk properly.

FRANCIS. What?

ERIC. Don't act up, stand straight and just walk properly so your mother and I can see you walk.

JUNE. Put your shoulders down Francis.

ERIC. Why do you have to make such a show of everything?

FRANCIS. Why can't I be left alone? I walk properly all right.

Don't I walk up and down that bloody road every day?

PETER *comes in.*

Eight years now, four times a day, twenty times a week, more than two hundred and fifty times a term.

PETER. You talking again.

FRANCIS. What's that?

PETER. Seven hundred and fifty times a year.

JUNE. They say the whole of South Street went last night.

FRANCIS. Oh it's all right though, that was only really old buildings.

ERIC. One good thing, and I'll tell you something now. There's not one in the West Quarter I wouldn't like to see gone. Let's keep all that to your exams and have a clean sweep of some of these old places.

JUNE. I'd rather it didn't have to happen this way.

ERIC (*to* FRANCIS). I don't see you so keen to refuse new boots when I offer them. Happy enough to ditch old ones then. What use old boots eh?

FRANCIS. They say you can make soup out of old boots!

ERIC. Don't talk soft boy.

PETER. I reckon they've given us six hours homework tonight.

FRANCIS. That's what it's been every night this week and I bet we'll need to carry on at this rate too.

JUNE. You two boys are exam-crazed.
Who's best at this who's worst at that.
As if it was all that matters.

FRANCIS. Don't you want us to get our exams?

FRANCIS *walks out of the door and leaves it open.*

ERIC. Door! Door!

FRANCIS *comes in.*

FRANCIS. Door! Table! Chair! Floor! Sink! (*He goes out.*)

ERIC. Shut the bloody door!

PETER *shuts the door.*

PETER. They were talking about Francis today at school.

The housemaster in the housemeeting this morning. He said 'There's one boy in this school who I would describe as the most aggressive boy here. That's Francis,' he said. And Francis grinned and acted like he was hiding under the table. 'Yes I would have no doubt in describing Francis as the most aggressive boy in this school.' That's pretty amazing isn't it?

JUNE. Francis will do all right, but he wants to watch his step at that school.

ERIC. He acts far too clever when he'd do better to do what he was told.

FRANCIS *comes in.*

FRANCIS. What they tell me?

ERIC. Don't you understand?

Why don't you do what they tell you?

You make life difficult for yourself.

Is it so difficult?

FRANCIS. Why should I do what they tell me?

Not if I don't want to, not if I think they're wrong.

ERIC. You think you know more than them, eh?

FRANCIS. Yes, well, in fact I do, about some things.

ERIC. Well you're just iggerant then . . .

FRANCIS. Iggerant? Ignorant!

Can't you even talk properly?

JUNE. Can't you see that if you constantly do what they tell you not to, people will dislike you.

FRANCIS. Either you live by the rules other people set you, or you set your own. I'm going to set my own.

ERIC. Another day over! (*He goes out.*)

FRANCIS. Another day over! Another year over!
Another meal over! He says it all the time you know.

JUNE. I know.

FRANCIS. I don't think he even notices. Another tea over! Another journey over!

JUNE. It's not stupidity you know, or meek acceptance of other people's rules, it's a satisfaction in what's complete, complete and satisfactory. He'll say 'anther job done', 'another row of potatoes planted'. A pleasure in modest achievement, not an all-suffering ignorance.

'Another war over', that's what I want to hear right now.

Francis, I don't enjoy having you here criticising. I don't enjoy hearing jibes at your father. Do you think he enjoys his only son always out to attack or undermine him?

Peter doesn't enjoy being here.

You may be clever, and don't we all know it.

We love you, but we don't always like you.

FRANCIS. You bore me.

JUNE *goes out.*

PETER. Friday night, I wish we could go somewhere.
Hey, why *are* you taking all these exams?

FRANCIS. Why?
So I can take higher school certificates, that's why.

PETER. I'd rather be out; out on the town; up the West End, on the
tiles, downing the beers!

FRANCIS. I need them so I can go to university.

PETER. It's not my cup of tea.
But perhaps that's right for you. You could do very well there.
You're lucky to be able to choose.

FRANCIS. Why?

PETER. Why what? Why so bitter, you could stop now. Why take all
these exams?

FRANCIS. Why, because if we're forced to play this bloody game
let's play it like a game, eh?

PETER. Fair dos for all? Or so that we can win?

FRANCIS. Neither. Let's throw the counters in the air and let the
people dive for them.
Sweep the board! Change everything!

PETER. Oh Yes.

How?

8

JUNE. Francis brought home a painting once
just before Christmas,
it was the three wise men
unfinished.
They were in a line,
red, orange and yellow,
with an incomplete background
in yellow also,
which stopped when it reached the yellow one.

He asked me what to do
and I said

blend the colour to red
behind the yellow figure

And the picture was a great success.

Three wise men coming
out of the rising sun.

9

PETER. I think I've arrived.

Three weeks and a bit and I think I am here now:

I know my way round.

This family, Francis and his mum and dad,
I feel they're my family now.

Though I'll be gone in the autumn, I know that too.

But while I'm here, it's as if I've always been here, now.

10

ERIC. I was out early this morning
the world seemed glowing,
green and white
There was mist, and dew,
which gave a shine to the leaves,
The river was grey
and the sky pale.

My mother is under the ground.

I stood and listened.

All the leaves heavy and shimmering.

Too much living and growing
only so much soil
only so much light
leaf on leaf on leaf.

11

Kitchen: April. JUNE *writing, books open.* FRANCIS *comes in.*

FRANCIS. They sent me home. (*She looks up.*) Hello.

JUNE. What's wrong with you?

FRANCIS. I broke my nose, in hockey.

JUNE. Oh no, not you Francis.

FRANCIS. It doesn't hurt at all.

JUNE. It looks all right anyway.
You're lucky to find me here, they changed the shifts, so I'm working at home this afternoon, on the Anglo-Saxon.

FRANCIS. I did it in hockey.
A ball hit me, wack! and it's broken.

JUNE. It's been here a thousand years that nose, you know, and you've broken it!

FRANCIS. It wasn't my fault! I was in goal and I defended by attacking so he hit it right at me.

JUNE. A Norman nose faced into the sea spray and crossed the channel, in history.

FRANCIS. I cried.
'Quit snivelling' said the master and it's broken.
I've broken my nose.
Look at it.
'Quit snivelling.'

JUNE. This nose pointed skywards, spanned the cathedral.

FRANCIS. You do talk nonsense sometimes!

JUNE. A hard look and a straight nose!

FRANCIS. Straight nose! Ha! Ha!
If you asked me to follow it now I'd walk in a bloody circle.

JUNE. Is there anything I can do for it?

FRANCIS. They say I've not to touch it, and it'll set straight on its own.

JUNE. Not so bad for a boy.

FRANCIS. That's all right then.

JUNE. Was it Peter who hit the ball?

FRANCIS. No. Might just as well have been though.
  I expect he's still there, battling up and down.

JUNE. Why is it a battle?
  You must be careful with him, Francis.

FRANCIS. I'm the one people have to be kind to.
  I'm the one that's war-wounded!

JUNE. That's not very funny, just now.

FRANCIS. Oh, he's all right.

JUNE. You know what I'm saying.

FRANCIS. We get on.
  What's this?

JUNE. Still the Anglo-Saxon.

FRANCIS. Is it interesting?

JUNE. I don't know, yet.
  Your father says he wants you two boys to go out with him in the
  raids.
  Taking messages between the firewatchers.

FRANCIS. How will we get our homework done?

JUNE. If you sit down as soon as you get home you could do it then.

FRANCIS. But, when will I get a break?
  When am I going to get some peace?

JUNE. Think of everyone else.

FRANCIS. I don't get much choice around here.
  It won't make much difference to Peter though.
  He doesn't do his homework most of the time.

  PETER *comes in.*

PETER. Hello June.
  Are you all right Francis?
  I tried to come back with you but they wouldn't let me go.
  What did the nurse say?

JUNE. It's broken, but it'll mend.

PETER. Hey, it'll make you look really tough!
  A broken nose.

FRANCIS. Better than Pinocchio.

PETER. What's this you're doing?

JUNE. It's Anglo-Saxon.

PETER. They didn't write very well.

JUNE. That's just a facsimile, of an original text.

PETER. What is it, exactly?

JUNE. It's riddles.
They're not comic though; not jokes.
Would you like to look at one?
You have to imagine your own answers here.

She hands him a piece of paper. He looks up.

PETER. Shall we get our own tea then?

FRANCIS. Mmmm, I'm hungry too.

JUNE. I'll do it for you.

ERIC comes in.

ERIC. What's wrong with you?

FRANCIS. I'm waiting for my tea.

PETER. He's broken his nose.

ERIC. Give the boy some tea Mother.

JUNE. You're early too.

ERIC. They shut the foundry, and as I'll be out tonight I knocked off.
No coal delivery this week, at this time!
And I caught one of the apprentices at the canal.
He threw a machine part in the water.
He'd made it wrong, I could've milled it back again.
I felt sorry for the poor boy, he was so ashamed. Just seventeen I think, same age as you Peter.

| PETER
FRANCIS | (*simultaneous*). | Could I be apprenticed now then?
I've broken my nose. |

| JUNE
ERIC | (*simultaneous*). | You'd do better to get your school certificates.
Doesn't look serious to me. |

| PETER
JUNE | (*simultaneous*). | But, I'm no good at them.
No one's to touch it. |

| ERIC
FRANCIS | (*simultaneous*). | Sciences will be useful.
What's this about messages? |

ERIC. They need some more boys to run messages between the

firewatchers.

FRANCIS. And you want us to do it?

ERIC. Yes.

PETER. I wish I could be an apprentice, doing something instead of
this.

ERIC. You could help me on the UXB's if you want.
I need a boy.
You'd have to keep right back while we did the defusing, but you
could help move the pieces.

FRANCIS. So I do the messages on my own?

PETER. Yes.

Eric, why did the boy throw the thing in the canal?

ERIC. I only noticed because I used to do it myself, we all did.

The apprentices have to make trial pieces and the materials cost
money, now no one likes to admit their mistakes; so they throw
them away where nobody will know and they try again. There
must be thousands of machine parts in that canal.

JUNE. One day they'll find them all.
God knows what people will think then!

12

PETER. It's cold this place.
Last night,
in the shelter,
it was wet.
I put my hand out to touch the mattress
and it was damp,
drops of water all over.
Every surface covered.

A wet hole in the ground.

It snowed on the sports field too,
and nearly May.
Bare legs in the snow,
and nearly May.

13

ERIC. I went to the last war as
     an engineer.
     Fuel tanks I built, underground,
     and I dismantled
     simple explosive devices.
     Now the war's here,
     with us.
     So I go to people's gardens
     and find incendiaries
     like vegetable marrows.

     I defuse them.

     It's not safe.

     Of course,
     I feel sorry for the boy:
     Peter, I mean.

14

In the bedroom, late at night. FRANCIS is still awake.

   PETER *comes in.*

FRANCIS. You're late, the all-clear was hours ago.

PETER. They say it was the worst raid yet, Eric sent me home, he's
     still out.

FRANCIS. How did you get on with him?

PETER. All right.
     He's a good chap, I like him.
     And I suppose I learnt a lot,
     mechanical things, that'll be helpful in the Force.
     Some of the devices are quite simple.
     Eric showed me one, it was just eight pieces.
     I reckon I could take one apart in no time and rebuild it.
     It'd not be difficult.
     And they're not all big either.
     I saw another
     it would fit in my bicycle basket.

FRANCIS. You know what your mother wrote?

PETER. You read my letter?

FRANCIS. Yes. I found it.

PETER. Francis!

FRANCIS. 'I hope you had an uneventful journey.'
I can't understand how anyone can wish someone that.
It's too dull.
Life shouldn't be that dull.

PETER. I don't agree.

FRANCIS. An uneventful journey.

PETER. How can you say that?
Christ, *four* raids this week.

FRANCIS. Choose.
Choose now.
Eventful or uneventful.
I choose the profoundly eventful.

PETER. Oh Francis, just now: I'm away from home.
Bombs drop.
People die and kill.
My mother wished me an uneventful journey.
That's not unnatural.

FRANCIS. But we have no choice, do we?

PETER. I try to get on with you, you know, but there you go, acting
up all the time. I'm so tired. Tell me what you mean.
What do you *mean*?
You need to smarten up your ideas, Francis.

FRANCIS. It's my house you live in.

PETER. Thanks, it's the middle of the night, that's marvellous.

FRANCIS. I'm glad you're grateful, City Boy.

PETER. Local yokel! Ha Ha Ha!

FRANCIS. Goodnight!

Goes to sleep.

PETER. Francis, wake up.

FRANCIS *wakes up.*

FRANCIS. I like the rustic impressions.

Pause.

I mean what I say.

We have no uneventful journey.

Pause.

PETER. Are we friends?
  We are friends.

  Aren't we?

FRANCIS. Yes.
  I think so.

  Pause.

PETER. It means a lot to me.
  I've been very lonely, but if I know that you are my friend then I
  can carry on and do it all, because I know you'll be there, and I
  can talk to you.
  Let's meet when we're old, shall we?
  Will you come to my funeral if it's first?
  I'll go to yours.

  Pause.

FRANCIS. You are a silly old thing.
  I didn't know at all.

PETER. I'm sorry.

  Pause.

FRANCIS. I was waiting for you.
  Will you help me?

PETER. Yes, of course.

FRANCIS. It's serious.
  You know you help my father now to collect pieces of the
  dismantled UXB's.
  I'd like to get enough pieces to make a bomb.
  I'd like to blow up the school.
  No more exams then!

PETER. That would be terrible.

FRANCIS. I don't see.

PETER. Francis, some things are good and some bad, everyone
  knows that.
  This is *bad*!
  Lots of people could be killed.

FRANCIS. Not if we timed it right.

PETER. Buildings destroyed, Francis.

FRANCIS. That's the idea.

PETER. Why now?
  Francis, making a bomb is *wrong*.

FRANCIS. We go out and do it to the Germans.

PETER. That's very different.
  The school is not our enemy, not like the Germans.

FRANCIS. Oh yes?

PETER. Look we know we're right, on the side of good, but the
  Nazis are wrong.

FRANCIS. Exactly.
  The things we like and agree with are *good* and those we dislike
  and disagree with are *bad*.
  Got it?

PETER. It's not so simple.

FRANCIS. Millions and millions of bombs drop every day, yesterday,
  tomorrow.
  How does one extra tip the balance.
  Right or wrong?
  We hate these exams, yes?
  You do.

PETER. Yes.

FRANCIS. Most of them will be no use.
  You want to be a soldier, yes?

PETER. Yes, I suppose so.

FRANCIS. And to me, well, they're a joke – a bad joke.
  None of us knows why we go through this charade.
  Who knows if the war will end, even if we win.
  So, let's choose; to sweep it all away.
  You're not convinced.

PETER. People might be killed, you and me.

FRANCIS. Look, I've worked it out.
  We assemble it under the stage in the hall, then we help to stack
  chairs one day and stay to switch the lights off and one of us goes
  to set it.
  After prayers the hall is always empty for an hour.

Peter, no one will get hurt.
It's a miracle the school's not been hit already.
It's monstrous, how could they have missed?

PETER. Are you really serious?

FRANCIS. I'm asking you to help me, as my friend, Peter.

PETER. Does this mean friends for ever then whatever happens?

FRANCIS. Yes.

PETER. I'll go with you.

FRANCIS. Everyone will be so sorry.
Poor boys, no exams.
Tragic, and they worked *so* hard.
Enforced school holiday.

PETER. How long have you been planning this?

FRANCIS. How often will you go out with him on the defusing lark?

PETER. Three nights a week from now on, perhaps.
As many nights as there are raids.

FRANCIS. Can you start collecting pieces, without him noticing?

PETER. Yes.

FRANCIS. You and I. Together.
Soon.

15

JUNE. Mostly when I look at Eric
He's still the man I love.
He cuts his sandwiches at night,
hovers in the bathroom
and lives in small ways.
Quite like a squirrel or a rabbit:
Squirrel man

The turn of his cheek,
line of his shoulder
and shine in his eye
that I love
are not always there.

When Francis was four,

he held his wrists together,
comparing cuffs.

Eric does that and
I cannot love him.

16

FRANCIS. The high point of the week
    that's Friday evening.
    This is Sunday afternoon
    the low.
    Last week's homework is there.
    Peter's gone out.
    We've not talked about it;
    Bombs.
    Everything goes on.

Bang!

I had a stupid idea
    there's not a chance it could happen.
    No fear
    Not us
    Not for real
    Not at all
    Not here!

That's certain.

17

Part of the north transept, Exeter Cathedral. The medieval clock is visible.
April: ERIC and JUNE are there.

ERIC. Do you know what I saw?
    Christmas trees, dozens of them, all dead and caught on the weir.
    It's a bit late isn't it? I'll show you on the way back.

JUNE. Do we need to walk that far in this weather?

ERIC. There'd be no point in us going back the way we came June.

JUNE. Can you hear the sleet on the boarding?
    It's so dark with the windows gone from the cathedral.

It's a wonder this place is still here.

ERIC. Sunday afternoon again. Such a week it's been.
I wish I could be in the garden more.

JUNE. Poor old dear man.
There's nothing we can do about the weather.

ERIC. The weather is the least of it. But I can't help thinking,
there's such a lot to be done out there.

JUNE. Now that you are out most nights, you and I, we have no
time.

ERIC. This is all we have.

JUNE. And there's little to say.

ERIC. There's nothing new at work.

JUNE. I know.

ERIC. Well you'd know, because I'd tell you.

JUNE. For a long time I thought I was unhappy but now I think I am
not.

ERIC. Thinking yourself unhappy. That's really soft, June.

JUNE. Now I feel as if I'd only just woken up.

ERIC. That's Sundays. We didn't get up till after eleven, did we?

JUNE. I was up earlier and left you to sleep you know.

ERIC. I wish you'd stay with me when I'm asleep.

JUNE. It's a blessing to sleep so long.

ERIC. It's no skill.

JUNE. Sometimes I'd like to sleep and not wake up.

ERIC. Don't fall asleep now, you've still got to walk home.
There's Peter.

PETER *has come in.*

PETER. Hello. How do you tell the time on this clock?

JUNE. Hello Peter. I thought you were revising.
You've only got three weeks; Peter you're soaked through.

ERIC. I didn't expect to see you here.

PETER. You two went out. Francis took his coat. I wanted to come
for a walk out as well.

ERIC. Come on Mother, tell us the time then.

JUNE. You both have watches, but since you ask:
     The top dial shows the minutes. It's been added later; and the
     outer ring on the main face shows the hours.
     It's a quarter to four.

PETER. What about the inner rings?

JUNE. In the centre, that's the earth, with the moon revolving.
     It shows the days of the month and phases of the moon.
     You can see the moon will be full at the end of next week.

ERIC. That's what I don't want to see.

PETER. And the motto beneath. What does that say?
     'Pereunt et imputantur.'

JUNE. It's Latin. I was told once; referring to the hours: 'They
     perish and are added to our account.'

ERIC. I'd like to know all I've done in my time.

JUNE. Is that what you think it means?

PETER. Do you know how this clock works exactly?

ERIC. Electricity.

JUNE. I'm cold. I'll sit by the heater at the west door and wait for
     you two boys.

ERIC. We'll light the fire when we get home June.

JUNE. All right.

     She goes.

PETER. Is June all right?

ERIC. It's the moon.

PETER. Moon?

ERIC. Bombers' moon. The thought of more raids has upset her.

PETER. I see.

ERIC. Looks like we'll be out most nights next week I'm afraid.

PETER. Just like last week?

ERIC. Yes.

PETER. I don't mind.

ERIC. Thank you Peter.

I've always wanted to say to Francis, but couldn't, so I'll say it to
you, about June. I've been lucky in love; and I don't care who
knows.

June and I, we've not always seen eye to eye, like now, but who
does? I'll tell you I couldn't have asked better.

And this Anglo-Saxon, it's useless, probably, even now, a waste of
time; but why shouldn't she do it?

She's an educated woman, my wife, you know. Not like you and
me; of course that's who Francis takes after.

PETER. I'd noticed. That's why he beats me in arguments, he knows
more words. It's not fair.

ERIC. Look before we go; see that window. The stained glass in it
had a panel of two boys fighting. Just like you and him.

PETER. Was it old?

ERIC. Oh yes, there's always been two boys fighting!

PETER. Where is it now then?

ERIC. Taken with the rest to be stored till after the war, against the
bomb damage.

PETER. Francis and me, we're not going to fight any more.

18

JUNE. I stood at the sink today
    and before I washed it,
    I held Peter's vest to my face;
    and I smelled his smell.

    He's a year older than my boy:
    Francis.
    Do we have children?
    How is that one mine?
    I wonder,
    what he tells me
    how much is it?

    These boys,
    we are theirs.

    Peter's vest, it was warm.

Francis wears two jumpers.

19

ERIC. The boy is too keen
    by half.

    Then tonight,
    when the raid comes
    he's not here.

    I've seen him
    up to something,
    taking things.

    Is he safe?

    The city
    it's burning
    and he's not here.

20

PETER. I never thought it,
    I never expected it to work,
    My God,
    I slotted the metal pieces in place
    and attached the detonator timer,
    it moved.
    I could have removed it
    perhaps.
    But I wasn't capable.
    I sat
    and looked at it.
    I
    did
    it.
    My God.

ACT TWO

1

FRANCIS. My first memory of the Exe,
 was walking on it.

 Next,
 Summer
 and paddling in the warm
 I put my foot through a salmon
 Dead
 and rotting in the mud.

 Now
 My mother says the word 'Exeter' means
 'a river abounding in fish'.

 Last year
 when the weir dried
 and salmon teemed in the pool
 boys came with air rifles
 shooting into the water.

 Now they spray the river
 on to the burning buildings
 in Salmon Pool Lane.

 The bombs leave us with ashes
 And last night
 our house was gone.

2

Next day. An allotment shed. PETER *curled up.* FRANCIS *comes in.*

FRANCIS. Hello, Peter.
 We thought we'd lost you.

PETER. How did you find me?

FRANCIS. I knew you'd be here.

PETER. That easy?

FRANCIS. Transparent.

PETER. What's happened?

FRANCIS. You know.

PETER. What now, then?

FRANCIS. They're all upset, it's horrible.
  We stay in a shelter tonight and go to my grandmother's
  tomorrow.
  It's miles out.
  The house has not been touched since she died.
  You must come.

PETER. Forget about me boy.

FRANCIS. Well sir, since Hitler, perhaps the only wholly evil man in
  the world, dropped a bomb on Salmon Pool Lane, you have
  nowhere else.

PETER. It wasn't Hitler's bomb.

FRANCIS. What?

PETER. It was ours.
  You know, the pieces.
  I put them together, like your dad showed me.

FRANCIS. In the house?

PETER. In the kitchen.

FRANCIS. The kitchen!

PETER. During the raid.
  And they worked, the last thing I expected.
  The timer gave me 30 seconds and I ran.
  I got your revision notes. (*Hands them to* FRANCIS.)

  FRANCIS *takes the pile of papers and throws them on the ground.*

FRANCIS. Gone! All gone.
  Whooah!
  Rubbish house, room, street!
  All gone!
  Whooah!
  No more exams, Peter!

PETER. We have to tell your parents, you know.

FRANCIS. No, we must never do that.
   No one must know.

PETER. But they're upset, it was their home.
   They took me in, you're their son.

FRANCIS. I'm still here.

PETER. How can we not tell?

FRANCIS. Because it would make nothing easier.
   Things would be more painful that way.

PETER. You're a coward.

FRANCIS. This will be more difficult.
   No one but you and me must ever know.

PETER. How can we go on as if we'd done nothing?
   Won't they know, won't they guess something's up?
   They know you too well, Francis.

FRANCIS. Everything is different now, we are no longer in that house.
   All the changes in our behaviour, they will account to what's happened.

PETER. I don't know if I can do this at all.

FRANCIS. Look, I'll help you.
   We're lucky not be dead, if you are wise you will work, as I shall.
   We have to keep doing the messages too.

PETER. You make it sound very easy.

FRANCIS. Soon, you'll get your call-up. What?
   Two and a half months, less.
   That's what you want, isn't it?
   You are not as tied as I am.

PETER. So we plug on and say nothing?

FRANCIS. Yes.

PETER. I'll try Francis, I promise you that.

FRANCIS. Come on, let's go.

PETER. Your revision notes, better take them.
   We will still have to go to school, take exams.

FRANCIS. Do you think so?

PETER. The school is still there.

What reason is there not to?
You said I should work as you will.
Isn't that what you meant?

FRANCIS. I don't know.
I didn't think.

PETER. Not like you Francis.

FRANCIS. You're not so stupid Peter.
Did you take anything of yours when you left?

PETER. No, I don't care about that.
It's all a mess.
In London, my sister may be dead, my mother gone, and I did
this here.

FRANCIS. It was our idea remember?
My fault as much as yours.
Perhaps our house would have gone anyway.

PETER. Perhaps.
Perhaps you're right.

3

JUNE. Eric keeps saying to me:
Nothing matters *that* much.
Nothing matters that much.
Nothing matters.

The saddest days of my life.

I go back to look.
I know there can be happier times,
but when?
The work,
and the discomfort of our lost home
envelop me.
Time will pass.
The Anglo-Saxon has all gone.
I'll forget that.

There's still our cathedral
almost untouched.
But I have no more words tonight.

4

ERIC. I'm rubbing my finger and thumb
    like this,
    and noticing it.

    I have a half pint
    and there I am
    rubbing my finger and thumb
    on the glass.

    I pick up the paper
    and I hear it:
    the paper crackling,
    and I see myself
    rubbing my finger and thumb.

5

FRANCIS. How do you paint the night indoors?
    I used to lie planning it
    part-closing my eyes
    deciding the colours of the darkness.

    I shut my eyes and see them.

    I paint the powder paint on the sugar paper.
    Colour and colour mixed in the pot,
    Greys streaked on the surface,
    Holes in the paper and drips on the floor.

    I've tried now, and used all the colours.
    What next?

6

ERIC's *mother's house: May.* JUNE *and* PETER *alone.*

JUNE. What are you going to do tomorrow, when the exams begin?

PETER. We've got to dig a trench, all round the school, so that we
    can defend it if they invade. All of us not taking the exams will be
    digging.

JUNE. I've been wanting to talk to you about your future Peter.
    I wish you'd not thrown away your chances of getting the

certificates. You see we feel a responsibility for you while you are with us.

PETER. I wasn't as lucky as Francis was I?
I didn't have all the notes in my satchel that night.

JUNE. All that work gone, when you could have shared his books.

PETER. I've had enough sharing.
You know, honestly, it never was my strong point, exams.
What good do they do you, when it comes to it?

JUNE. Obviously, exams only show who's good at exams, but people don't study simply for that.

PETER. None of this studying ever helps me to understand anything either. It's only by doing that you find out.

JUNE. And making mistakes?

PETER. Making mistakes, that's important too.
All these teachers, they've *taught* me all right but what I've learnt, I've learnt myself.
That's what I find.

JUNE. Like my correspondence course for the library exam.

PETER. Yes, that's right, you have to work it out for yourself.

JUNE. And when you have difficulty doing the exercises?
What then?

PETER. Then you invent the answers.

JUNE. That's no good Peter.

PETER. Not unless they're right!

JUNE. Then that's like cheating.

PETER. You won't invent the right answers unless you understand the questions.

JUNE. An educated guess.

PETER. Perhaps you can know more than you understand.
You can say more than you know.

JUNE. If you took these exams you'd find you only know what you learnt.

PETER. I know more than I've learnt.
And I know what I want to learn.

JUNE. But how is it you know what you want to learn; by reading?

PETER. Even reading though, it's all second hand isn't it?
   The world at two removes. My mother says it hurts your eyes . . .

JUNE. When you should be out in the fresh air?
   You won't get much fresh air in the machine shop.

PETER. Look at him then, cooped up in that room, learning it all
   off by heart and getting headaches and being sick.

JUNE. I'm sure that's more to do with the broken nose.

PETER. He'll need spectacles next. Now that's really desperate. No
   one's ever going to get me into a pair of them.

JUNE. In the library I see hundreds of people come every day to
   collect books from the shelves. At night they lie in the shelters
   and read them. People need something like that to keep them
   going.

PETER. Lucky we don't live in Germany where they burn the books
   then.

JUNE. What have you ever done?
   There's such a lot you don't know.

   Pause.

PETER. It's easy to say that. I could say it to you.

JUNE. It's experience I'm talking about.

PETER. Quantity or quality, which is it counts there?

JUNE. I don't think you understand what you're talking about.

PETER. I know what I'm saying.
   Why did you give up your exam?

JUNE. I don't know why I should tell you.
   It wasn't because I lost my books.
   It wasn't that at all. You don't get to read much at the issue desk,
   and though I'll stay as long as I can, I've found that if you love
   what's in the books, you don't work in a library.

PETER. What when you leave?

JUNE. Perhaps I should be out in the fresh air.
   There's a big enough garden.

PETER. This is more what I'd call country round here.

JUNE. Eric grew up in this house. It's safer away from the city.

PETER. It's just far enough out of town to be able to get in.

Along the canal, it's a good run.

JUNE. You three go the same direction now.

PETER. Just till the end of term; Eric will be on his own then, when Francis and me have to go up the hill to the Farm. Can't imagine what that'll be like.

JUNE. A couple of months farm work will do you no harm.

PETER. I'd like to go with Eric one day to the foundry.
At home I've seen the big machine shops in the dockland.
That's what I'd like to be, an engineer. The Forces will get me my apprenticeship. I'm keen to learn; because I know I can do it you see.

JUNE. I'm glad you know that at least. If you get the chance I'm sure you'll do well.

PETER. You've been kind to me and now I'm making the best of things until I go.

JUNE. I'm sorry you've had such a miserable time with us.

PETER. Don't say sorry. It's hardly your fault.

JUNE. Francis told me what happened.

PETER. Oh.

JUNE. After the bomb.

PETER. Bomb?

JUNE. After the bombs fell that night; how he found you in the allotment shed.
Why did you go there?

PETER. I was hungry, I wanted to lie down, that's all I could think. I must have panicked in the raid that night. I saw all the people leaving the city.

JUNE. We thought we'd lost you.

PETER. I'm sorry.

JUNE. There's something more isn't there?

PETER. No.

JUNE. Sure?

PETER. What?

JUNE. Tell me.

PETER. I don't want to go, you know.

JUNE. Poor Peter.

PETER. At least Francis can think about his exams.
   I've got nothing.

JUNE. Seventeen, and got nothing!

PETER. Please don't laugh at me.

JUNE. No one's really laughing.

7

JUNE. Today
   When Eric didn't come
   to meet me
   I waited for the bus, not minutes,
   two hours.
   I could have walked in half an hour.
   Everyone had gone,
   I was still there,
   When it never came.

   Now there's no study
   I sit down to write,
   letters to everyone.
   I think
   Most people spend their lives expecting to go on a journey;
   I'll not drown in this
   I walked home.

8

ERIC. She took a great pride in the flowers
   my mother and she did a big display at
   the end of the Great War. In the final
   year she grew these tall blooms; gladioli,
   in golden colours and all the same height.

   Then when I came back she borrowed my
   engineer's protractor to set them, at equal
   angles in wire.

It was to be a sunburst to go behind the altar.

When we got it there the angles were not so fine.

The sun burst skew-whiff behind the altar.

9

ERIC's *mother's house: June.* PETER *and* FRANCIS *are sharing a room. It is late.*

PETER. Last one tomorrow.

FRANCIS. The last one for now.

PETER. How are you?

FRANCIS. Terrible, stomach ache.

PETER. When did it start?

FRANCIS. In the afternoon. I was sitting here revising when it began: points of light, all colours and floating in space.

PETER. Like the flares falling.

FRANCIS. It wasn't in the air though, this was just pinpoints of light. I thought it was on the surface of my eyes, like dust. I splashed my eyes in the sink.

PETER. Perhaps it was the heat.

FRANCIS. I pulled the curtains against the light and it's gone. Now there's this headache and my stomach; it hurts in pulses and the ache keeps building up and fading.

PETER. The exams have not been that bad.

FRANCIS. It was so hot this morning in History I expected my hand to stick to the paper. And I walked out and I thought that's that: done History, forget History now.

PETER. So what have you been doing?

FRANCIS. I've just been lying looking at the cracks in the ceiling. Do you like this room?

PETER. I could be at home here.

FRANCIS. No use feeling that if you're leaving.

PETER. I may not have a home when I get there.

FRANCIS. Best to be at home in the world.
   Then you'll be at home everywhere.

PETER. I like this house a lot, even if it is run down.

FRANCIS. This must be more what you imagined coming to the
   country. Salmon Pool Lane was just the edge of the town.

PETER. It's so quiet here.

FRANCIS. Quiet? Not completely quiet. Listen.

   PETER *listens, then laughs.*

PETER. Apart from birds . . . and the cows, across the road . . . and
   that tree; it's fairly quiet. A lot quieter than my home.

FRANCIS. Home?

PETER. London.

FRANCIS. It must be very different.
   I can't imagine you there.

PETER. Another world, Francis.

FRANCIS. I can't imagine it at all.

PETER. I'll be able to think of you here, in this room in the country.

FRANCIS. That's right, in the country bored to death; in the
   country dying of boredom.

PETER. I think you should stay here.

FRANCIS. But we all have to go away.
   You just like it here because it's different.

PETER. Eric went away and came back.

FRANCIS. Be like Eric, like him!

PETER. I don't see that would be so bad, to be like your own father.

FRANCIS. No fear!

PETER. Watch what you're saying, he's just out there, creosoting
   the fence.

FRANCIS. Is that what the smell is?

PETER. Perhaps you should go then.
   You are just like your father, Francis.

FRANCIS. Would you come back here?

PETER. I'd come, for holidays and retiring.

FRANCIS. Still on about that.

PETER. It happens to us all.

FRANCIS. Like exams.

PETER. Not like exams.

FRANCIS. My stomach, it feels bad.

PETER *puts his hand on* FRANCIS's *forehead.*

PETER. I wish I could make you well.

FRANCIS *takes the hand, looks at it.*

FRANCIS. There's dirt beneath your nails.

PETER. A lot of exams inside your head.

FRANCIS. Your hands are filthy!

PETER. Dig in the day, dig in the night.
It's the story of my life these days.
Earthworks at school and gardening in the evenings.

FRANCIS. Some city boy.

PETER. You know, even though we started so late here Eric says the vegetables will be able to grow.

FRANCIS. And your runner beans? How are they?

PETER. They'll be up the pole!

FRANCIS. Perhaps you'll get to eat some before you leave.

PETER. Francis, why not go to sleep now? You can't do any more tonight.
I'll test you when we walk up the road tomorrow.

FRANCIS. Not long now.

PETER. Just tomorrow to get through.

FRANCIS. Everything will be all right when the exams are over.
I can forget everything then.

PETER. Apart from what we did.

FRANCIS. How do you mean?

PETER. A couple of weeks ago, I thought your mother knew.

FRANCIS. I should have thought that had all settled by now.

PETER. It's been easier for you.

FRANCIS. Leave it. It's all over Peter. Even the raids have stopped.

PETER. I'll never forget what I did.

ERIC *has come in.*

ERIC. You still worrying and moping about all that.

Pause.

I'm going to be fair to you boy. Just a few kind words.
I'm going to say it in front of Francis too so there's no secrets.
Don't turn scared.
That night you never turned up, I went home to find you.

PETER. You knew where I was?

ERIC. I knew you were too keen and I'd seen you taking those
   pieces. I guessed you were somewhere no one would go, larking
   about. Dangerous games, Peter.

FRANCIS. What's this?

ERIC (*to* FRANCIS). No doubt you were mixed up in this too.
   God knows what you were up to exactly.
   Something to do with that school I reckon. Split them and sell
   them round the classrooms as trophies, like shrapnel.

Pause.

Was that it? Near enough the truth?

Pause.

I know you boys.

(To FRANCIS.) Was this your daft idea?

FRANCIS. What are you asking?

PETER (*to* FRANCIS). Can't you shut up!

ERIC. I wouldn't trust either of you two.
   You're lucky, I'm not going to say anything to June about this.
   We don't want to go upsetting your mother now. And you
   (*To* PETER.) can count yourself fortunate, you were nearly out of
   the Force, before you were in.
   Now I'll not be able to trust you again Peter.

Pause.

We don't talk about this, understood.

Pause.

So you see, I knew everything, all along.

(*To* FRANCIS.) Leave it Francis, you can only do your best
tomorrow.
You want to stop getting anxious about these exams.

Pause.

You know your trouble boy: you've got too much fear. (*He goes.*)

FRANCIS *retches.*

FRANCIS. I'm going to be sick.

10

FRANCIS. When I woke at five
the sun had risen.
Last day of exams.
Peter was asleep.
I stood in the glass house
still in nightclothes.
Eric's tomatoes were red
when I ate them.
And the migraine
gone.
I'd like to think
Peter made me well.
But the truth is
it's all gone.

11

ERIC's *mother's house: August.* JUNE *is arranging lupins in a jar.* ERIC
watches.

JUNE. What happened to the summer? That's what I keep asking
myself.

ERIC. I expect Francis ate it along with my tomatoes.

JUNE. You'll get more tomatoes.

ERIC. Those are lovely.
I don't remember them.

JUNE. I found them in the garden.

ERIC. Are they a new sort?

JUNE. Just crossed in the wild I think.

ERIC. What have you been doing?

JUNE. Time to make a start I thought so I've been doing some weeding in the front.

ERIC. That's no way to do it.

JUNE. It's a wilderness that patch.

ERIC. She never touched it when she was on her own in the end. We should start clean.

JUNE. How are we going to do that?

ERIC. Peter and I, we could dig it over, turn all the soil.

JUNE. If I do a little weeding every day it'll be clear enough.

ERIC. The soil needs air, a clean start.

JUNE. There's always going to be weeds, Eric. It's not all weeds.

ERIC. They may not be weeds to you June, you know the names; but to me they're just weeds; that is, apart from the cultivated plants. But if it's what you want we'll do it your way. Obviously we ought to keep the pear trees.

JUNE. There's more than that, some shrubs and perennials too.

ERIC. I was thinking it might be worth moving some things from the garden at Salmon Pool Lane.

JUNE. It would be good to bring plants with us.

ERIC. We should go and have a look to see what the garden's doing there.

JUNE. I don't see why others should have what's left in our garden.

ERIC. Let's go over at the weekend.
Next year this place could be something.

JUNE. I'd love that.

ERIC. We've managed to get more done now that I'm out less evenings.

JUNE. So much has happened since she died.
I can still see the buildings you know.
I walk down South Street and though there's nothing on either

side, I can still see them there, on either side.
I can't even remember Francis taking his exams.

ERIC. There are envelopes out there I see, for both of them.

JUNE. Both at once.

ERIC. That's good.

JUNE. It'll put an end to the waiting.

I shall be glad to see the back of Peter. Having a boy like that
around all the time, it can't have been a good influence on
Francis.

ERIC. Didn't they tell you?

JUNE. What?

ERIC. Francis fell into one of the ricks this week, nearly suffocated
before Peter pulled him out.
Stupid boy.

JUNE. Peter was there first, no doubt.
I never took to him like you did. There was little good in him
coming here, I can't imagine it's been any safer than London.

ERIC. The raids stopped in May but they're still bombing London.

JUNE. I expected a little child, not a great big boy.

ERIC. You would have got your results by now too.

JUNE. If I'd kept on with it.

ERIC. You made the right decision there.

JUNE. Did I?

ERIC. There's been enough on, hasn't there?
Be honest now, you couldn't make head nor tail of it.

JUNE. I might have done.

ERIC. But who needs it?

JUNE. I'd liked to have persevered because I always wondered about
the Anglo-Saxon.

ERIC. How?

JUNE. What it was, I'd like to have known.

ERIC. If you don't know then there's no real loss.

JUNE. I'd like to have made sense of it.

ERIC. Look at it this way June.

JUNE. What?

ERIC. There's nothing around here more Anglo-Saxon than me.

JUNE. Well I've got you then.

He kisses her on the cheek.

ERIC. Is there any tea?

JUNE. It's here.

She lays out two cups and saucers.

ERIC. I wish we didn't have to use those cups.

JUNE. There aren't any others for every day.
They're your mother's.

ERIC. I know. I wish we had some proper ones we could drink out of.

JUNE. Look at them, they're not bad, they're Victorian, that's all.

ERIC. I wouldn't mind them being out on the dresser.
They'd look all right there, for show.

JUNE. No one would see them but us.

ERIC. I'd like a nice plain cup for my tea.

JUNE. Why go on, it's only cups.

ERIC. I don't fancy it June, when I think of all the dead people that have drunk out of these.

JUNE. Eric, why now? Why so fussy?

ERIC. I just noticed I don't like them.

JUNE. Just old cups. An ugly old cup. Look at it, Eric.

An ugly old cup.

She holds one up to the light and drops it.

ERIC. Why did you do that?
I didn't mean you to do that.

JUNE. Too late. An old cup gone.

ERIC *goes to pick up some pieces.*

ERIC. That's nothing really now.

JUNE. That's right, now really nothing.

ERIC. What's up with you?

JUNE. I don't know. I went home the wrong way yesterday, ended
    up at Salmon Pool Lane.

ERIC. Here's another. Let me pour you another cup.

JUNE. It's habitual.

ERIC. What is?

JUNE. This, us, here. Merely habitual.
    There is no reason.

ERIC. This is our home now, we live here.
    We have our son. Smart boy.
    Passed his exams, I bet.
    Eighteen years. You and I.
    Don't cry, June.

    PETER *and* FRANCIS *come in holding envelopes.*

PETER. I got my results and he got his call-up!

FRANCIS. He means I got my results and he got his call-up.

PETER. That's what I said.

FRANCIS (*looks at broken china*). What's this?

JUNE. Well?

FRANCIS. I passed them all.

ERIC. What will you do now then?

PETER (*to* FRANCIS). What shall we do now?

FRANCIS. Hey let's run to the river!

    They run out.

ERIC. They've gone.
    Remember June. (*He sits beside her.*)
    I am here.
    You are here.
    And the ground's beneath our feet.

JUNE. I know only one thing.
    This feeling of loss.
    It's growing.

    He holds her.

PETER. It will be an eventful journey.
   Leaving it all green.
   I know everything's going
   But I'll remember what's growing.

FRANCIS. There are no other colours,
   Do we know what we have?
   There's no use inventing new
   and making sense,
   if there's only loss
   and making non-sense.

LOW LEVEL PANIC ■ CLARE McINTYRE

Clare McIntyre's *I've been Running* was performed at the Old Red Lion in May 1986, directed by Terry Johnson. *Low Level Panic* which was commissioned and presented by the Women's Playhouse Trust was first performed at the Royal Court Theatre Upstairs in February 1988, directed by Nancy Meckler. Her next commission from the Royal Court is *My Heart's a Suitcase* and she is also writing another play for the Women's Playhouse Trust, as yet untitled. Clare McIntyre has an extensive career as an actress in theatre, film and television.

Low Level Panic was first performed on 11 February 1988 at the Royal Court Theatre, London, in association with the Women's Playhouse Trust. The cast was as follows:

JO, twenties	Caroline Quentin
MARY, twenties	Lorraine Brunning
CELIA, possibly older but not much	Alaine Hickmott
TWO MEN (voices only, in Scene Two)	

Directed by Nancy Meckler
Designed by Lucy Weller
Lighting by Stephen Watson
Sound by Christopher Shutt

Setting

The play is set in a bathroom and there are two scenes set outdoors in streets. There is no need to change the set for these scenes: lighting changes are enough. I do not want the set to be totally naturalistic. There needs to be a bath, an armchair, a door, a window that you can easily look out of and throw things out of, and a mirror. Nobody goes to the toilet in the play so there's no need to have a toilet in the set. Added to which it is a household where the toilet is separate from the bathroom.

Scene One

JO *and* MARY *are in the bathroom.* JO *is having a bath.* MARY *is washing her face with a flannel at the washhand-basin. There is a pornographic magazine on the bathroom chair.*

The scene takes place during the morning of a sunny summer's day.

JO. Are you going to tell me?

MARY. What?

JO. What's the matter?

MARY. Nothing.

JO. You've been crying.

MARY. I'm alright.

JO. Don't bottle it up.

MARY. It's nice out. (*She opens the window.*)

JO. Suit yourself.

MARY *sits in the armchair and looks through the magazine.* JO *sings 'Misty'.*

'Look at me
I'm as helpless as a kitten
Up a tree.
Da da di da da di da
Di dum dum di da
I get Misty
Di dum dum di dum.'

Read that bit again.

MARY. Which bit?

JO. The bit you were reading.

MARY. The woman coming all the time?

JO. Yup.

MARY. Why?

JO. Just read it.

MARY. '. . . Well, I fucked her for ages and ages and lost count of the number of orgasms she had. Okay, the rest of my body was falling apart while I was fucking her, but my cock was as powerful as ever . . . blah, blah, blah, blah . . . That woman seemed to be having an orgasm each time I pushed my cock into her and another orgasm each time I pulled it out.' That bit?

JO. Yeah . . . Fancies himself doesn't he?

MARY. Do you get off on it?

JO. It's for men, Mary. You shouldn't be looking at it at all.

MARY. It's a free country.

JO. Why did you buy it?

MARY. I didn't. I found it.

JO. Oh.

MARY. In the bin.

JO. What bin?

MARY. Our bin.

JO. Our bin?

MARY. Mnn.

JO. In our bin?

MARY. Yeah.

JO. Charming.

MARY. It was just sitting there.

JO. Trust you.

MARY. What?

JO. Nothing.

MARY. What?

JO. Well *I* didn't find it did I?

MARY. No.

JO. What's the matter?

MARY. I'm alright.

JO. You've been crying. You're all blotchy.

MARY. I've been in the sun.

JO. Sure?

MARY. Yes. (*Holds up a double spread of the magazine to show* JO.) Look at this . . . Why do blokes get off on this stuff?

JO. Who cares?

MARY. I do.

JO. Why? What's it to you? Bloody nerve.

MARY. What?

JO. I might put old sweetie papers or a bag of orange peel in someone else's bin. I wouldn't ditch garbage like that on someone else.

MARY. What kind of blokes get off on it?

JO. Fuck knows. Maybe they're just fucked up. It's not everyone.

MARY. How do you know?

JO. It's blokes who can't get it together with anyone. Relatively speaking they're from another planet. I wish baths were big enough to float in.

MARY. I'll bet it's more than you think.

JO. That's what I'd do if I was really rich: I'd get a huge bath.

MARY. I'll bet you half the blokes in the world read this stuff.

JO. Sod the water bed: I'd go for a huge bath.

MARY. Are you listening?

JO. Yeah.

MARY. Well?

JO. What?

MARY. It's not just the odd freak. It's half the people you've ever met. Isn't it?

JO. I don't know. How should I know?

MARY. It is. I know it is.

JO. So what?

MARY. 'Long, leggy Barbara reveals all and hopes all you guys out there like what you see.'

JO. 'Course they do.

MARY. She's not that pretty.

JO. She's thin though isn't she?

MARY. Not really.

JO. She's thinner than me.

MARY. How d'you know. You haven't even looked.

JO. I don't have to.

MARY. You're not that fat.

JO. I'm not seventeen either. (*She sings:*)

'She was just seventeen
Well, you know what I mean
And the way she moved
Was way beyond compare.
I couldn't dance with another
Ooooooooo
When I saw her standing there.'

MARY (*looks out of the window*). I wish there was a garden out here at the front of the house.

JO. Ummn.

MARY. Might be quieter.

JO. Than what?

MARY. The back.

JO. Doubt it.

MARY. Might be more peaceful

JO *stretches both her legs vertically out of the bath and looks at them.*

JO. What do you think?

MARY. What?

JO. My legs?

MARY. What about them?

JO. They look really good.

MARY. Why?

JO. Like this.

MARY. Do they?

JO. I think so.

MARY. They don't look any different.

JO. 'Course they do. Don't you look at pictures of yourself upside down?

MARY. No.

JO. I look amazing.

MARY. You're obsessed.

JO. If I could grow six inches and be as fat as I am now I'd be really tall and thin. I could stretch out all the fat on my legs till they were long and slender and I'd go to swanky bars and smoke menthol cigarettes and I'd wrap my new legs round cocktail stools and I'd smooth myself all over with my delicate hands and I'd have my hair up so you could see my neck. I'd save all the pennies I see lying about on the streets in an old whisky bottle then I'd go out and buy silky underwear with lots of lace on it and suspenders and that's what I'd wear. I wouldn't wear anything else because that would spoil it. I'd wear that and a lot of make-up and I'd snake my way around bars and hotels in Mayfair and I'd be able to drink whatever I like. I'd have cocktails and white wine out of bottles with special dates on them in tall glasses that were all dewy with cold and I'd smile a lot. I wouldn't laugh. I wouldn't guffaw. I'd just smile and show my teeth and I'd really be somebody then.

MARY. They wouldn't let you in. You'd have to have a coat.

JO. Some sort of wrap.

MARY. You'd need a coat. A proper coat. Done up.

JO. I'd have a fur. As soon as I got inside I'd take it off.

MARY. In the lounge?

JO. They don't have lounges. Where've you been?

MARY. They do.

JO. They'd see me approach. Just my feet in 'fuck me' stilettos and the door would open like magic and uniformed men would be bowing. They wouldn't look at me: their eyes would be averted. I'd be able to get through doors without even turning the handles.

MARY. Could be like at airports where you just stand there and the doors open.

JO. No. There's nothing glam in that. That's just 'cos people have got luggage.

MARY. You could have a case couldn't you, if you were going to stay over?

JO. No. It's all unplanned. On the spur. That's the whole point. It just happens. I'm just there.

MARY. Could be a revolving door.

JO. It's got to be liveried doormen bowing, moving about like shadows, getting doors opened and stopping taxis. I want all of that.

MARY. You'd have to pay them. They expect tips you know.

JO. Pooh.

MARY. You'd need a lot of money. I'm telling you.

JO. I wouldn't need anything, I wouldn't even have a bag. I'd have my lipstick on a chain round my neck. I'd play with my drink a bit, wiping the dewy bits off the glass and feeling my way up and down the stem with my fingers. Then I'd go to the loo and do my lipstick.

MARY. Then what?

JO. I'd meet someone.

MARY. Who?

JO. Someone.

MARY. He might be gross.

JO. Then I'd meet someone else.

MARY. He might be foreign. Mightn't he? In a place like that.

JO. He might be.

MARY. Could be hard to talk to.

JO. We wouldn't talk. Christ. We'd be really . . . We'd just *be* there.

MARY. He might ask you to dinner and you wouldn't know.

JO. I wouldn't want dinner.

MARY. You might.

JO. No. We'd just drink: play with our drinks and look at each other. We wouldn't really drink them. We wouldn't get pissed. We'd sit while the ice melted in them and they got all watery and we'd look at each other. He'd look at me that is. I'd know he was looking at me and I'd look at myself in the mirror behind the bar. The whole place would be mirrors and he'd be looking at my legs . . . Then we'd leave. People would crash their cars when I got out in the street. There'd be cars jumping over each other to pick me up, men running towards me, desperate to get a closer look and try and touch me, touch my fur. But I wouldn't give anything away. I wouldn't get involved. I'd be wearing sunglasses, enormous, dark ones so they wouldn't see into me. I'd just be an amazing pair of legs, in sunglasses getting into a car.

MARY. A limousine.

JO. Yes. A great big American limousine.

MARY. A Cadillac. A Pontiac. An Oldsmobile.

JO. Maybe just a Jag.

MARY. A Rolls.

JO. Nah. I hate them.

MARY. A Lamborghini.

JO. That'd do.

MARY. A Chevrolet.

JO. I don't know. Some car big enough for eight people across the back seat.

MARY. He'd probably be an American wouldn't he?

JO. Might be.

MARY. Tall. With a moustache.

JO. No moustache, he'd be in a suit.

MARY. Then what?

JO. We'd go to his place.

MARY. You'd have to talk.

JO. Not in the car.

MARY. Sooner or later you'd have to talk.

JO. I can talk.

MARY. He might be a biochemist.

JO. I can talk.

MARY. Not about money and international banking and

horticulture you can't.

JO. There's other things.

MARY. What?

JO. Chit chat.

MARY. What other things?

JO. I don't know . . . the route. The English countryside.

MARY. Pull the other one. You're in a big car with smoky glass windows with an internationally famous, gambling millionaire and all you can talk about is roads and flora and fauna.

JO. He doesn't want me to talk to him.

MARY. Dead right he doesn't.

JO. I can talk.

MARY. What about for God's sake? What about?

JO. I'd be an astonishingly beautiful, mysterious, fascinating woman. The kind of woman men dream about but hardly ever see. I wouldn't need to talk.

MARY. You could put your foot in it though couldn't you?

JO. I could be dumb. I could be a mute. He might like that.

MARY. Yeah, he probably would.

JO. We'd be a beautiful couple.

MARY. A couple of dumbclucks.

JO. But rich.

MARY. Yes.

JO. And glamorous. Going somewhere. Speeding off into the night.

MARY. Where?

JO. I don't know . . . Just somewhere else.

MARY. You might not even like it.

JO. What?

MARY. Having sex with him.

JO. He might have a yacht. I could lounge about and go swimming. I'd dive in off the side of the boat. I'd be really good. I wouldn't have to hold my nose or hang on to the side. I'd go right under with my eyes open, do somersaults and all sorts just to get cool, go right down, dive down a long way and then float back up looking at the bright, bright blue above and my air bubbles bursting on the surface.

MARY. You might not even want to touch him.

JO. I'd climb back on to the boat, dry off, have a Campari and a smoke and listen to the music wafting up from below deck out into the open sunshine.

MARY. You might find him repulsive.

JO. Christ it would be amazing. Christ. Think of it. All that blue and sea.

MARY. He could have a revolting body and push you around.

JO. He might have a sense of humour. There's a chance. We might grow to like each other after a while.

MARY. How do you know?

JO. I don't. I don't know anything do I?

MARY. You'd hate it.

JO. We'd be a glamorous couple with a lot of money and a yacht. I wouldn't mind fucking that.

MARY. It's horrible.

JO. Oh shut up. Stop being such a killjoy. It'd be phenomenal. I'd feel brilliant about myself. I'd get really thin and I'd get tanned all over, even my armpits. That would be my sole occupation, getting tanned without any strapmarks. I'd love every single minute of it.

MARY. Of what?

JO. The life. That kind of life.

MARY. He might give you the creeps.

JO. Well if he did I'd tell him to piss off. The whole point is he wouldn't. I'd fancy him to death.

MARY. How do you know? You wouldn't necessarily.

JO. Oh for Heaven's sake what's got into you today?

MARY. I don't know.

JO. Fucking makes the world go round. It's the only thing that makes being grown-up worthwhile (*She stands up in the bath.*) You've spoilt it.

MARY. It wasn't real.

JO. So what? (*She gets out and dries herself.*)

MARY. You've gone all wrinkled.

JO. The water's cold.

MARY. Celia's going to love you.

JO. Why?

MARY. You've used all the hot water haven't you?

JO. She's going to storm in here any minute with every toiletry in the land and give us advice isn't she?

MARY. Do you think blokes waste as much time worrying about their figures as you do?

JO. Don't talk soft. Men don't have figures. They've got jobs and flash cars and important things to worry about.

MARY. They worry about their looks too.

JO. You don't talk about their legs though do you?

MARY. I don't talk about your legs either.

JO. Exactly. (*She goes off to her bedroom.*)

MARY. How do you know you'd fancy him?

JO (*off*). What?

MARY. How do you know . . .

JO (*off*). I've been eating all day.

MARY. Why?

JO (*off*). I got up this morning and knew I was going to do it. I went downstairs and bit all the handles off the mugs: I was that pissed off.

MARY *starts tearing pages out of the magazine, screwing them up into balls and aiming them out of the window into the dustbin beneath.* JO *is standing in the doorway wearing a towelling bathrobe.* MARY *shouts to her as if she were in the other room.*

MARY. Jo!

JO. What?

MARY. Oh . . . Go and move the bin will you.

JO. I haven't got any clothes on.

MARY. You have.

JO. I haven't.

MARY. Go on.

JO. You go.

MARY. I can't.

JO. Why?

MARY. Oh go on. No one'll see.

JO. Why can't you go?

MARY. I'm doing the aiming.

JO. No.

MARY. GOAL!

JO *gets on to the bathroom scales.*

JO. I'm going to kill myself.

MARY. *And another!*

JO. The trouble is I don't really find my body disgusting enough. That's got to be the answer. If I was stones and stones overweight it would be clear as day. I've always thought that. It's much easier to do big things like realise there's nothing for it but to wire your jaws together and stop eating completely. You could psyche yourself up for that, get religious about it. No, I definitely do not have enough self-loathing. It's either that or I just can't be bothered to face it every day. I want to be so repulsively fat that I can go on a diet and lose the whole lot once and for all. What I can't face is the fact that that's never it. I'm not repulsive but I'm not right either. It's a constant, gnawing, boring distraction. I don't know whether to treat myself or whip myself. Lose a pound and buy a woolly or go to the pictures and eat chocs and indulge how much I hate myself. What a stupid waste of time and effort. I'm not bloody perfect and that's that. (*She is looking at her face in the mirror.*)

MARY. Stop picking. You'll have no face left.

JO. I'm not picking.

MARY. If you were really fat you wouldn't be able to cross your legs would you?

JO. I dunno.

MARY. You wouldn't. You wouldn't be able to cross your legs. You wouldn't be able to bend over and do up your shoes. You'd get all out of breath when you went up the stairs. You're not fat at all.

JO. I feel fat. I feel enormous. I feel ugly and a mess. I don't feel right.

MARY. Do this. (*She crosses her arms in front of her and joins her hands, pushes one elbow through the other one keeping her hands joined. Then she puts her arms over her head still keeping her hands joined.* JO *tries to do it and can't.*) There, all you've got is a fat head.

JO. I've got bunions and an unattractive clitoris.

MARY. How can you have an unattractive clitoris?

JO. I can.

MARY. I want to be somewhere else at Christmas.

JO. Can you get genital herpes on your hand?

CELIA (*off*). Jo? Mary?

JO. What?

CELIA (*off*). There's a deckchair burning in the garden.

JO. What?

CELIA (*off*). Some kids have set fire to one of the deckchairs. Little buggers.

JO. I haven't got any clothes on.

CELIA (*off*). Mary?

MARY. I'm coming. (*She goes out.*)

CELIA (*off*). I've just done my nails.

MARY (*off*). Doesn't matter. I'll go.

CELIA (*off*). Sorry. (CELIA *comes in.*) Little buggers. Honestly what a . . .

JO. What a weird thing to do.

CELIA. It's completely ruined.

JO. Little shits.

CELIA. You've been ages.

JO. Have I?

CELIA. What have you been doing?

JO. Having a wank. Picking my nose. You should have been here.

CELIA. What *has* happened to your face?

JO. Why?

CELIA. I mean . . .

JO. What?

CELIA. I'm sorry.

JO. What's wrong with it?

CELIA. Nothing.

JO. Spots.

CELIA. It isn't really.

JO. Great oozing sores.

CELIA. I shouldn't have said anything.

JO. No, go on: annihilate me completely.

CELIA. What do you use?

JO. What do you mean?

CELIA. To clean your face?

JO. I wash it.

CELIA. You shouldn't.

JO. I'm not dead yet.

CELIA. Never, never, never wash your face.

JO. I know, 'cleanse and moisturise and make a habit of it'.

CELIA. Have you finished?

JO. Ummn? . . . Yes. (*She picks up the magazine and starts browsing through it.*)

CELIA. I just want to . . .

JO. Sure. Go ahead.

CELIA. You know it makes sense.

JO. What does?

CELIA. To look after your skin.

JO. I know. I know.

CELIA. I think you should make the most of yourself. I've got green eyes so I have to be careful. I like to use a powder shadow. Greasy eye make-up just smudges in the creases and you have to repair it all the time. But if you get the right powder it can last all day. It's hard to get a shade that will compliment green eyes you know: you wouldn't believe it but it is. It has to be a brown, obviously, but the dark browns tend to look black which just looks dreadful and the lighter browns are all far too yellow so I can't use them either. And I do think your eye make-up should look subtle. It's so easy to overdo it. But I knew when I'd found the right colour. Oh, I knew straight away. I think you do. No hesitation. To hell with the cost. It was such a relief. Because I do want to make the effort to make the most of myself. I need to. I think you should. You're no good to anyone if you don't like yourself. We're none of us perfect. I don't look like anything at all without make-up.

JO (holding up a double spread of the magazine at CELIA). Do you think she makes the most of herself?

CELIA. I don't know. I . . .

JO. She'd better because she wants to be a model when she grows up.

CELIA. Why don't either of you like me?

JO (reading from the magazine). '. . . . I ended up in bed with all three, in a scrum of arms, legs, fingers, mouths and cunts. Apart from having to pee a few times I had an absolute orgy, poking in hole after hole, being licked and sucked, spraying tits and buttocks with come, whitewashing wombs – I think I came five times, a personal best. I know you think I'm boasting but you did ask. Yours Simon. From Bletchley.' Well, thank you Simon.

CELIA. That's disgusting.

JO. 'Whitewashing wombs'? . . . Men are bloody barmy aren't they? Really.

CELIA. It's disgusting.

JO. No it's not. It's just silly.

CELIA. It's disgusting. He could have AIDS.

JO. Terrific.

CELIA. He could have.

JO. Yeah and he could have killed his Granny the night before and he could die in two years time of sclerosis of the liver and one of the girls could have . . .

MARY *comes back on. She stands in the doorway.*

Well?

MARY. I just stood and watched. I couldn't do anything.

CELIA. Never mind.

MARY. I was too late. It's all spoilt. The canvas bit has gone completely and it's just smouldering round the edges now. I've ruined it.

CELIA. It was past saving anyway.

MARY. Why did he have to choose our bin? I mean why don't people leave me alone? Why do they have to include me in their horrible, messy lives? I don't want to look at that stuff. I don't want to think about it. I don't want to get involved. It's got nothing to do with me has it? What's it got to do with me? I don't want to listen to those two opposite rowing either. Why don't they shut the window if they want to have a row? Why don't they shut the window when they're having sex and when they're hitting each other and screaming? Why don't people keep themselves to themselves? Why can't they keep their gross, messy, ugly lives private? What are you meant to do on a lovely sunny day? Sit hiding under the bedclothes? How do you get a bit of peace? All I wanted to do was sit in the garden and daydream in the sun for a while. Is that such a lot to ask for? I can't bear listening to that stuff. I don't want to hear it. It's got nothing to do with me: all their worry about money and how much they hate each other. What's it got to do with me? I can't make head or tail of any of it and it's such a lovely day for England we should all be out there having fun.

CELIA. It doesn't matter Mary. We can easily get another deckchair. We could get one this afternoon.

MARY. I get so bloody confused. I didn't know I was doing any damage. I didn't plan to set fire to it. I was just sitting there watching this cigarette burn. I couldn't smoke it with all that going on. All I could do was sit there and try not to listen, and try not to think about it and try not to try and make sense of it and try to daydream about a quiet life in the sun. But they won't let me.

They interfere all the time. Why me? Why my dustbin? Why my garden? Why doesn't it all just disappear and leave me alone?

JO. I knew you were in a state. Why wouldn't you say?

MARY. Say what?

JO. What's going on inside your head Mary? What are you doing looking at this stuff if it upsets you? (*She throws the magazine out of the window into the bin below.*)

MARY. I've got to.

JO. Why?

MARY. Because that is how I feel.

JO. What is?

MARY. A thing. I'm a thing.

JO. Nobody's a thing.

MARY. We're all just things to fuck.

CELIA. That man opposite does say the most awful things.

MARY. 'Are you going to suck it or fuck it or what?' I don't want to listen to that.

CELIA. Quite.

JO. Who does?

MARY. It's the whole world, the whole world of men obsessed with schoolgirls' knickers. (*She goes out.*)

Pause.

CELIA. I remember walking up the hill from the station with my friend Beverley Stratton. We must have been about twelve and we found this pornographic magazine on the pavement. So we took it into the woods. We didn't say much but we were everso excited. It was really cheap and nasty, pages and pages of it. It was like a very, very cheap outsize paperback: very cheap print that makes your hands all grubby, like newspaper, all black and white and murky.

I remember us staring at this thing, looking at it for ages. The pictures were all of women in black underwear: black bras, black suspender belts, black fishnet stockings. Some of them weren't even wearing that much. And they all had fantastic long hair. masses of it. And they were wearing those shoes with huge platform soles and high, high heels. And they were playing around with these feather boas. They looked like they were pretending to tie each other up or something . . . There weren't any men in the pictures. I don't remember there being any men, at all.

So we looked at this thing for ages . . . and then we buried it.

JO. Well, muck's good for the garden isn't it?

Blackout.

Scene Two

One evening at midnight some weeks earlier. MARY enters wheeling her bicycle. She is wearing a summer skirt and blouse and has a luminous plastic belt around her waist. There are lights on the bicycle both front and back. There is a bicycle lock round the handlebars and another one round the seat pillar. MARY holds onto the bicycle throughout the scene.

There are two men in the scene but they will only be heard, they will not be seen. They are indicated in the script only as A and B. This scene takes place at midnight in a street which is now deserted. The only light is street light.

MARY. Maybe if I'd been wearing trousers it wouldn't have happened. I was only wearing a skirt because I'd just come from work and it's the kind of place where they like you to wear a skirt, that or smart trousers. Well I haven't got any smart trousers so I have to wear a skirt. You're better off on a bike in trousers I know. It's obvious. But it's not as if I was going on a marathon. It takes ten minutes to cycle home at the outside. More like five. If that. I'm not really comfortable on a bike in a skirt: it just makes people look at your legs. But who's around at that time of night to look? Anyway I wasn't even on the bike: I was *going* to get on it. I was going to. It's not as if I was cycling along with my skirt up round my ears. I wasn't. I don't do silly things like that. I could have been getting into a car in a skirt. Would that have made a difference? I could have cycled to work wearing a pair of jeans and had my skirt folded up in one of the panniers but then it would have been all squashed and that wouldn't have gone down well at all with the management. Or I could have come to work on the bicycle wearing a skirt and could have changed into trousers to go home given that you're meant to be alright in the daylight but you're not safe at night. Or I could have walked to work and got a taxi home and I could have worn whatever I liked. But I'd still have been there, on the edge of the road at midnight, about to get on my bicycle or into a car or just been stuck there waiting for a taxi whether I'd been in a skirt or not, whether I had good legs or not, whether I was fifteen or menopausal or lame, I'd still have been there.

MARY *switches on the bicycle lights, front and back. She then fumbles with her keys undoing one of the locks. As she is doing this A speaks.*

A. Is this your bike?

MARY. Yes.

A. Is it?

MARY. What?

A. Your bike?

MARY. Yes.

A. It's nice.

MARY. Yes.

A. It's a nice bike.

B. I'd like a bike like that.

MARY *laughs.*

MARY. Mnn.

A. Are you going to give us a ride?

MARY. I can't.

A. Why not?

MARY. Sorry?

A. Let me have a go on it.

MARY. I'm going home.

B. Give him a go.

MARY. I'm going home.

A. Go on.

MARY. It's late.

A. Will you give him a go on it tomorrow?

MARY. I don't know.

B. Give us a go.

MARY. I'm going home.

A. It's a nice bike.

MARY. Look I'm sorry I'm . . .

B. She's going home.

A. The lady's going home.

MARY. Yes.

A. You live round here?

MARY. Not far.

A. Where do you live?

MARY. It takes about five minutes.

B. Do you ride fast?

MARY. I don't know.

B. I'll bet you ride fast don't you?

A. It's a nice bike.

MARY. Yes.

B. You could ride fast couldn't you?

A. Where do you live?

MARY. Not far.

A. Where?

   MARY *doesn't answer.*

B. You got lights?

MARY. Yes.

B. Can I have a look?

MARY. What?

B. I just want to have a look.

MARY. They're the same as any others.

B. I only want a look.

A. Give him a look.

MARY. What for?

B. I'll give it back.

MARY. I need it now.

A. What kind of a lock's that?

MARY. I don't know.

A. Can I have a look?

MARY. I'm going home.

A. Why have you got two locks?

MARY. So it doesn't get nicked.

B. Do you think we're going to nick it?

MARY. I don't know. Are you?

A. Where are you from?

MARY *doesn't answer.*

A. Eh?

B. You're not English are you?

MARY. Yes.

B. You don't sound English.

MARY. Don't I?

A. You're Swedish or something aren't you?

MARY. No. I'm English.

B. You don't look English.

A. Where are you from?

B. You look Swedish or German or something.

MARY. Well I'm English. I come from England.

A. You been working?

MARY. Yes.

B. You been with your boyfriend?

MARY. No. I've been working.

B. She's been fucking her boyfriend.

MARY. Can I . . .

A. Look at this.

MARY *lets go of her bicycle. It crashes to the floor. The man behind her*

*puts his hands on her hips and pushes his fingers up her vagina. The
other hand rides up her body onto her breasts. The actress should enact
these things using her own arms and hands. The movements are forceful
and deliberate. The actress should carry out these actions until is is crystal
clear that she is not being felt in a tentative way but is being sexually
assaulted. She then holds her arms away from herself, disassociating
herself from what is happening to her and screams. She is screaming for
everything: to be helped: to release her anger and her fear.*

Blackout

Scene Three

*A little time after Scene One. CELIA enters carrying her towel and
spongebag. She shuts and locks the door. She crosses and closes the window.
She takes various things out of her spongebag in preparation for her bath.
She checks that the bath is clean. She decides that it isn't. She gets the liquid
bath cleaner and cloth and is about to set about cleaning the bath when there
is a knock at the door.*

CELIA. Yes.

JO. Sorry Celia I think I've used all the hot water.

CELIA. Oh no.

JO. Sorry . . . You can have a bath this evening can't you?

CELIA. Yes but . . .

JO. Sorry.

CELIA. Honestly you might have . . .

JO. Sorry.

CELIA. Oh that's alright . . . Jo, do you think I could . . . Jo? .. .

*There is no answer. The lights fade as CELIA gathers her bath things
together and returns them to her spongebag.*

Scene Four

*One night. JO is sitting in the armchair. She is wearing a pair of men's
stripy, baggy pyjamas. She sits with her legs tucked up and her arms round
them.*

JO. I sometimes wish I could tell someone that sometimes I just come home, go upstairs and masturbate. I might roam around the kitchen a bit first, pick at a couple of things, have a look in the fridge. Sometimes I'll find myself checking out the house. I'll be in someone else's room for no reason at all, 'cept I suppose to see they're not there: looking for signs. I'm not nosey really. I'd never read anyone's letters.

I like to go upstairs and take all my clothes off and get under the bedcovers. I close the curtains but not completely. I like to see the daylight creep through. I lie there and think about what my body is like and about being somewhere else: somewhere hot and abroad. But my body feels soft and cool. I'm not sweaty at all. I'm quite, quite cleaned and perfumed.

I think about hitchhiking in a flowery skirt and a very sexy top and wedge canvas shoes that have ties round the ankles. I always imagine my body a different shape to the way it is. I'm always very thin and light and what I think people think is the most desirable thing possible.

I always get picked up by two men in a lorry. I've tried imagining other things like military uniforms and all that but I don't get so whooped up about it. No, I get in this lorry and it's quite clear what the atmosphere is straight away. Then I'll do something provocative like shut my eyes and be half asleep and the bloke who isn't driving starts making love to me and it's all incredibly fast in my imagination and we get into the back bit of the lorry where they sleep at night and we make love as if we adore each other.

There's never a moment of worry. The men are never mean or anything. They both just want to make love to me. It's all very serious and passionate. I think they are very male. I don't really know what that means but . . . The one who's driving must stop driving because then he is there as well and then it gets muddled because I think I've really had enough but I like to think of him watching us.

Then that's it. It never ends. There's no conclusion. We don't introduce each other and drive on. I mean I've never worked out what happens then. I've never had to. It just ends and I start thinking about something else.

I try to think about something else but I usually feel upset. I always feel upset actually and I'll hang on to my pillow and wrap myself in the sheet and cry a bit. Then I'll get up and wash my face and think 'Thank God no one knows what I think.'

I don't feel guilty. No one knows what goes on inside your head anyway. I just feel sad about everything that I do not have.

But it's awful to think like that. Isn't it? I mean it's completely untrue for a start. I've never actually felt that in my life. I haven't often hitched rides from lorry drivers on my own but when I have I haven't felt like touching them. I haven't really felt anything at all other than scared and thankful that they weren't trying to do anything.

I can't imagine for the life of me what I thought I was doing when I was hitchhiking. I think now I must have been mad. I could have got myself killed.

JO *remains sitting there while the lights fade to a recording of the Evening Prayer 'When At Night I Go To Sleep' from Humperdinck's opera* Hansel and Gretel, *sung in English. The last part of the song is in darkness during which she goes out.*

When At Night I Go To Sleep
When at night I go to sleep
Fourteen angels watch do keep
Two stand here beside me
Two stand there to guide me
Two are on my right hand
Two are on my left hand
Two more come to wake me
Two more come to take me
Two more gently beckon
And light the path to Heaven

Scene Five

Early evening in the present, i.e. later in the day of Scenes One and Three. MARY *enters wearing a party dress. She is virtually ready to go out but is making the finishing touches.*

JO (*off*). Mary!

MARY. What?

JO. Where are you?

MARY. In here.

JO. Are you dressed?

MARY. Yeah.

JO. Put some music on.

MARY (*going out*). Like what?

JO (*off*). Something boppy.

MARY (*off*). What?

JO (*off*). Anything.

MARY (*off*). Name something.

JO (*off*). Anything. Use your head.

JO *comes in. She is also in her party gear. Both women are dressed in things they have bought specifically to go out in.* JO *is also nearly dressed and doing the finishing touches.* MARY *has put on a record: it is something good to dance to.* JO *has painted her nails and the varnish is drying.*

Shit. I meant to do my toes . . . Louder! . . . . Mary . . . Turn it up.

JO *goes out.* MARY *turns up the music. It is incredibly loud.* JO *comes back on with a mirror which she props up against the bathroom wall.* MARY *comes in.*

MARY. How do I look?

JO. What?

MARY *goes out to turn down the music. She comes back on.*

MARY. What do you think?

JO. Brilliant.

MARY. Do I need anything else?

JO. It suits you down to the ground.

MARY. Do you think?

JO. I *know* it does.

MARY. Doesn't it need something round the neck?

JO. No. It looks exactly right as it is. Don't play around with it.

MARY. I don't know I like it.

JO. Oh Mary don't say that. We spent hours finding it.

MARY. I know.

JO. You liked it in the shop.

MARY. I know.

JO. You did didn't you?

MARY. Yes.

JO. So what's happened?

MARY. I don't know.

JO. It's just 'cos it's not what you're used to buying.

MARY. Ummn.

JO. But it looks terrific on you.

MARY. I don't know.

JO. Honestly.

MARY. I thought I might . . .

JO. It suits you. Believe me.

MARY. I'd never have bought it if you hadn't been there.

JO. I know. You wouldn't even have tried it on.

MARY. Would you wear it?

JO. I couldn't get into it could I?

MARY. These shoes are killing me. No wonder you never wear them.

JO. Take them off when you get there. You won't want to dance in them anyway will you? No one in their right mind dances with their shoes on . . . You should have worn them round the house, broken them in a bit.

MARY. Haven't you ever worn them?

JO. Yes . . . No. They're too small.

MARY. Were they expensive?

JO. Not really.

MARY. They look expensive.

JO. I know. I love them.

MARY. Christ! (*She takes one off.*)

JO. Put bits of plaster on where they hurt.

MARY. They're killing me. I can't walk.

JO. They're flattering though. They make your feet look right. If I get shoes that make my feet look small they make me look enormous. Those look perfect on me and I can't bloody walk in them.

MARY. They're agony.

JO. Are they?

MARY. Ummn.

JO. Shit . . . Seriously?

MARY. I think so.

JO. They're not too small are they?

MARY. I don't think so. They just hurt.

JO. Where?

MARY. Here.

JO. Stick bits of cotton wool in there. They'll soften up. So long as they're not too small you'll be alright.

MARY. No they're not too small. They're definitely not too small.

JO. They'll soften up. All you've got to do is stand around in them.

MARY. They're the right sort of thing aren't they?

JO. They're perfect.

MARY. I'll just have to grin and bear it then.

JO. Take some cotton wool with you in case. We look brilliant.

MARY. Yeah.

JO. Fucking ace.

MARY. Mnn.

JO. We'll knock 'em dead.

MARY. Ummn . . . Do you like the colour?

JO. Oh God yes. You can wear stuff like that . . . I don't look right in a mirror.

MARY. You look fine.

JO. Do I?

MARY. Yeah. You look great.

JO. Sure?

MARY. Yes. Now stop looking at yourself or you'll start wanting to change everything.

JO. Right . . . This really is what you need you know. You need to get yourself out of yourself, forget who you are and have a good time . . . *Do* I look alright in this?

MARY. 'Course you do.

JO. Do I?

MARY. Yeah.

JO. I'm not sure.

MARY. Well if it's not comfortable don't wear it.

JO. It is comfortable. I mean it fits. I got the right size. It's not too small. I just don't know I like it . . . on me. Does it make me look attractive?

MARY. I don't know. It looks nice though.

JO *goes out to turn up the music.* MARY *stays looking at herself in the mirror.*

MARY. Jo!

JO (*off*). What?

MARY. Come here a minute.

JO (*off*). Where's your perfume?

MARY. Come in here.

JO (*comes back on*). Where is it?

MARY. I don't want to go.

JO. What?

MARY. Really I don't.

JO. Why?

MARY. I feel sick.

JO. You look really nice.

MARY (*takes her dress off and sits down holding it*). I hate it.

JO. You can take the shoes off when you get there.

MARY. It's not the shoes.

JO. You've got to go.

MARY. I haven't.

JO. You can't.

MARY. I can.

JO. But why?

MARY. You go.

JO. For fuck's sake. (*She goes out.* MARY *shouts after her. She turns off the music.*)

MARY (*as* JO *comes in with a bottle of wine*). I feel like a tart. I feel disgusting.

JO. You don't look like a tart.

MARY. I feel it.

JO. What's a tart anyway?

MARY. I don't know.

JO. You don't look like a tart. You look French.

MARY. So what?

JO. Why didn't you say any of this in the shop?

MARY. I can never think straight in clothes shops . . . You can see straight through it.

JO. You can't. You can't see anything. I'd have told you.

MARY. We're going to walk down the street and get whistled at by blokes who'd stick their fingers up your vagina as soon as look at you and they don't even know who I am.

JO. We'll get a taxi.

MARY. I feel like somebody else.

Pause.

JO. Those blokes were dickheads. It was just one of those things. It's never happened before. It won't happen again. And why let it wreck this evening?

MARY. They're not just anything. They're out there in their thousands and their heads are full of rubbish and you don't know who the hell they are.

JO. You can't stop yourself having fun. It'll drive you mad.

MARY. I am mad.

JO. You're not. You're screwed up. We're all screwed up.

MARY. What's the point? What are we going for?

JO. Fun.

MARY. What fun?

JO. Anything.

MARY. Like what?

JO. Oh come on.

MARY. What?

JO. What the hell do you go to parties for? You know.

MARY. Yes.

JO. Have a bop. Meet someone.

MARY. It's all the same thing.

JO. It's not the same thing. They were stupid idiots.

MARY. Why me?

JO. Because you were there.

MARY. My body was there but I was somewhere else.

JO. You were alright though weren't you? Nothing broken? Nothing spoilt?

MARY. No.

JO. They wanted to frighten you.

MARY. I wasn't frightened.

JO. Take the piss out of you.

MARY. I was angry.

JO. Right.

MARY. I was terrified.

JO. They didn't know what they were doing.

MARY. I wouldn't know them if I passed them in the street.

JO. It's not everyone: not by a million miles it's not everyone.

MARY. I don't even dress up much.

JO. That's got nothing to do with it. You've just got to be born female.

MARY. Great.

JO. You're one in a million.

MARY. Everyone's one in a million.

JO. It won't happen again.

MARY. What if they'd had a knife?

JO. They didn't . . . Now something nasty's happened to you it'll happen to someone else next.

MARY. It wasn't nasty enough.

JO. You might fall out of a helicopter next, get drowned in a boat. Why worry?

MARY. I'm a sitting duck.

JO. You've sailed along so far.

MARY. I'm going to sit in this bathroom for the rest of my life and go out every so often for a sandwich. (JO *crosses to the door.*) Where are you going?

JO. I'm going to watch telly: some American rubbish with people in big cars who live by the sea. (*She goes out.*)

MARY. Fat lot of good that'll do you. (*She takes a couple of large swigs from the wine bottle, which she hangs onto for the rest of the scene.*)

JO (*coming in*). If you don't come to this party I'll kill you.

MARY. It was because I was dressed up.

JO. We've been over this before Mary: you weren't dressed up.

MARY. I was more dressed up than usual.

JO. You were wearing a skirt.

MARY. For me I was dressed up.

JO. You weren't dressed up at all. You never dress up. And what if you were?

MARY. I remember being all dolled up.

JO. I can't remember ever seeing you all dolled up.

MARY. I am now.

JO. Apart from now I don't.

MARY. I was wearing those enamel bracelets I've got. I can't remember why . . . but I was looking nice. I know I was. I just felt it. Sometimes you do feel that don't you? Sometimes you just know you're looking okay. It's not like I was looking like anything in particular. I just felt nice. That's more it. I'd felt nice when I'd been cycling to work: all cool and breezy. I don't remember what I looked like but I remember how I felt.

JO. But you weren't dressed up.

MARY. I wasn't concentrating.

JO. You weren't.

MARY. No.

JO. You always wore a skirt didn't you?

MARY. Had to.

JO. You were just dressed ordinary.

MARY. They didn't think so.

JO. Boys like that don't think, not with their brains that is. They might think a bit with their dicks but not with their brains they don't. Not at all. They don't even know where their brains are.

MARY. I'm sure I was looking nice . . . for me, that is.

JO. You are nice looking.

MARY. I must have been looking sexy but I didn't know it. They must have thought I was looking all dressed up and sexy.

JO. What's wrong with looking sexy?

MARY. I want to look like I feel.

JO. You do. You must do. You just look natural.

MARY. Not in a bloody party dress I don't. Not all done up in a party dress. It makes me feel like I did then, all flimsy and open and . . .

JO. And women love it.

MARY. What?

JO. Being sexy.

MARY. Do they?

JO. 'Course they do.

MARY. And what's being sexy?

JO. Oh come on.

MARY. Feeling like this?

JO. Yes. What's wrong with that?

MARY. It feels horrible.

JO. Why can't you enjoy it?

MARY. Because . . .

JO. You won't let yourself will you? Just relax.

MARY. I'm trying.

JO. You've got to feel good about yourself or nothing'll happen.

MARY. Nothing like what?

JO. I'm going to count to ten and then I'm going to *scream*.

MARY. So this looks sexy does it? (*Holding her dress up against her.*)

JO. 'Course it does . . . No, it doesn't. It doesn't look sexy at all. Okay?

MARY. No. I feel like someone else. I feel funny and peculiar and a million miles from confident and that's fine and terrific and just as it should be and I'm to go out and enjoy myself. Right?

JO. Yes.

MARY. That's what you want me to do?

JO. Yes. 'Cos you will. You're just nervous. I'm nervous for Heaven's sake.

MARY. Are you?

JO. Yes. No.

MARY. Which?

JO. I don't know.

MARY. But what . . .

JO. Stop asking questions. You'll disappear up your own bum.

MARY. I think I'm in a coma.

JO. Well rally round or we'll be late.

MARY. 'Pornography's the tip of the iceberg.' Somebody said that.

JO. Oh my God. Cut my wrists. Cut my wrists.

MARY. They were right.

JO. And we've all got to learn to live with it.

MARY. I can't . . .

JO. In the course of a day, a day without too much effort put into it you'll see more pictures of naked breasts than you will naked bollocks. Breast for breast, bollock for bollock, breasts will come out on top.

MARY. Is that . . . ?

JO. Try and stop thinking for once will you? For five minutes, however long it's going to take you to get yourself out of this house and on to the street. (*She goes out.*)

MARY (*has to shout to be heard*). What matters then? Things do matter, you know. We've got to understand why we think whatever it is we do think otherwise how are we meant to live with ourselves? I mean that's what we are. We are what we think about things.

JO enters carrying her coat – ready, apart from final touches of make-up, to leave.

Most of the time you know what you think. You know if you like oranges or not or what you feel like having for tea. But none of that matters. And you can't say that everything that does matter somehow has got nothing to do with you 'cos it has got something to do with you whether you like it or not. It has. 'Cos we're all alive and we all walk down the street and see things and you can't pretend those things don't get inside your head somehow because they do. Even if you're not aware of it they do. So they're there for you to make sense of. You've got to decide what you feel about them and you can't just say you feel whatever it is you do just because that's the way you do because that isn't true. You're not born thinking the way you think. Things happen which make you think like that. You're making decisions all the time even if what you're deciding to do is not to think about something. That's a decision. I mean there are some people who don't think they think at all, who think they're just thick, but they are thinking because all that stuff they see is getting into their heads just like it's getting into mine. It's part of them like it's part of you and me. It's there for them to think about. It's hopeless to say you don't have to think about things because you do. You've got to.

JO. You're pissed aren't you?

MARY. Yup.

JO. Aren't you?

MARY. Yup.

JO. Coming?

MARY. Yup.

JO. Bloody liability.

MARY. Yup.

CELIA *comes in, also in her party gear.*

CELIA. Right. I'm ready. (*Seeing* MARY *not yet dressed.*) Aren't you coming?

Blackout.

Sound cue: Some boppy, party music. The lights come up. MARY, JO *and* CELIA *observe themselves in three imagined mirrors straight out front.*

The light and the music fade and the characters go out.

Scene Six

A road. Early one evening. MARY *comes in wearing the clothes she was wearing in the previous scene plus a jacket. The light is fading daylight and street lights. At the top of the scene there needs to be the sound of traffic. This should fade to almost inaudible as* MARY *speaks.*

MARY. I was walking past a poster one day.

It was an absolutely huge poster.

It was like the size of one of those ones that's on the way out to the airport, you know, like, like for Concorde or something.

But it wasn't sort of long across it was long upright.

And it looked ever so weird 'cos it just sort of stood out of the skyline.

And I just stopped and looked at it. I suppose it was advertising something but I didn't really see that. I just saw what it was, what was in the picture.

And there was a gorilla in the picture and he was holding on to a woman in a bikini.

He had one hand through her legs and gripping on to a thigh and his other arm was right round her and clutching on to her ribs and he had one thumb which was sort of half pulling off her bikini top.

And I looked at the woman and she looked like she was just mucking about really, you know, she, you know, her arms were just sort of thrown up in the air and her body was all sort of shiny. It didn't look like it was wet. It just looked like it had years and years of suntan oil on it. She was hairless and shiny and silky, like she would, you know, tall and thin.

And I looked at her and then I looked at her face.

And she had absolutely no expression at all.

There was no expression on her face at all.

I couldn't detect any expression.

I couldn't see that she was looking like anything.

At all.

She just, she didn't, it wasn't, she wasn't scared, she wasn't aroused. She just didn't look like anything at all.

She didn't even look as if she was in a daze.

And then I looked . . .

Her body. She didn't in her body look like anything at all either.

She didn't look like she was trying to get away. She just looked like she was posing there and the gorilla was holding on to her.

And I just wanted to ask her what she felt. I really, really wanted to ask her what she felt.

So I got into the picture. I walked up to it and as I got close to it I realised it was one of those relief pictures.

And I climbed up on the hoarding that was beneath it and I got my feet on her feet. And actually when I was close up to it it was absolutely huge. It was really big. I mean as I was standing up, you know, I got to about her kneecap.

So I climbed up on this picture and I was standing on her knees and I could just use all the relief bits to get me right up. And as I got towards the top I had to hold on to the gorilla's hand and I was levering myself up and finally I was standing on her breast and hanging on to her neck and then I got one knee on one of her shoulders.

And as I got up there I was face to face with her and her eyes were absolutely huge and they were com . . . they weren't focused. I wasn't sc . . . scared because they weren't focused. They weren't looking at me. I don't, I don't think they were looking at anything at all.

And as I got up there her head gently fell back and her mouth opened.

So I pulled myself up on both of her shoulders and looked into her mouth. And I just screamed and screamed and I nearly just fell off the picture because inside there wasn't anything at all.

She was completely empty.

And all I could see was the gorilla's thumb stuck through her crotch and he was wiggling it.

And as I looked away her head came back upright and her eyelids closed and opened and they were exactly like a doll's when you tilt the head of a doll back the eyelids open and shut.

Well I got off and on to the ground as fast as I could.

In some ways I was, I felt a lot happier they hadn't used anyone real to make the picture.

MARY *goes out.*

Blackout.

Scene Seven

Later that night after the party. JO *comes in to the bathroom which is in virtual darkness. Any light there is in the room is coming through the window from outside as the light in the room itself is out.* JO *switches on the light to reveal* MARY *kneeling beside the bath with both her arms in the tub. She is wearing daytime clothes and has on a pair of rubber gloves.* JO *is still in her party clothes.*

JO. Jesus Christ you gave me a fright!

MARY. Hello.

JO. What are you doing?

MARY. Umnn?

JO. What are you doing?

MARY. Seeing what my sheets'll look like in the dark.

JO. What?

MARY. I'm just seeing what my sheets'll look like in the dark.

JO. What on *earth* are you doing?

MARY. I'm dyeing my sheets.

JO. Bloody Hell. (*She goes out switching off the light as she does.* MARY *swirls the sheets round.* JO *comes back. She has changed into her slippers.*) Do you know what time it is?

MARY. No.

JO. It's the middle of the bloody night.

MARY. Is it?

JO. Just thought I'd mention it.

MARY. I couldn't sleep.

Pause.

JO. God I always do it. I always bloody do it. I always guffaw at parties. Always. I don't know why I can't seem to keep a check on myself. I can't seem to see what a twit I'm being until I'm out on the street, on my own, on my way home. Then I have instant, total recall of every stupid, awful, embarrassing thing I said . . . I wish I didn't have such a loud laugh. It's deafening. Even in a room full of people shouting it's deafening. I can't seem to keep quiet and enigmatic and let other people do the approaching. But what if nobody does? What then? What if everyone avoids me all evening . . . ? Nobody talks more than me at parties. As soon as I feel unrelaxed my mouth opens and out come a million questions. I just come across as terribly, terribly interested in everyone there. That's why people want me to go to their sodding parties. At least I'll talk. Am I terribly loud?

MARY. No.

JO. Do I act the fool?

MARY. I don't think so. (*She holds up her party dress out of the bath. She has been dyeing it along with the sheets.*) What do you think?

JO. Is that your . . ?

MARY. Yeah. I've dyed it.

JO. So I see.

MARY. What do you think?

JO. You've ruined it.

MARY. Why?

JO. Look at it.

MARY. I haven't ruined it.

JO. What have you gone and done that for?

MARY. I didn't like it.

JO. Ask a silly question get a silly . . .

MARY. It's a nice colour isn't it?

JO. What are you trying to prove?

MARY. What do you mean?

JO. That we shouldn't have bought it?

MARY. No.

JO. Sure?

MARY. Yes. I'm not trying to prove anything.

JO. Aren't you?

MARY. No.

JO. It might be a nice colour. You can't really tell when it's wet . . . (*Feeling her armpits.*) God I'm sweating. There's a swamp up here. Was I sweating like this all evening?

MARY. I'm going to wear it with a sweatshirt over it. It'll just look like a skirt.

JO. I must have been sweating non stop. Look at the tidemarks.

MARY. It'll look alright.

JO. That's nerves you know.

MARY. What is?

JO. Sweating like this.

MARY. Is it?

JO. You should have got someone to do it properly if you wanted to do it. You can never get the colour even yourself and it's 'dry clean only' isn't it?

MARY. I don't know. I didn't look.

JO. That sort of thing always is.

MARY. Never mind.

JO. I'd never have let you buy it if I'd known you'd ... .

MARY. God I'll wear it now. I'd never have worn it again like it was.

JO. I really thought you'd wear it.

MARY. No way. Clingy party dresses aren't really my thing are they?

JO. They could be.

MARY. I'm going to look like I feel, not like someone else's idea of what they think I'm feeling like.

JO. Come again.

MARY. Ummn?

JO. You're going to look like your idea . . .

MARY. If you're comfy in jeans and a T-shirt wear jeans and a T-shirt. Why make yourself miserable trying to be something you're not?

JO. Ah yes. Now that sounds more like it.

MARY. More like what?

JO. You *are* trying to make a point.

MARY. Who to? I've dyed the dress so I'll wear it because I'd never have worn it how it was because I don't like wearing things that make me feel naked.

JO. Did you hate it?

MARY. What?

JO. The party?

MARY. It was okay.

JO. What you don't like in the world isn't going to go away because you go and do something weird like dye a party dress.

MARY. Why are you trying to turn this into some kind of big gesture?

JO. Well it is isn't it?

MARY. No.

JO. It looks like a big gesture to me.

MARY. Why?

JO. 'Cos it's such a bizarre thing to be doing. It's the middle of the night and you're sloshing this stuff around in the bath, in the dark and you've gone and deliberately ruined a very nice dress.

MARY. Will you stop saying that. It's going to look fine. You wait.

JO. It is a weird thing to do though you must admit.

MARY. I suppose so.

JO. I mean I don't usually come back from a party and throw my dress into a bath full of dye.

MARY. Nor do I.

JO. I suppose it might look alright with a sweatshirt.

MARY. It will. I know it will. (*She wrings the dress out and puts it on a hanger.*)

JO. Well I did my best. I got you all glammed up and looking fabulous and . . .

MARY. Oh I enjoyed the party. I mean it was alright. I didn't hate it or anything. 'Cept there wasn't any food.

JO. You only stayed ten minutes.

MARY. No I didn't. Honestly I stayed . . .

JO. Twenty.

MARY. Did you enjoy it?

JO. I didn't meet anyone if that's what you mean. Nothing happened. I don't know if anyone met anyone but I know I didn't. There didn't seem to be anyone there that I could see: nobody that you'd want to . . .

MARY. No.

JO (*inspecting her face in the mirror*). People are different now aren't they? Maybe parties aren't where you meet people any more.

MARY. It was very loud.

JO. Maybe you've got to join a club or have hobbies or something. It's weird to think about isn't it?

MARY. What?

JO. Whether to be worried or not . . . Whether to do it or not. Mind you I don't know what I'm talking about 'cos there wasn't anyone there to do it with was there?

MARY. Now admit it it looks alright.

JO. Maybe.

MARY. Not a streak in sight.

JO. No but it's shrunk.

MARY. Has it?

JO. But you'll wear it. I can see you wearing it. You've gone and wrecked it but you'll wear it won't you?

MARY. Yup.

JO. And you're happy now aren't you?

MARY. Yup.

JO. It's still a shame.

MARY. I don't think so.

JO. You looked so good in it. (*She is inspecting her face in the mirror.*)

MARY. Where would you be without a mirror?

JO. Dunno.

MARY. You'd really be at a loose end wouldn't you?

JO. Shut your trap. You're getting as bad as Celia.

MARY. She met someone.

JO. What?

MARY. She met someone.

JO. How do you know?

MARY. She came back with him.

JO. How do you know?

MARY. She did.

JO. You're kidding.

MARY. Sh.

JO. Jesus.

MARY. Shh.

JO. *Jesus.*

MARY. Shut up.

JO. Who?

MARY. I don't know. Some bloke.

JO. Who?

MARY. How should I know?

JO. I don't believe it . . . Really . . ? You're taking the piss.

MARY. Yes. Really.

JO. But there wasn't anyone there . . . Bloody hell. She wouldn't even have been there if it hadn't been for me, if I hadn't invited her. I don't know why I did. Sometimes I feel sorry for her I suppose.

MARY. There's no need to feel sorry for Celia.

JO. How did she meet someone? There wasn't anyone there apart from a bunch of pricks.

MARY. Maybe she met a prick.

JO. Are they noisy?

MARY. I don't know.

JO. Go on.

MARY. I don't know. Why don't you go down and ask them?

JO. Go on say.

MARY. Say what?

JO (*opens the door and listens*). I wonder if you can hear them from here.

MARY. I don't know.

JO. If they were really noisy you could.

MARY. I'll bet they can hear you.

JO. Sh.

MARY. You're the one who's making all the noise.

JO. Listen.

MARY. Why are you so interested?

JO. I'm not.

MARY. You could have fooled me.

JO. Sh.

MARY. You're jealous.

JO. 'Course I am.

MARY. Beats me.

JO. Sh. Sh.

MARY. Don't be so childish.

JO. What beats you?

MARY. What makes you tick?

JO. Why?

MARY. You don't know what you do want do you?

JO. Oh come off it. I'm not jealous really. All the men at that party were repulsive.

MARY. Exactly.

JO. But . . .

MARY. But what?

JO. Nothing.

MARY. What?

JO. Sometimes I'd rather be with anybody than nobody I suppose. That's all.

MARY. You wouldn't really.

JO. Yes I would. Believe me I would.

MARY. Even somebody you didn't like?

JO. Yes.

MARY. Even somebody from that party?

JO. Yes.

MARY. Somebody you didn't even find attractive?

JO. Yes.

MARY. You don't mean that.

JO. I do.

MARY. Why?

JO. Because I would.

MARY. How can you possibly say that? You wouldn't enjoy it at all.

JO. I would.

MARY. How?

JO. You're so bloody naive, Mary.

MARY. I don't understand you at all.

JO. I just would.

MARY. It doesn't make sense.

JO. Since when do things make sense . . ? I can't understand why you've got to make everything so complicated.

MARY. I haven't.

JO. Then why are you making such an issue out of a dress? Nothing you can do is going to change . . .

MARY. You're the one who's making an issue out of it. I'm not. I'm not trying to make what I don't like in the world go away; I'm dyeing a dress. What I don't like isn't going to go away anyway so why bother trying? Things don't go away. They stay put and you learn to live with them. There's nothing I can do about the world. I can't control people's hearts and minds. They're going to go on saying one thing and feeling another whether I like it or not. They are going to say you can do whatever you like but they won't mean it because what they'll actually be thinking about is a fifteen-year-old in suspenders jerking them off in a railway carriage with no expression on her face at all. There's nothing I can do about it. And sometimes it'll make me unhappy and sometimes I won't think about it. Sometimes I'm going to be walking down the street feeling fine and sometimes I'm going to be walking down the street feeling horrible. That's just the way it is.

Pause.

JO. There have been times when I have been fucking someone and I've been lying there imagining I'm with someone else. I've pretended I'm with some bloke I've never met, a bloke who doesn't even exist, some bloke who's got a brilliant body. A bloke who'd never look at me twice.

And I've imagined myself good enough for him, beautiful, sexy, desirable. And we've both been fabulous and greedy for each other and we haven't cared about anything other than what we've both been getting and what we've already got. We've been in a competition and we've both been winning and it hasn't been about love at all. And it's made me cry . . . See? We're all fucked up.

MARY. I always thought you liked it.

JO. What?

MARY. Sex.

JO. I do.

MARY. With that going on in your head?

JO. I don't know. I don't know why I said it. I don't always think like that. Just sometimes.

MARY. When?

JO. Just sometimes. Sometimes I find I'm thinking weird things like that. Maybe it's just when I'm bored . . . I just imagine really getting off on myself, that's all.

MARY. With someone you hate?

JO. It isn't real. It isn't happening. I make it up.

MARY. Why?

JO. It makes me feel raunchy.

MARY. But you're not like that.

JO. Thanks.

MARY. You wouldn't want someone like that.

JO. I wouldn't really but . . .

MARY. But what?

JO. What does it matter? It's just stuff going on in my head. What's the harm in that? Thinking can't kill you can it? Or can it now? Is that the latest? Now you can't even think. *Sh.*

MARY. What?

JO. *Shh.*

MARY. Why?

JO. Someone's coming.

MARY. Lock the door.

JO. Ummn?

MARY. Lock the door. He'll come in here. He'll think . . .

JO. Sh. Sh. (*She peers out of the door.*).

MARY. Lock the door. We don't want him coming in here. He'll think it's the loo.

JO. I was sure I heard someone.

MARY. Didn't you?

JO. Can't have.

MARY. I wish you weren't so unhappy.

JO. Me?

MARY. Yes.

JO. I'm not unhappy. I'm knackered. (*She looks in the mirror.*) God I
look dreadful.

MARY. What's so awful about your face and your legs and everything
else?

JO. Umnn?

MARY. You always want to be somebody else.

JO. Don't you?

MARY. No.

Pause.

JO. I wish I was in a couple. Life'd be so much easier in a couple.
You'd have someone to go with and someone to come home with
and . . .

MARY. You'll meet someone.

JO. I could have met someone this evening if I'd put my mind to it.
You can always meet someone. Always. But sometimes I suppose
you just think 'why bother?' There are always going to be blokes
who've just split up with someone who want to talk about it all
night long but don't even notice what you look like. And there
are the quiet quiet blokes who get to show signs of life eventually
if you really work at them. And the blokes with terrible skin who
are embarrassing dancers. And the fat blokes who are never going
to get it together with anyone. There's always someone if you've
got the energy.

MARY. Parties are horrible. That's a fact.

JO. Yeah. (*She goes to the door.*) What's the betting I don't fall asleep
for an hour?

MARY. Aren't you going to wash your face?

JO. Can't be bothered.

MARY. Go on, clean your face. You'll feel better.

JO. 'Cleanse and moisturise and make a habit of it.'

MARY. Go on. (MARY *goes out.* JO *takes her make-up off at the mirror. We hear her giving the following speech through the speakers. It fades out over the last line during which the lights also fade and she goes out.*)

JO (*on tape*). 'I want all the men in the room to want me. I want them all to be dreaming of having me, one after the other. They are all beautiful and they all want me because I am beautiful. And each one tears off my clothes. He comes up to me, silent and clean and brave looking and he's wearing a black suit and ever such a white shirt and black tie and he lifts me on to the table and he tears a slit in my dress up to my waist and the diamanté shoulder straps snap as he clutches my breasts and sucks and sucks and I arch my back and watch them all watching us. And my diamond necklace flickers in the light. Then the next one pushes me on to the floor and he has to tear my dress all over again. He comes down on me hard and strong and urgent and no one can take their eyes off us and . . .'

Scene Eight

The next morning, i.e. after the night of Scene Six. Morning light. CELIA *comes in. She has everything for her bath. She begins her face-cleaning routine then spots the bath full of dye in the mirror.*

CELIA. Oh for Heaven's sake. (*She resumes her face-cleaning routine and then goes out abruptly.*) Jo! . . . . Jo! (*She knocks on* JO*'s door. . . .* Jo! (*She knocks again.*)

JO (*off*). What?

CELIA. Could you come and move this stuff from the bath please, whatever it is.

JO (*off*). Eh?

CELIA. Could you come and do something with this stuff in the bath.

JO (*off*). What stuff?

CELIA. Whatever it is that's in the bath. I don't know what it is.

JO (*off*). Can't you do it?

CELIA. *Please* Jo.

JO (*off*). I'm asleep.

CELIA. I'd like to have a bath.

JO (*off*). It's the middle of the night.

CELIA. It's a quarter past eleven and I've got to, I've *got* to have a bath. I really have. I've got . . . I'm . . . honestly I'm really in a hurry. It's getting on for twelve. Please Jo . . . Jo . . ? I'm . . . er . . . Jo? (*She knocks on her door.*)

JO (*off*). What?

CELIA. I'm sorry to get you up but I can't have a bath until . . . I'm going to open the window and throw it out. I don't care what it is or what it's doing there. I want a bath and I'm damned well going to have one. (CELIA *comes in.*) I've had it up to here with sharing a bathroom: up to here. I can never get into it and when I do, finally, I find it's filthy, disgusting and completely unusable. (*She opens the window.*) It's going out. This minute. Everyone tramples on me; absolutely everyone and I'm sick and tired of it. (*She is now attempting to wring out the sheets.*) You can jolly well have a dose of your own medicine and see if I care. This bathroom is just as much mine as it is yours and *I want to use it now.* You can kindly put your smelly old, rotten, ugly, nasty, horrible, nasty, nasty, smelly . . .

JO (*comes in wearing nightclothes*). Alright. Alright. Keep your hair on.

CELIA (*gets up*). I'm sick of this. Sick of it. There's no consideration in this house: none whatsoever.

JO. Just calm down. It's not the end of the world. It's a couple of old sheets.

CELIA. You're selfish. You live in your own little world don't you? What am I supposed to do? Jump in the bath with them? Does it ever occur to you that someone else may wish to use the bathroom apart from you? Or is that too stupid a question for words? I don't know what you find to do in here all the time but you manage to monopolise this room almost every day. Every single day. It's so inconsiderate. You live in a trance Jo, a complete trance, without a thought for other people. . . (*She sees the dress hanging up.*) Isn't that Mary's dress?

JO. Yes.

CELIA. So these are . .

JO. Exactly.

CELIA. I'm terribly sorry.

JO. Mary's sheets.

CELIA. I really am sorry.

JO. Forget it.

CELIA. Honestly I . . .

JO. Doesn't matter.

CELIA. I really wouldn't have . . .

JO. Don't go on about it.

CELIA. No, but I *am* sorry. I'd never have woken you. I wouldn't have dreamt of it. Really I wouldn't. I'd never have woken you unless . . . It never crossed my mind it might be Mary's. I'm terribly sorry. I feel absolutely awful.

JO. Alright.

CELIA. I'm a bit hung over to be honest. I think we must have drunk an awful lot last night. I just flew off the handle.

JO. Yes.

CELIA. I'd rather have a bath now because . . . well, I'm meeting . . . I don't know what I was thinking about. I just assumed it was yours; I don't know why. You see I'm in rather a hurry because I'm meeting . . . I mean someone's picking me up. But you do monopolise the bathroom sometimes you must admit.

JO. What's he like?

CELIA. Who?

JO. Romeo.

CELIA. Oh, very nice.

JO. What's his name?

CELIA. Mark. He's gone to pick up the car and we're . . Did somebody spill wine over Mary's dress?

JO. Not that I know of.

CELIA. I thought maybe that's why she's gone and dyed it.

JO. Don't think so.

CELIA. She looked so nice in it.

JO. She didn't think so.

CELIA. Didn't she?

JO. She thought she looked like a tart in it.

CELIA. Oh.

JO. I think she's mental.

CELIA. It hasn't stained the bath has it?

JO. Hope not.

CELIA. I shouldn't think it has. Mary's usually very careful isn't she?

JO. You are meant to use the bath.

CELIA. Yes.

JO. I don't know you're meant to leave the stuff in there a week but you are meant to use it.

CELIA. Or you can use a washing machine.

JO. We haven't got a washing machine.

CELIA. No I know but . . . She's managed to get the colour nice and even hasn't she?

JO. She's wrecked it.

CELIA. Did you two get to bed terribly late?

JO. Suppose so.

CELIA. Thank you for inviting me. I did enjoy myself.

JO. Good.

CELIA. Did you?

JO. Sure. You'd better get on with your bath then hadn't you?

CELIA. Yes. Do you think Mary'd mind if I . . .

JO (*shouts*). Mary . . ! Mary . . ! Mary!

MARY (*off*). What?

JO. Come and clear this stuff out of the bath will you?

MARY (*off*). What?

JO. Celia's chucking your sheets out of the window.

MARY (*off*). Ummn?

JO. Celia's in a terrible temper and she's chucking your stuff out of the window. She's got your sheets and your party dress and your toothpaste and your flannel and your loofah and your verruca cream and your dental floss and your fabric conditioner and your bucket and spade and your (CELIA *goes out.*) plastic frog from

Mikanos and your bubble bath and your 24-hour cream and your 8-hour cream and your overnight cream and your handcream and your odourless underarm hair-removing cream and your salad cream and your . . .

MARY (*comes in, wearing nightclothes*). Ha ha ha. Very funny.

JO. Celia wants a bath.

MARY. So she tells me. (*She wrings out the sheets and puts them in a plastic bucket.*)

JO. She's in a rush. She's got a date.

MARY. Alright. Just give us a second, will you.

JO (*watches MARY wringing out the sheets. She closes the door*). Fuck me if it isn't 'The Royal We' already. She's only known him half an hour.

MARY. Shh.

JO. It is. Believe me. 'We this. We that. We drank rather a lot. We plan to. We're going to'. God!

MARY. Shh.

JO. Bloody Hell, she gets on my wick.

CELIA (*coming in*). Thanks very much Mary. I'd have done it myself only I didn't really know . . .

JO *goes out.*

I didn't want to spoil it. Sorry, I've got you both up now.

MARY. Doesn't matter.

CELIA. Your dress looks very nice.

MARY. It's a bit out of shape I think.

CELIA. It looks more you now though.

MARY. Oh.

CELIA. No, I mean it looks more practical.

MARY. Oh . . . Right.

MARY *goes out.*
CELIA *approaches the bath. There is the sound of a car horn outside.*

CELIA. Oh God! (*The car horn repeats.*)

MARY (*off*). Celia!

CELIA. Coming. (*She gathers her things together.*)

MARY (*off*). Celia!

CELIA. Yes. I'm coming. (*She leaves.*)

(*Off.*) I'm coming.

There is the sound of the front door bell.

(*Off.*) Hang on. Just a minute . . . I won't be a minute.

JO *comes in and crosses to the window. She opens it a fraction and looks out. She crosses and gets on the scales.*

JO. I'm going to shoot myself. I didn't eat a thing all evening and I haven't lost an ounce: Not One Single Ounce. And I danced like a lunatic and talked until I was hoarse and I'm exactly the same as I was yesterday . . . When am I going to wake up and be different?

MARY (*comes in*). What are you muttering about?

JO. Nothing.

MARY. Off in a trance somewhere?

JO. No.

MARY. So what's his car like?

JO. Nothing to write home about.

MARY. Not a huge American convertible with quadraphonic sound and a dashboard like an aeroplane?

JO. No.

MARY. That's a pity.

JO. The last word in dull to be honest.

We hear CELIA run down the stairs and go out.

MARY. Not your style then?

JO. No way. On a day like this I'd like a man with a car with a sunroof and those big squashy tyres that mean you can drive across the beach and one of those iceboxes in the back with two bottles of pink champagne and . . .

MARY. Have you ever had pink champagne?

JO. No.

Blackout.

Winsome Pinnock was born in Islington in 1961 and attained a joint-honours degree in English and Drama from Goldsmith's in 1982. Over the next four years she worked as a marketing assistant for a unit trust organisation and then as a sales support supervisor. In September 1986 her first play *A Hero's Welcome* was presented in a rehearsed reading at the Royal Court Theatre Upstairs and in the following year her second play *The Wind of Change* was presented at the Half Moon and toured thereafter. Later in the same year *Leave Taking* was produced at Liverpool Playhouse Studio, and from February to June 1988 *Picture Palace,* a play commissioned by the Women's Playhouse Trust, toured nationally. She is currently working on two commissions for the Royal Court: a play for the Theatre Upstairs and a second play *Claudia Jones* for the YPT (Young People's Theatre). She has also been commissioned by the National Theatre Studio. Her first work for television, an episode for the BBC series *South of the Border,* was broadcast in November 1988. *A Hero's Welcome* will be produced at the Theatre Upstairs in February 1989 by the Women's Playhouse Trust.

Leave Taking was first performed at the Liverpool Playhouse Studio on 11 November 1987 with the following cast:

ENID MATTHEWS, early fifties	Ellen Thomas
DEL MATTHEWS, early twenties	Natasha Williams
VIV MATTHEWS, late teens	Lisa Lewis
MAI, late sixties	Lucita Lijertwood
BRODERICK, early sixties	Tommy Eytle

Directed by Kate Rowland
Designed by Candida Boyes
Lighting by Les Lyon

'These grandmothers and mothers of ours [were] driven to a numb and bleeding madness by the springs of creativity in them for which there was no release . . . Throwing away this spirituality was their pathetic attempt to lighten the soul to a weight their work-worn, sexually abused bodies could bear'

Alice Walker – *In Search of our Mothers' Gardens*

'[A mother accepts] a daughter with the bitter pleasure of self-recognition in another victim, and at the same time feels guilty for having brought her into the world'

Simone de Beauvoir – *The Second Sex*

ACT ONE

Scene One

MAI's bedsit. Very messy. The table centre stage is covered in papers, playing cards scattered all over, a glass of water and the remains of a half-burnt white candle. At the table, two chairs. In the middle of the table a large Afro wig. MAI sits in the armchair; she's very tatty, wears a tatty cardigan over an old dress. She's slumped in the armchair drinking from a bottle of stout. She sucks from the bottle then burps softly and rubs her stomach. On her lap is a notebook which she picks up, finds her page and tries to read, having to hold it away from her and close her eyes tight. She picks up a pen and starts to write in the book, slowly, then throws her pen down.

MAI. Lord, see my troubles now.

Curls and uncurls her fingers and bends her arm at the elbow, then stops to pick the pen up again. There is a knock at the door. This startles MAI who sits up abruptly and gives another soft belch. Knocking continues. MAI quietly puts down the stout bottle. The knocking is persistent.

MAI. What the . . . (Calls, polite.) Who is it?

ENID (off). Enid Matthews.

MAI (puzzled, to herself). Enid Matthews? What you want?

ENID. I did make appointment.

MAI. Come back on Thursday.

ENID. After I come so far?

MAI. Is Bank Holiday.

ENID. I pay five pound more.

There is a slight pause, then MAI puts the wig on.

MAI. The Good Lord did say that money isn't everything. But when duty call, it call.

MAI opens the door. ENID comes in followed by VIV and DEL.

MAI. I sometimes regret the day Mother discovered I had the gift. Since I was eighteen I ain't had a moment's peace.

ENID. I bring me daughters with me.

MAI. Some people don't like that.

ENID (*downcast*). Oh.

MAI. But I don't mind it – I have a absentee son.

ENID. Them tell me you have the gift good.

MAI. These days people does want me to help them win on the *Mirror* Bingo.

(*To girls:*) Unno ever read before?

No reply from VIV *and* DEL.

Unno scared a' me? A so young people does scared a' obeah woman. Can't keep any secret from me. (*To* ENID:) Tha's ten pounds extra. On top a' the five pound special Bank Holiday price.

ENID. Long as we get a reading.

MAI (*the hostess*). Sit down nuh?

They do so, ENID *in the armchair, the girls at the table.* MAI *picks up the stout bottle.*

Excuse the mess. Today is suppose to be me day off. Unno want a cup a' tea?

The girls open their mouths to speak but ENID *is there first.*

ENID. We all right.

MAI. Eager for you reading ennit? I like to get to know me client first, have a cup a' tea, a biscuit an' a chat. You relax, I relax. Is more pleasant that way.

ENID. We ain't really got much time. Straight after this I got to run home, got people coming.

MAI. Jus' one cup a' tea?

ENID. All right.

MAI. Put the kettle on. (*She goes out carrying the stout bottle.*)

DEL. She stinks.

ENID. Shush.

DEL. End up paying fifty quid time she's finished with you.

ENID. That any a' your business?

DEL. Mumbo jumbo.

VIV. I'm hungry.

DEL. Maybe our hostess'll rustle you up a little something – At a price.

VIV. Spooky dooky. She's not going to read me on me own is she?

ENID. I want to hear what she got to say about you two.

DEL. That's not fair, thought it was supposed to be a very private thing.

ENID. I'm the one paying.

DEL. Don't even want one.

ENID. Then why you come?

DEL. Because . . .

VIV. She wants to prove you wrong. You two make me laugh.

DEL. Don't know why you couldn't just carry us to the doctor's.

VIV (*to* ENID). She really read the future? She tell me what grades I'll get in the exams?

ENID. Member that car accident with Miss Pannycook? A she predict that.

DEL (*stands and looks round the room*). Stinks in here.

ENID. When she bring the tea jus' pretend you drinkint it, then let it get cold. Man could pick up all sorta' disease from these bedsit places.

DEL (*holding a glass from the table up to the light*). Reckon she does what you do and nicks holy water off the Roman Catholics?

ENID. You want people hear you?

DEL. Fancy nicking holy water to practise voodoo.

ENID. You go too far, Miss Delores.

VIV. It's not voodoo.

DEL (*puts on accent*). Obeah.

VIV. Sit down Del, you're making me nervous.

Pause. ENID *taps her feet.*

Like a doctor's waiting room.

ENID. I might get a bath if she don't charge too much extra.

VIV. You had one this morning.

DEL. A holy bath. Stinks.

ENID. The older you get, the more you find out you got to protect you'self. You'll learn.

MAI *puts her head round the door.*

MAI. Lady, you can help me with the tray?

ENID. Of course. You two sit and behave.

ENID *and* MAI *go out.*

VIV. Still feel ill?

DEL. I'm all right now.

VIV. Try not to make a fuss, Del. Just do what she says.

DEL. Anything for a quiet life. Stop staring at me.

VIV. Sure you're all right? You should see a doctor.

DEL. I'm fine.

VIV. Might be . . .

DEL. It's not, all right?

VIV. Some girl in school . . .

DEL. Shut up. Smells like pigs in here.

VIV. Shall I open a window?

DEL. It's supposed to stink. Part of the atmosphere.

VIV. I like it.

DEL. You would.

VIV. There's as many obeah women in the West Indies as priests.

DEL. How d'you know that?

VIV. Uncle Brod said.

DEL. What's he know?

VIV. He was born there. (*Picks up an African figure.*) Look at this.

DEL. What is it?

VIV. There's writing on the bottom.

DEL *reads then drops it.*

VIV. What's up? (*Picks it up and reads, laughs.*) You believe that?

DEL. (*sheepish*). No.

VIV. You believe it. (*Putting the figure back.*) I want to go to the West Indies, do a grand tour.

DEL.. Fucking dreamhead.

Cock crows.

DEL. What's that?

VIV (*dashes to the window, looks out*). Chickens.

DEL.. What?

VIV. Have a look.

DEL *goes to the window.*

VIV. Look at the fat one.

DEL.. Fucking farmyard.

VIV. He's trying to eat that little one or something.

DEL. Trying to get his leg over you mean.

ENID *and* MAI *come in holding tea cups.*

MAI. I think that one mad you know. All midnight he crowing.

VIV. You allowed to keep chickens in London?

MAI. Why not? Is a free country.

DEL. Yeah?

MAI. I couldn't live without a few fowl in the backyard.

VIV. Do you use them for . . .

MAI. That was the old time obeah. We leave your tea in the kitchen.

ENID. Go and get it.

MAI. I got business to do with Mam.

ENID. Go on.

VIV *and* DEL *go out.*

MAI (*direct*). Look, lady, if is man you come 'bout you might as well go straight home. So many black women over here does come see me 'bout man: how to catch him, how to get him back, how to get rid of him. Mostly them does want to get him back. So many a'those women lef' lonely on them own. Some a'them gone mad over man. They think I can work miracles.

ENID. My husban' lef' me gone, yes. But I don't want him back. I bring up those two girls on me own.

MAI. I glad to hear it. So what I can do for you?

ENID. I want a reading an' maybe a healing bath.

MAI. I don't do bath any more. Damn' fool landlady keep complaining how I was bringing complete stranger in she house use bath. Think she going catch something. An' I know say all my clients does hundred times cleaner than she.

ENID. First, I want you to read between the lines for me.

MAI. What?

ENID (*reaching inside her bag, takes out a letter*). Me sister send me this letter a month ago. Since that time I ain't been sleeping at night. The woman so lie. I don't know whether to believe she or not. I thought that you could be able to give me some guidance.

MAI. Cost you extra.

ENID *nods and hands* MAI *a letter.* MAI *holds the letter away from her and closes her right eye. No good. She searches around the table, then takes a pair of glasses from under some papers and puts them on. She reads. After a while she puts the letter on the table.*

MAI. You send money home?

ENID. Regular.

MAI. When last you go back there?

ENID. Five years ago.

MAI. And you' mother?

ENID. If the woman didn't climb tree, pick coconut give me.

MAI. Even so. . .

ENID. Woman strong as she don't suffer from disease like that.

MAI. They bring doctor to her?

ENID. So them say. But like I tell you, them so lie you don't know if is true. My sister so bloody lazy. And greedy. Want the whole a'me pay packet. She must be want me and the children to starve.

MAI. We have more than them.

ENID. They think I'm a millionaire. Not as if I ain't write them tell them how hard it is over here. (*Scornful.*) Mother on dying. (*Kisses her teeth.*) We a long-lived family. Me gran'mother live till ninety-five.

MAI *takes up the letter, folds it and hands it back to* ENID.

MAI. Send them what them ask for. You mother could do with it anyway.

ENID. Can't you tell, by reading it, whether them lying or not?

MAI. M'dear, that not the way the spirit work.

ENID (*agitated*). Everything fall on me. How must I know what to do? (*Calmer.*) All right. Thanks for the advice.

MAI. You ready for you' reading?

ENID. You can do the older girl first? She badly in need of a reading.

MAI. Call her in nuh?

ENID *goes to the door, calls.*

ENID. Del. Come here.

DEL *comes into the room.* ENID *returns to the armchair.*

MAI (*scratching her wig so that it rides up a bit*). Sit nuh?

DEL *sits.*

DEL. This is stupid.

MAI. You don't like read? What you want? Palm or card?

ENID (*quickly*). Palm.

MAI (*takes* DEL's *hand*). A mother force her daughter into reading is usually something she want to know about the girl. What you want to know Enid Matthews?

DEL. She wants to know if I'm pregnant.

MAI (*lets go of* DEL's *hand and stands*). Then she come to the wrong place.

ENID. Who tell you that? You see how the little bitch stay?

DEL. I see you watching my stomach, making what you think are discreet enquiries about my menstrual cycle. (*To* MAI.) She keeps this diary.

MAI. I'm not a doctor.

ENID. See how the girl shame me in front a' people. (*To* MAI.) She suppose to come straight home after work. Girl don't come back till midnight. Say she working late. Till midnight? Working late my arse.

MAI. That don't mean anything.

ENID. A mother know these things.

DEL. She makes me sick. Her eyes are everywhere.

ENID. Look at her palm and see if is lie me telling.

DEL. Can't have a bath without her poking her nose through the keyhole.

MAI. I can only predict and protect.

ENID. I asking you to protect my daughter.

MAI. They have these clinics. . .

ENID. I paying you good money.

DEL. Wasting your money on mumbo jumbo.

ENID (*raising her hand to* DEL.). If I had the strength, you would. . .

MAI. Girl, step outside for me nuh? I want to talk to Mam on she own again.

DEL. She's disgusting.

> MAI *gently touches* DEL*'s shoulder.* DEL *goes.* MAI *sits again, takes off her wig and scratches her head thoughtfully. To* ENID, *understanding.*

MAI. It hard bringing up two young girls on you own.

ENID. Them father never give me a penny, just kick the womb out a'me an' go him own sweet way. The small one a study for big big 'A' level an' thing. Them think the world at them feet. They not going to end up like the old woman: no getting down on them knee an' scrubbing hospital floor for them. But this is white man country, a black woman less than nuttin', I shoulda' had boys. Least boys can fight, throw licks.

MAI. And petrol bomb.

ENID. Give me something to save them.

MAI. I can't . . . Maybe you can save them you'self.

ENID. How?

> MAI *shrugs.*

ENID. You a obeah woman an' you can't tell me nuttin'?

MAI. Go home and send that money to your folks.

ENID. That all you have to say to me? After I come all this way, all you can tell me is to give away what little I have? (*Rising*.) I'm going somewhere where I can get a proper reading.

MAI. I hope they tell you what you want to hear.

ENID. Predict and protect, my foot.

MAI. The rest is up to you.

ENID (*rising, getting her things together to leave*). My mother always say to me, never you trust a obeah woman or a priest.

MAI. You shoulda' listen to she.

ENID. Is always the same damn thing. Unno jus' a look money.

MAI. A woman got to live.

ENID. I must give away all my money? Chuh.

MAI. You not a happy woman, Enid Matthews.

ENID. How you know? (*Sarcastic.*) Read me mind?

MAI. You can't conjure happiness outa' thin air.

VIV *looks in.*

VIV. Is it my turn yet?

MAI. Not finish wit' Mam yet.

ENID. Get outside Viv.

VIV. You all right?

ENID. I said get outside.

VIV *moves away. Pause.* ENID, *calmer, reaches inside her bag and takes out notes, which she hands to* MAI.

ENID. For you time. (*She moves to the door.*)

MAI. Anytime you need someone to . . . tell things, I always here.

ENID *hesitates in the doorway then goes out, closing the door behind her.* MAI *sighs and throws the notes into the Afro wig, then returns to her armchair.*

Scene Two

ENID*'s living room. Evening.* ENID *puts the finishing touches to the table she's setting.* VIV, *wearing a dress, sits on the sofa, books balanced on her lap.* VIV *works, yawning from time to time.* ENID *looks at her watch then fidgets* *with her collar.*

ENID. Del come home yet?

VIV. You know she hasn't. She told you she was going out.

ENID. She never say anything about staying out all night.

VIV. You're not going to argue again?

ENID. Is my house. She got to learn to have respec'. Pastor an' him wife did say them want to meet all me family.

VIV. She'll be back before they get here.

BRODERICK *comes in. He wears a suit, his tie hangs around his neck. He carries a letter.*

BRODERICK. Do this tie for me nuh Enid?

ENID. You can't do it yourself?

BRODERICK (*behind his hand, loud whisper to* VIV). You mother wasn't always so clean cut, you know. In the old days she could throw a drink to she head.

VIV. I don't believe you.

ENID. I warning you, Brod.

BRODERICK (*suddenly taking her hand and spinning her round*). I like it when you speak rough like that. Come, do it again, nuh, lash me with you tongue.

ENID (*pulls away from him*). One day, Brod, you going get what you asking for. God going teach you a lesson. And you won't be laughing neither. I will. (*Referring to the letter.*) What that you got there?

BRODERICK. Is for you. When I did come in yesterday morning . . .

ENID. Drunk.

BRODERICK. Don't chastise me, Enid. Poor man not suppose to be sober. Last time I sober, I thought I was in hell. When I come in I musta' pick it up by mistake.

ENID (*takes the letter*). From me sister. (*Still looking at the letter.*) Wonder what she want this time. If that woman did spend as much time working as writing begging letter she would be a rich woman. So would I. (*Puts the letter down.*)

BRODERICK. Pastor know how to play gin rummy? Or you think I should get out that white rum I was keeping warm under me mattress? Just to give the man a little sniff.

ENID (*warning*). Brod.

BRODERICK. Is jus' a idea. How else we going entertain the man?

ENID. Talk to him.

BRODERICK. Boy, we really turn English now.

ENID. Guess who I see today, Brod? Gullyman.

BRODERICK. Gullyman? Good time now I ain't see Gullyman. You talk to him?

ENID. Man mad walk street no shoes, no socks, shirt open down to him navel. In the cold. Man a walk an' shake, walk an' shake. Beg me fifty pence for a cup a' tea. Didn't even recognise me.

BRODERICK. Gone mad eh?

VIV. Who's Gullyman?

ENID. Before your time.

BRODERICK. Wild days. Remember those days Enid? (*To* VIV:) You' mother was wild, you see.

ENID (*warning*). Brod.

BRODERICK. Wonder what happen to the rest a' those folks.

ENID. There was that man who was always getting into fight with white man over woman, what they used to call him?

BRODERICK. Drink. It was then I learn how to drink. We needed a lot a drinks to get through. Rough times, I tell you.

ENID. Cassius! Wonder what happen to Cassius. You think Gullyman remember Cassius? I remember one time them two catch a fight right in that backyard. (*Laughs.*)

BRODERICK. Gullyman let England fly a him head.

VIV. What?

BRODERICK. Gullyman come over here with two dollar in him pocket. But Gullyman could work, an' he had a talent for saving. Within three years Gullyman buy car – old car granted, but car all the same – an' house. Gullyman forget everybody, all him friends, him people back home, just cut everybody off. You meet him in the road, him wouldn't see you. Remember how him used to talk Enid?

ENID. Like him have cork in him nosehole.

BRODERICK. English. An' he was always correcting people – remember Enid? (*Imitating.*) 'Don't say wartar, man, say worter'.

ENID. Now he can hardly talk broken English.

VIV. That's very sad.

BRODERICK. Man get what him deserve. English.

ENID. He was right. You come here, you try to fit in. Stick to the rules.

BRODERICK. Who tell you that?

ENID. England been good to me. To all of us. I love England an' I bring up the girls to love England because they English.

BRODERICK. She love England. Up until two years ago I woulda' say the same thing. Then them send me letter say if I don't get my papers in order they going kick me outa' the country.

VIV. They said that?

BRODERICK. Words to that effect. Throw all sort a' insult at me. Call me a alien. As if I spend the last thirty years on Mars instead of in a dirty car factory. Fifty odd pounds I had to pay. After I had spent the whole a' my life standing to attention whenever I hear the national anthem.

ENID (*takes a piece of paper out of her pocket, unfolds it*). You see this?

VIV (*embarrassed*). Mum.

ENID. Viv school report. All 'A's. My daughter going to university. How many a' my sister children back home going to university?

BRODERICK. And you know why? Is history ennit? They ain't going to university because there ain't no resources, there ain't no resources because for hundreds a' years those islands been suffocated by all those big nations. Only now they starting to recover a little.

ENID (*folding the report, putting it back*). Them weak because them too damn lazy. If them did get up off them backside . . .

BRODERICK. Lazy? Enid, don't you remember? (*To* VIV.) You ever look at you' mother footbottom see how it crack?

ENID. Shut up you' mouth man.

BRODERICK. Back home she used to rise with the dawn, an' she was on them feet, bare feet, all day: climb high hill, work in the field, walk over big stone to fetch water from gully.

ENID. Brod, what the use you telling her that? She don't know that way of life, she don't understand.

BRODERICK. Well she should, you teaching those children all wrong.

ENID. What you think I should teach her?

BRODERICK. Where she come from. These girls ain't English like them newsreader, them people got English stamp on them like the letters on a stick a' rock, right through English. These girls got Caribbean souls.

ENID. Don't talk foolish.

BRODERICK (*To*VIV). Girl, tell me what you know about Nanny a' the Maroons.

VIV. I don't know.

ENID (*triumphant*). See.

VIV. But I want to know.

BRODERICK. Nanny is a heroine. When the English invade she fight them off. Bullets used to bounce from she shoulders back onto the men who was trying to destroy her. Nanny kill plenty people that way. Strong. That why black women so powerful. Is in the blood. Look at you mother.

ENID. Man, you talk so much nonsense. And you . . . (*To*VIV.) You intelligent. You shouldn't encourage him. What you know about back home?

BRODERICK. You going mix these children up.

ENID. Mix up what? They know who they are. She know who she is. Tell him who you are.

VIV (*stands, recites*). A dust whom England bore, shaped, made aware . . . A body of England's breathing English air, washed by the rivers, blest by the suns of home.

ENID (*not quite sure how to take this*). You see . . . See. *That's* all you need to know, English.

ENID *goes into the kitchen.* VIV *throws down her pen. Pause.* BRODERICK *takes* VIV*'s book from behind a cushion and starts to turn the pages.* VIV *sits at the table, staring into space.*

BRODERICK (*reading*). 'Jeff put his hand on her knee and squeezed. Her lower lip filled with blood and started to quiver. Jeff's hand started its slow and thrilling ascent up her leg and rested on her – '.

Them never teach this sorta' thing in my day.

VIV *rushes over to the sofa and snatches the book from* BRODERICK.

VIV. That's my private property.

BRODERICK. They examine you on that?

VIV. It's for relaxation.

BRODERICK. Better not let you mother see it. Think you some kind of maniac.

VIV (*putting the book away under her papers on the table*). She means well you know Brod?

BRODERICK. You telling me? I know you mother long before you was born. Them days she did like to fire fire: always moving, laughing, doing something. Plenty men did want her. You' father was a lucky man.

VIV. Think she misses him?

BRODERICK. She ain't been the same since he left.

VIV. She's been good to me Brod, to me and Del.

BRODERICK. She's a good woman.

VIV. Only hope I can live up to it.

BRODERICK. She very proud a' you.

VIV. Only wish I deserved it. The way she's worked so hard and everything.

BRODERICK. She think you deserve it. Make her happy and accept that.

VIV. Just I feel like I got to live out something she's missed out on.

BRODERICK. All parent live through them children.

VIV. But what if I fail?

BRODERICK. You won't fail.

ENID *comes in, wiping her hands on her overall.*

ENID. I did leave a list a' things to remember somewhere.

BRODERICK (*teasing*). See how English you mother get? What she did know about list before she come here? List and queue. Back home we keep everything in we head.

ENID. And don't it show?

VIV. Come on, you two, I'm trying to do some serious studying here.

ENID *picks the letter up from the table.*

BRODERICK. Enid, why don't you let the girl go out a bit more?

ENID. She got enough on her mind with the studying.

BRODERICK. But if she is a (*mock accent*) Hinglish girl like how you say she is, she should be with her boyfriend every single night like all the other Hinglish girls.

ENID. Brod, I know what I'm doing. (*Waving the letter.*) Want to place bet as to who me sister going say sick, need doctor this time?

BRODERICK. You too hard, Enid.

ENID. There ain't nobody in she big family she ain't send to me for money to fetch doctor for. She must think me fool. She must think I . . .

Sound of front door opening and slamming shut. Silence.

BRODERICK. Enid, you want me and Viv to go upstairs?

ENID. Stay you bound, Brod.

VIV. Mum, please don't make a row.

DEL *enters dressed for a party.*

DEL (*taking in the atmosphere*). This an ambush or what?

ENID. Where you been?

DEL. Busy day. Had to work late.

ENID. You never come home last night.

DEL. Got held up, decided to stay where I was. (*Moving to the kitchen.*) Dinner in the oven? I'm starving.

ENID. You never got to work today, Del. I did ring them up.

DEL. I was too ill to go in. Slept on someone's floor last night and caught a chill. Better now though. (*Coughs.*) Just about.

ENID. Don't lie to me girl.

DEL. You're not going to believe anything I say are you?

ENID. Tell me where you been.

DEL. I don't have to tell you anything.

BRODERICK. Enid, the girl come home now, you don't have to fight.

DEL. Leave her Brod. What she really wants is all the sordid details. Well, I'm not going to play her game. I'm going to bed cos I'm exhausted. (*Pointed.*) I haven't slept all night. (*Walks towards the door.*)

ENID. Future, I want you in this house by twelve.

DEL. All right Mummy. Anything you say.

ENID. Don't you laugh at me girl.

DEL. I'm not some kid. You can't tell me what to do any more.

ENID. Long as you live under my roof, you abide by my rules. If you don't like it . . .

DEL. All right.

ENID. Now get upstairs, take off those clothes and come back down and eat your dinner.

DEL. Yes Mummy. (*She walks to the door, then stops at the doorway.*) I spent all last night dancing. The music just picks you up and throws you around the room. You can't stop. I always feel like me when I'm dancing. You can't pretend. Why don't you want me to feel like that? Just because you've given up on life, doesn't mean that I have to. (*Slight pause.*) I think you must be really frightened. And lonely.

ENID. You not too big I can't hit you.

DEL. Try it.

BRODERICK. Don't talk to you mother like that, Del.

ENID. You think you turning into woman? This house too small for two of us.

DEL. Who cares? I hate it here. I hate my life, everything.

ENID. Ungrateful . . .

DEL. What I got to be grateful for? A greasy job in some greasy café where they treat me like shit, a couple of quid at the end of every week and a few hours off I can't even call my own. What's that to be grateful for?

ENID. I slave for years just so you wouldn't go without. It's not easy for a woman on her own. You don't know half the sacrifice I make for you. All you know is you get food in your belly, roof over you head and nobody could ever say that you were worse off than those who had fathers.

DEL. But you don't give us anything we can use out there. Every day we go out and they can do what the hell they like with us. You're always telling us to be grateful. For what? You move around with your back bent, dancing attendance on some illusion that was exposed years ago. You ain't given me nothing worthwhile. (*Slight pause.*) You pretend to love but you don't know how to. You don't even love yourself. You despise life. Make you happy to see me and Viv as sad as you are. But I'll never be like you. I'm going to have everything: life, love, sex – everything that you wanted but were too frightened to enjoy.

ENID *slaps* DEL *hard. For a moment it looks as though* DEL *is going to retaliate, but she manages to restrain herself.* DEL *goes out.*

VIV. Del.

ENID. Leave her.

VIV *goes out.*

BRODERICK. Miss Enid . . . She a young woman, they all the same that age.

ENID. People grow up in England, think they can treat you anyhow. Well, they can't.

Pause. BRODERICK *looks at his watch.*

BRODERICK. Pastor soon come.

ENID. Yes.

BRODERICK. You all right Miss Enid?

ENID (*annoyed*). Yes, yes, Brod. Jus' leave me.

BRODERICK *hesitates a bit, then goes.* ENID *sits on the sofa.*

Scene Three

Three hours later. Late evening. ENID *sits on the sofa with a glass in her hand while* BRODERICK *takes a pile of plates from the table and goes into the kitchen, then comes back.*

BRODERICK. That go all right, Miss Enid.

ENID. You think so Brod?

BRODERICK. They seem to have a good time. You think they like me?

ENID. You look sharp, Brod. Thanks for helping me out.

BRODERICK. The hard part was to drink in little sips. Pastor does always take little sip like that?

ENID. He's a high man.

BRODERICK. Notice how him wife look round the place? Shock to see how nice we keep it. (*Slight pause.*) You all right Miss Enid?

ENID. Viv did go out?

BRODERICK. I think so. Don't be too hard on the girl.

ENID. I brought them up to behave properly, not to be rude to people.

BRODERICK. She wasn't exactly rude, Miss Enid.

ENID. You call not answering people when them talking to you polite?

BRODERICK. She upset. She's a sensitive girl.

ENID. You would be on their side. Think I'm some kind a' monster. And Del. She shoulda' come down. I was so 'shame when Pastor ask me where she was. You think he could see I was lying?

BRODERICK. Pastor Trent have many quality, but I don't think he have the gift a' sight.

ENID. When I need my daughters' support they running wild.

BRODERICK. Those girls ain't wild, Enid.

ENID. You ain't got a hard word to say about anything. Long as you have your glass a' whisky or white rum, everything roses.

BRODERICK. I can be tough when I need to be.

ENID. At least it wasn't disaster.

BRODERICK. The church important to you, Enid.

ENID. Wasn't I brought up in the church?

BRODERICK. So what? After this evening Pastor going allow you to take round the collection box or what?

ENID. What you talking about Brod?

BRODERICK. I don't understand the church business these days. They seem to care more about social position than souls.

ENID. Don't mock, Brod. It very important, the church. Is at the centre, the heart a' things. Is there to support you when you need it. If I didn't have my Bible . . .

BRODERICK. Is just when the Pastor start talking about saving souls I start to wondering what special occasion they saving them for. Is all pay now and enjoy later.

ENID. Draw the curtains for me nuh, Brod.

BRODERICK (*doing so*). Pastor Lee is a very nice man. But him put me in mind a' Gullyman. You notice the resemblance? All the time he talking he making excuse: the man keep rubbing him hand and walking backward, walking away from people like me an' you. Him an' him wife just want a easy life, discuss the Bible over tea in china cup. All that talk about discussion group. In my day it was about throwing youself right on the edge of life, it was jumping and shouting and feeling the damn' thing, feeling the spirit flame up inside you.

ENID. That why you does drink so much rum, these days? To feel the fire flaming up inside you again?

BRODERICK. Don't make fun, Enid. I drink my drink and dreams does come before me.

ENID. Spend half you' life flat out drunk.

BRODERICK. I can see things that Pastor could only dream of. Visions. (*Scornful.*) Bible reading. The man dry and dead, trying to talk like one a' them white priest, you notice? Why don't we love ourselves? Why we so quick to give up what we are? The man an' him wife backing away from themselves, from us. Way she looking round this house. It good enough? These people good enough? We walking backwards from ourselves. We losing so much; walking backward you can't see where you going. I need a drink.

ENID. You already have enough, Brod.

BRODERICK. I know I have enough when a beam a' light stretch down an' bathe everything in a deep glow, dazzle me eyes, make me feel like Moses.

ENID (*smiling despite herself*). Moses? Brod, you got to stop this blasphemy.

BRODERICK. What happen, Enid? You don't want me to lead you back out of the Promised Land?

ENID. Shut up, Brod, and get you drink.

BRODERICK. You a understanding woman, Enid. (*Picks letter up from the coffee table.*) You forget you' letter.

ENID. I feel too exhausted for my sister's nonsense.

BRODERICK. Give us both a little laugh.

ENID *puts the letter to her nose and takes a deep breath in.*

What you doing Enid?

ENID. Think it smell a' back home?

BRODERICK *takes the letter and smells it.*

BRODERICK. My nose don't work any more. (*Hands the letter back to* ENID.)

ENID. Sometimes when I'm at work I can smell Mooma's cooking.

BRODERICK. Now, Mooma could cook. Thas the thing about them old time woman, them really could an cook. Even so-so food they turn into a feast.

ENID. Christmas time, remember.

BRODERICK. A whole loaf a' hard dough bread to you'self.

ENID. And chocolate tea.

BRODERICK. See Mooma grating chocolate in mortar.

ENID. Rolling it up in little balls.

BRODERICK. Hear her nuh 'Come on Birdy' – a so she used to call me, Birdy – 'Roll it up *small*, like little dumpling.' Mooma.

ENID. One day she tek me on a long walk. I don't know why. Tek me to all she secret place. Places she would just sit, think and dream. That was the closest I ever get to really know her.

BRODERICK. 'Member Mooma singing?

Pause. Both are lost in nostalgia. ENID *wakes up.*

What's wrong Enid?

ENID. Nuttin'. Jus' thinking. (*Slight pause.*) You know, the day I leave home, she never say goodbye to me. She must be never want me to go. I did think she woulda' understand: in the twenties she leave home go Cuba fe cut cane. But the day I was to leave I couldn't find her, search everywhere. You know where she was? In the field, as usual, working hard like this was jus' any other day, cutting away with she cutlass. 'Mooma' I say 'I gone now.' She never turn round, jus' carry on working, chop chop chop, play deaf. In the end I had to give up, walk away. (*Slight pause.*) I had this . . . big, dark hole inside.

BRODERICK (*gently*). Miss Enid. Gregory never know how lucky him was. A should an' me. I woulda' make you happy.

ENID. Water under the bridge. We too old for all a' that.

BRODERICK. Life in the old dog yet, Enid.

ENID. They write messages on walls over here – 'Grow old gracefully: let sleeping dogs lie.'

BRODERICK. You know is true, Enid.

ENID. Where you wife, Brod?

BRODERICK. That ain't fair, Enid. The woman was a whore.

ENID. Iris tek other man because you never look after her.

BRODERICK (*squirming*). I was a young man.

ENID. So was Gregory. (*Slight pause.*) I don't need a man, Brod. I'm too old. I do all right on me own.

BRODERICK. Don't talk fool. Come to me 'bout you don't need man. Remember, I know you, Enid.

ENID. Brod . . .

BRODERICK. I know what you use to be like. Gregory wasn't the sorta' man keep things quiet.

ENID. He had no sense.

BRODERICK. So what wrong with me?

ENID. You a good man, Brod.

BRODERICK. Not good enough for you, though. Seem to me, Enid, England spoil you. If it was back home you woulda' pick you'self up an' carry on living. Here, you just give up. You burying you'self alive. All right, carry on.

Sound of front door.

BRODERICK. You still want that drink?

ENID. Let it stay. Get one for you'self.

BRODERICK *goes into kitchen.* VIV *puts her head round the door and looks in.*

ENID. Them gone.

VIV (*comes in*). Thank God for that.

ENID. What make you so rude?

VIV. I wasn't. (*Slight pause.*) They annoyed me. Way she talked, like a little bird.

ENID. She talk nice.

VIV. That's what she thinks. They annoy me these people, come here like they doing us a favour.

ENID. Them was doing me a favour. I feel better now the house bless.

VIV. They never come round before.

ENID. They didn't know who I was before. Now they see I'm decent from the way I bring unno up. None a' their children going university.

VIV (*understanding*). I see. You been moved a step up on the social ladder. Talk about Christian charity.

ENID. Where you went?

VIV. For a walk. It's nice outside.

BRODERICK *comes in with his drink.*

BRODERICK. You call this weather nice? Still, you was born here.

VIV. Didn't notice the weather. Just walked about, best way to think.

BRODERICK. Walk it out, tha's what I always say.

ENID. What you got on you mind you have to walk it out?

VIV. I want to go to Jamaica.

ENID. What?

VIV. I want to see for meself. What it's like and everything. It must be part of me.

ENID. Don't talk nonsense.

VIV. Who knows? I might like it so much I won't want to come back.

ENID. Wouldn't survive two minutes. You don't know what it like out there. (*Waving her letter about.*) They start begging you for this that an' the other, you soon come running back. You know, Brod, last year she did write ask me for eight million dollars.

BRODERICK. Is what you saying?

ENID. A true. She did want me to buy her a house with swimming pool.

VIV. Probably just confused.

BRODERICK. Open this one nuh. Give we a joke.

ENID (*opening the letter*). Maybe this time she want me to fix up a castle for her.

BRODERICK (*laughing*). Or buy her a limousine. With chauffeur. (*Laughs.*)

ENID *stands slowly, reading the letter. She walks upstage and stops. Something seems to drain out of her, she sags a little at the knees.* BRODERICK'*s laughter trails off.*

What happened Enid? (*Takes letter from her and reads. Doesn't know what to do with himself, whether to touch* ENID *or not.*) I sorry, Enid, she was a mother to me as well.

ENID. A them kill her. All them got 'pon them mind a money. Them never look after her properly.

BRODERICK. Is what you saying? Nobody kill her. Her time just come.

ENID. What you know? Time just come . . . A them kill her, I know these people.

BRODERICK. You can't say . . .

ENID. Then whose fault it is? Mine?

BRODERICK. Is nobody fault, Enid.

ENID. A lie them a tell, them just want me to . . .

BRODERICK. What?

ENID *doesn't answer.*

Is not lie, Enid. Mooma dead.

ENID. No.

BRODERICK. Yes.

Pause while it sinks in, then:

ENID (*listless*). Go look money send for funeral.

BRODERICK. You don't have to do that now, Enid. It can wait.

ENID. No, Brod, nuttin' ever wait.

ENID *goes out, leaving* VIV *and* BRODERICK *on stage.*

Scene Four

Very late night. ENID *'s living room.* ENID *sits on the sofa with a drink. The lights are out but the room is lit with lights from outside.* ENID *sips her drink, then knocks it back.* VIV *appears in her nightdress.*

VIV. Mum. (*Moves into the room.*) En't you tired yet?

ENID. Go back to bed.

VIV. You can't sit in the dark all night. Let me . . .

ENID. Don't turn the light on.

Pause. VIV *stands and watches her mother, worried.*

VIV. You all right?

ENID. I'm used to sitting in the dark. You think me mother could afford electricity? Hot an' cold running water? Flush toilet? (*Laughs.*) You ever been hungry?

VIV. Yes.

ENID. Not that little nibbling English lunchtime hunger. I talking 'bout the sort what roar in your stomach like a blazing fire night and day so sometimes you going mad wit' the thought a' food. You think is easy living off the land? The land fail you, you might as well be dead.

VIV. You don't live off the land any more.

ENID. Oh, I did escape, din' I? Lucky me. We was the poorest family in the whole a' the distric'. People used to laugh on us, pick at us. An' we still use to walk around like the royal family. (*Laughs at herself, bitter.*) Escape. To what? Where I going run to now?

VIV. Why should you want to run anywhere?

ENID. Sometime I feel like a cat chasing him own tail. Going round and round and getting nowhere but dizzy. (*Slight pause. Deep in thought.*) My uncle did go to America.

VIV. Did he?

ENID. I never tell you? Him did come back visit with him wife. I did think she was the most beautiful woman I ever seen in me life. She straighten she hair an' red up she face. You shoulda' see she underclothes – pink an' silky. I did feel ashame' that all we had was to put her up in we little run-down house. Long after, I couldn' stop dreaming about her. An' America. I did read everything I could get me hand on. I knew I was going there one day.

VIV. Never knew you wanted to go to America.

ENID. I did cry for days when them say they wasn' taking any more people.

VIV. All your dreams up in smoke.

ENID. I wanted to die. I didn't want to grow old in that blasted slow pace distric'. (*Pause.*) You want a drink?

VIV *shakes her head and watches her mother as she pours a drink into cup.*

VIV (*suddenly noticing something in her mother*). You drunk?

ENID. Me? Miss Holy Drawers? A so you father use to call me. Miss Holy Drawers. Because I didn' want to end up like all the other girls in the distric'. I had plans, I tell you. I wasn' going let no blasted man breed me up. (*Sips from the glass, a bit nervous, spills some.*)

VIV (*cleaning* ENID *up*). Take it easy, Mum.

ENID. You a good girl.

VIV. Don't go all maudlin on me. Don't think I can cope with another Uncle Brod.

ENID. You' Uncle Brod all right. But he don't understand what it is to want things. The man never want nuttin' in him life. You' Uncle Brod happy here, Jamaica, on a desert island. Is all the same to him 'cos he ain't got no wantin' in him head.

VIV. Not like you?

ENID. Got too much in me head.

VIV. Like Del.

ENID. That girl heading for big trouble. I try to warn her but she won't take telling. She think she know everything, think she a woman. She ain't so big I can't . . . (*Trails off. Pause. She rises slowly. Though she's not noticeably drunk, she wobbles a bit.*)

VIV. You going up to bed now?

ENID. I had was to give you something . . . (*Takes a Building Society passbook out of her bag and hands it to* VIV.

VIV (*takes the book and looks inside it. Quietly*). You musta' bin saving ages.

ENID. Once I put me mind to something . . . (*Shrugs.*)

VIV. I can't take this.

ENID. You deserve it. After you work so hard to pass you exams.

VIV. I ain't got them yet.

ENID. But you will.

VIV. So this is a down payment.

ENID. What?

VIV. I'm a sort of investment.

ENID. You're my child.

VIV (*holding out the book*). Spend it on yourself.

ENID. What I would buy for myself? I'm not a dreaming seven-year-old any more. I'm a big woman.

VIV. I don't wanna let you down.

ENID. You won't never let me down.

DEL. *comes in carrying a suitcase. She's wearing the same clothes as in Scene Two. It seems as though she may have been crying.*

ENID. Where the hell you think you going this time a' night?

DEL. As far away from you as I can.

ENID. Go back upstairs.

DEL. No.

ENID. I said . . .

DEL. You can't make me.

ENID. A so you think?

ENID *makes a grab for the suitcase. There's some rather clumsy pushing and shoving as DEL drags it away from her.*

DEL. Take your fucking hands off me.

A moment passes. Something's changed between them. ENID gives in and DEL goes out.

VIV. Mum, don't let her go.

ENID (*hard*). Why not?

VIV. What's happening? What do you want?

ENID. I want . . . I want to go home.

ACT TWO

Scene One

A few weeks later. MAI*'s bedsit, midday.* MAI *carries a saucer on which is a heap of salt. She walks round the table slowly and mutters something under her breath. She sprinkles salt around the room.* DEL *appears wearing only an outsize T-shirt; she's just woken up. She rubs her eyes.*

DEL. What's going on?

MAI. Sssh!

DEL. You gone mad or something?

MAI (*a bit out of breath, stops to rest*). Go back upstairs.

DEL. Done yourself a mischief.

MAI. Now see what you done.

DEL. What?

MAI. See how you make me spill it?

DEL. It's only salt . . .

MAI: Only salt . . .

DEL. I broken the spell or what?

MAI. I have to start again. (*Mops her brow.*) I getting too old.

DEL. Another fugitive husband?

MAI. I said is none a' your business.

DEL. Don't know why they bother.

MAI. You going spend the day naked?

DEL. Only just got up.

MAI. What if somebody call round?

DEL. They come to see you.

MAI. What sort of impression you going give?

DEL. I couldn't sleep.

MAI. No?

DEL. Those pictures on the wall . . . I had nightmares I was being crushed by a pair of gigantic pink tits.

MAI. My husband was the same.

DEL. Can't think of you married.

MAI. I done many things you wouldn't think. (*Searching cupboards.*) Salt, salt.

DEL (*picks up the cards from the table and starts to play with them*). You'd be surprised if that stuff really worked.

MAI. You doubt it?

DEL. Don't you?

MAI. Mind those cards.

DEL. Why? Burn my fingers or something?

MAI. Stop playing with my things.

DEL. Just looking.

MAI. Few nights you been here an' I can't find a damn thing.

DEL. Scared I'll find out you're a phoney?

MAI. Look girl, you want to stay here in *my* house you abide by my rules, y'hear. You got to learn to respect . . .

DEL. Here we go again. I'll make breakfast.

MAI. Don't turn you' back on me, girl!

DEL *turns round holding the cards, still shuffling them.*

I was talking about respect.

DEL. I need a sermon I'll go to church.

MAI. Don't speak to me like I'm your mother.

DEL *drops the cards.*

You do that on purpose.

DEL. Sorry Mai.

MAI. This evening you pack you' bags and find somewhere else.

DEL. All right, I will.

MAI. Everything you touch, falls in pieces. (*Stoops to pick up the cards, her back goes. She groans a bit,* DEL *walks her over to a chair.*)

DEL. I don't mean to spoil things.

Cock crows.

Shut up.

MAI. He want him breakfast.

DEL. *goes over to the cupboard, takes out some grain which she puts in an enamel basin.*

Remember to talk to him.

DEL. Shit.

MAI. Softly.

DEL *stands and sullenly throws the contents of the basin out to the yard; the hens go for it.* DEL *stands in the doorway looking out.*

MAI (*watching her, then gently*). Put some grain in you' hand.

DEL *turns round and puts the basin away.*

DEL. Breakfast?

MAI. What you plan to do today?

DEL. There's no milk.

MAI. I can't afford to feed the both of us on me pension.

DEL. I'll sign on.

MAI. Make sure you do.

Knock at the door.

What they want with me at this time?

DEL. One of the husbands wants you to get off his back.

MAI. You put on some clothes.

MAI *goes out.* DEL *sits in a chair, looking round the room.* MAI *comes in with* VIV.

MAI. Didn't I tell you to put on some clothes?

DEL. What you want?

VIV. En't I allowed a visit?

MAI *drags on her wig and puts on her coat.*

MAI. I going to the shops. What we need? Milk . . .

DEL. And salt.

MAI *smiles and goes out.*

VIV. En't you gonna offer me a cup a' tea?

DEL. We run out a' tea.

VIV. Glass a' water then.

DEL. *grudgingly fetches a glass of water and hands it to* VIV.

VIV. How you living?

DEL. I got friends.

VIV. You don't look well.

DEL. Worse I went back with you and that crazy woman.

VIV. You be crazy you carry on like this. Can't have a baby here.

DEL. 'Least it's quiet.

VIV. Different at home now.

DEL. Council're gonna get me somewhere. Priority if you're single parent. Might get a garden.

VIV. I'm not gonna let you have my niece here.

DEL. Aunts ain't got rights.

VIV. You got milk yet?

DEL. Pervert.

VIV. Wouldn't surprise me if you don't.

DEL. I look after meself.

VIV. Don't look like it.

DEL. Leave us out.

VIV. I want to be there when it comes.

DEL. Hold my hand? Be escaping yourself in – what? – coupla months? You'll be going to wild parties, there'll be men – sex, drugs, booze.

VIV. I won't.

DEL (*gentle*). No. (*A bit angry with* VIV.) Good thing you're clever else I could just see you staying in that house for the rest a' your life, letting her tell you what to do: one a' them spinster virgins in sensible shoes what gets her kicks rubbing up against doorknobs. You got to grow up, sus out what it is you want out of life, not what'll please her. I feel sorry for you, you don't know nothing 'cept for what you learnt off by heart from some text book.

VIV. That what you think?

Pause.

So what you do all day then? Play patience?

DEL. There's loads to do.

VIV. You give up your job.

DEL. Don't hassle me, Viv.

VIV. Place smells damp. Be horrible in the winter. Baby'll get fungus on its lungs. (*Slight pause.*) They're dropping like flies in the sixth form: one by one all the black girls are falling pregnant. It's like ten little Indians, everyone's placing bets about who's going to be next. One girl's so far gone she couldn't fit the desk in the exam. They had to get her this stool. Humiliating. Then she had to go to the loo every five minutes.

DEL. Probably had the answers written on her stomach.

VIV. What's it feel like?

DEL. You wanna try it. (*Slight pause.*) They should teach it in schools. I'm only three months gone and my body don't belong to me no more, it's all out of control. I was up half last night, fantasising about strawberry jam and pilchard sandwiches.

VIV. It's all in the mind. I read it. (*Looks down at her feet, embarrassed.*)

DEL. I'm the centre of a universe. Believe it? You get sick, tired and scared.

VIV. Come home with me.

DEL. Let me get on with my life can't you?

VIV. You got a new man?

DEL. I'm finished with men.

VIV. What happened with you and Roy? Did you beg?

DEL. Don't be stupid.

VIV. Some girl in my group got down on her hands and knees up Oxford Street. He just left her there. Makes you wanna laugh. Or cry.

DEL. Loads a' black women bring up children on their own.

VIV. That's the problem.

DEL. But not you, eh? You're cut out for better things. End up reading the news on the BBC.

VIV. Leave us out Del.

DEL. Or married to some politician. One a' those blokes what goes on telly with his fists clenched, then goes home to the little woman who's preparing genteel lunchtime drinks for their Hampstead neighbours.

VIV. You don't know fuck.

DEL. Oooh she's started swearing – a bad sign.

VIV. Stop laughing at me, Del. None of this is my fault. You and the old woman can't keep using me . . .

DEL. Who said anything about the old woman?

VIV. I've had it up to here with you two. What about me?

DEL. What about you?

VIV (*gently mocking herself*). My one act of rebellion and I'm shitting myself.

DEL. What?

VIV. Anyone else would just shrug it off, light up an illegal fag in the school lav and swank about it. But not Miss I-get-my-kicks-rubbing-up-against-doorknobs. Oh no. For me it's some big moral dilemma: I walked out on an exam.

DEL. What for?

VIV. I knew all the answers. I'm like a machine – pat me on the head and they all come tumbling out. Rely on me to say exactly what the examiners want to hear. It doesn't change anything. (*Slight pause.*) I sometimes feel like I need another language to express myself. (*Smiles.*) Swahili perhaps.

DEL. You're really stupid. You want to end up some galley slave in a burger bar? You had a chance. You shoulda' been grateful.

VIV. You sound just like . . .

DEL. You better go home. She'll go spare.

VIV. Kicking me out?

DEL. Yes.

VIV (*rising*). All right. (*She takes a fat envelope out of her jacket pocket and hands it to DEL.*) For my niece.

DEL. (*looking inside the envelope*). Where d'you get all this?

VIV. Secret.

DEL. You got a Saturday job or what? (*Truth dawns.*) The old woman? (*Bitter.*) For being a good girl?

VIV. Just take it.

DEL. Go and sit your exam, Viv.

VIV. Don't blame me.

DEL. Fuck off.

VIV *goes out leaving the envelope on the table.*

Scene Two

That evening. MAI's bedsit. There's a lighted candle on the table and a glass of water. The table is cluttered as in Scene One. ENID sits at the table with her palm held out. MAI, frowning, holds her palm and looks at it. There's also a bottle of stout on the table.

MAI (*peers closely at ENID's palm*). You going on a long journey. (*Lets go of ENID's hand and picks up the stout bottle.*) So you better look out you passport. I could do with a bit a' sunshine meself. (*Slight pause.*) That will be four pounds. (*She takes a swig from the bottle and burps, rubbing her stomach.*) Cash.

ENID *rummages in her bag and takes out some money, hands it to MAI who pushes it up under her wig. ENID sits, handbag in lap. MAI watches her as if waiting for her to do something.*

You want a bottle a stout?

ENID. My mother died.

MAI. So did mine. Eighteen years ago now. I still miss her.

ENID. I wasn't a good daughter. When she was alive it was like I had something to fall back on. I used to blame her . . .

MAI. My son blames me for the weather.

ENID. Our children are right to blame us. If we can't protect them we shouldn't have them.

MAI. But we have such faith you see. Every birth is a renewal, a second chance. We make sacrifices to make sure it is. My mother worked so hard she went blind. You should a' hear how she did curse God.

Soon after she discovered that I had the gift. My mother's blindness was the sacrifice for my sight.

Pause. MAI *watches* ENID, *who looks away.* MAI *looks at her watch, rises.*

ENID. Now I have nothing.

MAI. There's always something.

ENID. No.

MAI (*hinting*). Boy, time you look round the day over.

ENID (*taking the hint*). Tekking up you time . . .

MAI. Don't worry lady. Just have to put the chickens to bed.

ENID. Chickens?

MAI. I have five. Put me in mind a' back home, you see.

ENID. You keep them here?

MAI. And why shouldn't I? Is there any law against it? If the woman upstairs didn't take out a court order on me. I give her court order. If I set one big duppy 'pon she . . . Though of course, I couldn't do that. I use my gift only to do good.

ENID. If I did send that money home she wouldna' die.

MAI (*taking* ENID's *coat from the hook on the door*). We all got to go sometime. Is in the book: 'A time to born, a time to die'. (*Hands* ENID *her coat, which* ENID *takes, although she doesn't move.*) You want something else lady?

ENID (*still not moving*). No. (*Standing, she stares straight ahead, then her face contorts and her mouth opens in a soundless scream. She starts to sob, terribly embarrassed and trying to hold back.*)

MAI. Let it out lady.

ENID (*getting herself together, wiping her eyes*). Sorry.

MAI. Feel better ennit?

ENID. Weeks now I ain't sleep.

MAI (*sitting* ENID *down*). You bin to a doctor?

ENID. What doctor know about our illness? Just give you few pills to sick you stomach and a doctor certificate. What they know about a black woman soul.

MAI (*understanding*). What you want me do for you?

ENID. When I kneel to pray in church, I feel a pressure all round here. (*Holds her head.*) Like something want to crush the life outa'me. I can't work like before. I can't talk to people any more. Take this evil spirit off me.

MAI. If this was back home I woulda' say bring me two a' you best fowl as a sorta' sacrifice. Over here I don't think the blood a' two meagre chicken going make you better.

ENID. Is this I come here for? Look at me. (*Smiles, bitter.*) Miss English.

MAI. Is not easy turning you back on a way a' life and building another. You mustn't think we failed. Why, I have a son somewhere. He don't come home any more . . . (*Moves to cupboard and takes out a small bottle, which she gives to* ENID.) Take these. Make a sign a' the cross on you' forehead with this one in the morning and this one at night. The pressure soon ease. Soon you notice life picking up again.

ENID (*reaching into her bag*). How much?

MAI. Nuttin'. I give as a friend.

ENID *stands and waits. There's something frail about her now, in contrast to the strong woman in earlier scenes.*

Anything else you want me to do for you?

ENID. Give me back my daughter.

MAI. I can't conjure up bodies from outa' thin air.

ENID. I know she staying here.

MAI. Enid Matthews.

ENID. Just bring her come.

MAI *takes off her wig, scratches her head, snuffs candle on table and goes out.* ENID *moves upstage and composes herself.* DEL *comes in.*

DEL. Mum?

ENID *turns and looks at her. For a moment one might think she will embrace* DEL. *She can't. Instead she opens her handbag and takes out a couple of notes. She gives them to* DEL, *who doesn't move.*

ENID. Tek it.

DEL. You always give money.

ENID (*looking round room*). Rather take things off a stranger.

DEL. *takes the envelope from the previous scene off the table and hands it to* ENID.

DEL. Viv left this behind.

ENID. What I have is yours.

DEL. Send it to your family back home.

ENID. So you're a rich man's daughter?

DEL. You let your mother die.

ENID. She was a' old woman.

DEL. You always said how strong she was. A doctor coulda' give her a few more years.

ENID. What for?

DEL. I can't believe that you could be so selfish and cruel.

ENID. You don't know nuttin'. Go an' sen' the money home. Let them feast today. What about tomorrow? You think one little gift going make their life all right? You poorer than they are. Least them all in it together. When I was a girl you kill a cow, you share it up, everybody in the distric' get a piece. Here, you poor an' you by you'self. Nobody cares. Send it home. (*She tears the notes and scatters them about the room.* DEL *tries to restrain her but* ENID *just shrugs her off.*) What I have is yours. Nobody else.

DEL. Why did you come here? I don't wanna' see you. I'm doing all right here. There's nothing I want from you.

ENID. You really think you something, ennit? You soon find out what it like. You soon wake up.

DEL. I have. Into a fucking nightmare.

ENID. You an' you' bastard picknee. You nuttin', y'hear me? Nuttin'.

DEL *slaps her mother, then recoils. A moment passes where each stands, shocked.* MAI *comes in.*

MAI. Please, the landlady want to know what going on. She ain't see so many people pass through here since Carnival.

ENID (*quietly*). Nuttin' going on . . .

ENID *goes out. Pause.* DEL. *takes her jacket from the hook on the door and puts it on.*

DEL. Need some fresh air.

MAI. Don't you feel for her?

DEL. *doesn't reply.*

She as lost as you are.

DEL. Who says I'm lost?

MAI. Then why did you come here?

DEL. Just . . . needed a place to stay.

MAI (*angry*). Come here, expecting me to give you the answers –
palm reading, herbal bath, tricks with cards, read the bumps on
you head – expect me to look into your lives and alter the future for
you. You have sucked me dry. I've come to the end. My battery
dead. Finished. I have had enough.

DEL. I don't believe in that stuff.

MAI. Then what you want from me?

DEL. Don't know.

MAI. That's a start.

DEL. Maybe I am lost.

MAI. You want a stout.

DEL *nods.*

(*Opening the bottle, handing it to* DEL.) You should be helping each
other survive.

DEL. She let her mother die.

MAI. Don't we all let our mothers die? She's just one woman. (*Starts
moving off.*) I'm going to bed. I need a good long sleep.

DEL. You said this morning I should find somewhere else to stay.

MAI. You got a place?

DEL. (*downcast*). I got friends.

MAI (*rises, looks for something on the table*). Drink you stout. Give you
strength. You need to be strong. (*Takes up sheets of paper.*) Take
these.

DEL. What is it?

MAI. I sometimes write things down.

DEL. Like magic spells?

MAI (*smiles*). I want you to have my thoughts. I don't have a daughter
to pass them on to. And that boy, he won't listen. (*Slight pause.*) We

keep fighting, shadow-boxing they call it. Looking in mirrors and throwing punches on thin air. What are you fighting?

Pause.

DEL. How d'you get it? The gift?

MAI. When I was a girl mother got down on her hands and knees each night and prayed to God to save me.

DEL. What from?

MAI. There was nothing for a woman – no job, nothing but babies. Mother had her first child when she was fourteen.

DEL. Her prayers were answered.

MAI. When she had a headache I had only to touch her forehead and she was cured. You don't believe me? Maybe you right.

DEL. You don't know how much I'd like to believe you. I want things to work out. Like when you was a kid playing pretend and things got out of hand you could conjure up a fairy godmother to wipe the slate clean and pretend none of it happened. I'd love to live my life like that: pretending none of it had ever happened. I'd love for you to give me something. I don't want a baby: I'm scared I'm gonna' hate it like she hates me. I'm not in love with it now – it's sucking me dry, taking me over. I don't want it.

MAI. Then why did you get pregnant?

DEL. What?

MAI. You want it all right.

DEL. Yes.

MAI. I need a holiday. Some sunshine before I die.

DEL. Go home.

MAI. Home is like a figment a' my imagination. You know, sometime I think our people condemn' to wander the earth. Is a sorta' punishment.

DEL. What we done wrong?

MAI. What anybody done wrong? The world full a' people think that life is a hit and run driver and that they jus' innocent bystanders. I'm telling you to grasp life by the reins, and to ride it. And don't you dare let go.

DEL (*puts down the bottle*). I'm going.

MAI. Where? (*Smiles.*) Home?

DEL *returns the smile.*

I thought that this was the last journey, that I would settle here. Then I look at my boy: he English as they come – a Cockney – though he don't think so. All the time he roaming in him mind, round and round like he want to escape, but where the hell he going to escape to? If he could find some peace in himself – journey inside himself – everything would be all right. You at peace with yourself, you at home anywhere.

DEL. That true?

MAI. No.

DEL. Then what is?

MAI. I'm an old woman.

DEL. You make sense by not making sense.

MAI. Why not just go home to you' mother? Run and catch her up.

DEL. I can't.

Pause.

I think we probably come from a tribe of nomads: it's in the blood – from Africa to the West Indies. You know, my grandmother travelled to Cuba to cut cane in the twenties. Then my mum came here . . .

MAI. So, now, where you going?

DEL *stands for a short while, smiles and shrugs.*

DEL. For a walk. (*She goes out.*)

Scene Three

Very early morning the next day. BRODERICK *lies stretched out on the table.* DEL, *in her T-shirt, is looking down at him quizzically. She puts her hand to his face, checks his breathing, lifts his hand and lets it flop back to his chest. She puts her ear to his chest.* MAI *stands beside her, carrying a mug of water.*

MAI. Him dead?

DEL. Not quite.

MAI. Good.

MAI *tips water from the mug into* BRODERICK's *face. They watch him as he blinks, then slowly comes to life, groaning. He sits up and blinks, then stares at* DEL *and* MAI.

BRODERICK. This heaven?

DEL. We look like angels, Uncle Brod?

MAI. You know this old tramp?

BRODERICK. Old tramp?

DEL. He's my uncle – family friend. What happened?

BRODERICK. Woman gone mad. If she didn't turn me outa' the house.

DEL. Why?

BRODERICK. Say she carry too many people for too long, then throw me an' Viv outa' the house.

DEL. Where's Viv?

BRODERICK. Staying with a friend.

DEL.. She shoulda' come here.

MAI. Here? The landlady think I up to no good in here as it is.

BRODERICK. Fancy, all the years I know her an' she kick me out into the street with nowhere to go.

MAI. So the man spen' the evening in public house. Then after, come knocking on my door, waking up my neighbours in middle night a shout say how him gone blind.

DEL.. Blind?

BRODERICK. If you did drink a bottle a' rum to you'self, you could see anything?

DEL. When you gonna' learn, Uncle Brod?

MAI. Look what him do to me table. Why him choose this house? You can tell me?

BRODERICK. I wanted to speak to my young friend. There was something I had was to tell her.

DEL. What?

BRODERICK. My mind gone blank.

MAI. Minute I set eye 'pon that Enid Matthews I did know say the woman was trouble. I did read it in she palm.

BRODERICK. You do reading?

DEL. Palms, cards, tea leaves, you name it she does it.

MAI. I was thinking a' retiring.

BRODERICK. You does heal?

MAI. Only by appointment.

BRODERICK. I can make appointment now?

MAI (*nodding at* DEL). See my secretary.

DEL. You what?

BRODERICK. You see I have this . . .

MAI. Sunday is my day of rest.

BRODERICK (*disappointed*). Oh. (*Rubs his throat.*) I thirsty.

MAI. You want some water?

BRODERICK. I would prefer a . . . (MAI *gives him a look*.) A drop a water would an' nice.

MAI *goes out.*

DEL. Poor Uncle Brod.

BRODERICK. Poor Broderick James. A doomed man.

DEL. You still drunk?

BRODERICK. Always playing the fool. I was the same at school.

DEL. Behind every clown . . .

BRODERICK. Take off the mask to reveal another an' so on an' so forth. (*Holds his head.*)

DEL. Want an aspirin?

BRODERICK. The pain feel good: I like to pay a penance.

DEL. You drink too much.

BRODERICK. It help me forget.

DEL. What?

BRODERICK (*raises his eyebrows*). I forget.

DEL. Old joke.

BRODERICK. You expect a' old drunk like me to create new ones?

DEL. You're not an old drunk.

BRODERICK (*looking down at himself and getting down off the table, stretches*). You think you Mooma would an' let me in if I serenade she under she window?

DEL. Better play it cool Brod.

BRODERICK. I said some things to you mother last night, heat a' the moment you know.

DEL. Hope you told her a few home truths.

BRODERICK. I shouldna' get involve.

DEL. She'll get over it.

BRODERICK. It not nice to see you mother hurtin'. She must be tired by now.

DEL. I could understand if she put up a fight. She lets life overwhelm her.

BRODERICK. And you don't?

DEL. I can stand up for meself.

BRODERICK. That mus' be why you looking so well. (*Indicates her stomach.*) The father visit you?

DEL. I don't want him to.

BRODERICK. I have a wife and children.

DEL. I never knew you had children.

BRODERICK. They don't want to know me.

DEL. Why?

BRODERICK. I don't talk about it.

DEL. Why not?

BRODERICK. Because . . .

DEL. What makes men so allergic to the sound of a baby crying?

BRODERICK. You're a child, you don't understand. These things happen when we were young.

DEL. You love my mum or what?

BRODERICK. What sorta' question that?

DEL. Do you?

BRODERICK. No. Not in the way you talking.

DEL. Why not? Tell me.

BRODERICK (*joking*). Black women so hard to love. They do every damn' thing by themself. Them so blinking self-sufficient they don't need a man for anything.

DEL. Leave us out, Brod.

BRODERICK (*squirming*). It's hard to love black women. To do so you have to . . .

DEL. What?

BRODERICK. Love you'self.

DEL. Yeah? (*Retreating.*) Just wanted to know, that's all.

BRODERICK (*can't bring himself to look* DEL *in the eye*). I was no good for my wife. I couldn't love her and yet she was the most precious thing . . . I wanted to kill . . . I hated her because she could see what it was I wanted to kill. I hated her intelligence, her beauty because I felt none a' these things in me. I wanted to destroy them. (*Slight pause.*) This is a confession.

DEL. I can't absolve you.

BRODERICK. I don't want you to. I was never as bad as some a' these men.

DEL. Good old Uncle Brod.

BRODERICK. You' father, he was a mad man. One time I go to the house an' he . . .

DEL. I don't wanna' know.

BRODERICK (*almost to himself*). I never see a man eyes look so empty. Him never use to behave them ways in Jamaica. What do that to us? Englan'?

Slight pause.

You mother did really love him. She didn't want anybody else from the time when we was young.

DEL. You come here to tell me all this rubbish?

BRODERICK. You soon be a mother you'self.

DEL. So everyone keeps reminding me as if it's some big deal. It's not gonna' change me.

BRODERICK. The tragedy a' parenthood is that you bring up you children as if you preparing them to live the perfect life that you never had. Only thing is, you got to send them out into an imperfect world. You mother can't change the world.

DEL. I never asked her to.

BRODERICK. Her life hasn't been easy.

DEL. She's made a martyr of herself. I'll never do that.

BRODERICK. A person can't fight through life without stopping to lick them wounds. She not Nanny a' the Maroons. You got to try and understand her, what she been through.

DEL. All right, but when will she ever understand me?

MAI *comes in with some water.*

MAI. Is you was playing with that tap?

DEL. No.

MAI. Damn thing stick.

BRODERICK. I gone.

MAI. So quick?

BRODERICK. I got things to do.

DEL. What?

BRODERICK. Little joke . . . serenade you Mooma under she window. (*He goes out.*)

MAI. But what a man mad. Oh well. (*Raises mug.*) Cheers.

MAI *drinks water and the scene ends.*

Scene Four

MAI*'s bedsit, a few days later. The stage is quite dark. A broom is propped against the table.* DEL, *wearing an apron, sits at the table. A lighted candle is in the centre of the table.* DEL *stares at the naked flame, then chants.*

DEL. O wonderful and bountiful Goddess of Harmony. Bring me money and prosperity. Shine your radiant and benevolent face down on my finances today. Bring me all the riches I desire today. Thank you, Vesta, for your generous help.

MAI *appears in the latter part of her speech and watches her, then:*

MAI. What you up to?

DEL *quickly blows out the candle, gets up and switches on the light. We see that the room is much tidier than in previous scenes.* DEL *takes up a duster and proceeds to polish the table.*

I hope you ain't using my equipment for you' own selfish ends.

DEL. I was just mucking about.

MAI. You muck about in you' own time in future.

DEL. This place look clean or what? Feel like Cinderella.

MAI (*runs her finger along the table to test for dust*). Not bad.

DEL. First time this place's been cleaned in years.

MAI (*picks up the candle*). You use the last a' the candle begging Vesta to make you a millionaire?

DEL. I'll go out and get some more in a minute. (*Sweeping now.*) You need a new coat.

MAI. I like old things.

DEL. So do I.

MAI *keeps her coat on and sits wearily.*

MAI. I ever tell you about pocomania?

DEL. That's when the women back home dressed in white and huffed and puffed themselves into the spirit world and ended up talking tongues. Why don't we have a poco session? I fancy a trip to the twilight world.

MAI. You need wide open spaces.

DEL. We could go on Hampstead Heath or somewhere.

MAI. You want to end up in gaol?

DEL. We wouldn't.

MAI. Didn't they put Pastor Perry in gaol for breaking into Highgate Cemetery and sprinkling fowl blood over this Marx man tombstone?

DEL. Serves him right. Silly old fool.

MAI. Yes. The old ways are dying.

DEL. About time too.

MAI. What you doing here if you ain't keeping them alive?

DEL. There's enough older people around who need all this mumbo jumbo. 'Sides it's a laugh. Better than that burger bar. Things people tell you.

MAI. I ever hear you repeating what go on in here to anybody outside is me an' you.

DEL. As if I would.

MAI. You sick this morning?

DEL. Bit.

MAI. You never drink the tea I did leave you?

DEL. It's too strong. Only makes me worse.

MAI. You expect everything to come to you easy. What time is it?

DEL. Quarter to.

MAI. We got a client arriving in fifteen minutes.

DEL. You shoulda' told me. (*Takes cardbox file from table.*) What's the name?

MAI. You an' your file. I got all the information I need up here. (*Touches her head, yawns.*)

DEL. Tired?

MAI. Not me. (*The following is a regular routine.*) You practise with the cards?

DEL. There's so much to remember. On its own a card means one thing, then alongside another it can mean any number of things. I can't get the hang of it.

MAI. Keep practising. (*Holds out her palm to* DEL.) Read.

DEL (*staring at* MAI*'s palm frowning, struggling to remember what she's been taught like a child learning to read*). I can't.

MAI. Can't. Can't. Can't is your favourite word. Come on, girl.

DEL (*after a while*). You're going to have a long life.

MAI. You think I going cross you' palm with silver for that piece a flannel?

DEL. One day you'll be rich.

MAI. How many times must I tell you? (*Pulls her hand away*.) You see everything you need to know in their eyes.

DEL. Sorry Mai.

MAI. Miss Etta call this morning?

DEL. I gave her two bottles of protection oil and told her to come back next month.

MAI. She pay you?

DEL. She never has enough.

MAI. Old fox got it hide away somewhere.

DEL (*undoing her apron*). Go and get those candles.

MAI. Later. I want you to deal with this client.

DEL. On my own?

MAI. I can't always hold your hand.

DEL. I'll screw up.

MAI. You won't.

DEL. (*starting to prepare for the meeting. Putting holy water on the table, lighting a candle*). Will you stay an' listen to me?

MAI. I'm going to visit a friend a' mine. Make a change to visit a friend in she living room rather than a cemetery.

DEL. You're morbid.

MAI. I'm a realist. A very tired realist. I'll soon start forgetting things.

DEL. I'll look after you.

Pause. MAI *looks at* DEL *fondly.*

MAI. You're a good girl. You' client soon come. I gone.

DEL. Don't go. I'm nervous.

MAI. You be all right. See you later.

MAI *goes.* DEL *fiddles with the table, then tidies herself up and looks in the mirror. Moves back centre stage and lays out the cards. There's a knock on the door.* DEL *crosses to open it. The door opens to reveal* ENID. *The women stand in the doorway.*

ENID. I have a' appointment. I can come in? Mai did say you would be in.

DEL *lets* ENID *into the room.*

ENID. This place look different.

DEL. I been spring cleaning.

ENID. At home you couldn't boil water.

> DEL, *still standing, looks down at her feet.*

Sit down girl.

> DEL *remains standing.*

I never know say a daughter a' mine woulda' turn obeah woman.

DEL (*snaps*). I'm not going to apologise.

ENID. I ain't come here to fight.

DEL. Then what you come for?

ENID. You're my daughter.

DEL. So it's a duty call?

ENID. No.

> *She turns away.*

I never thought I see the day my child raise her hand to me. Many times I was angry with Mooma but I never hit her.

DEL. Am I supposed to feel guilty? Well, I don't.

ENID. I'm the one feel guilty. It ain't easy to let you' mother die. I knew she was dying. When I went out there you could just see it. She wanted me to put a' end to it. Come from big big England mus' have something that would put a' end to the waiting. I could hardly stand to watch her. Her skin was always smooth, no wrinkles – she did look like a big fat baby, like somebody doom to live forever. She would sit at the window and watch life growing, decaying, a pig dying, a goat strangling itself on it string – and pray that she would be next. She made me promise that I wouldn't send anything out for her, said that I was Miss English, that I should forget them and get on with my life here . . . How can a person forget? To do that you would have to tear your heart out.

> *Slight pause.*

When I was young Mooma never like me. I never do anything right for her. I was too black, my hair too dry – all the things that she was and didn't want to be. And I was never strong enough. All her life she worked like a man.

DEL. You're strong.

ENID. I have to seem strong because you an' Viv so weak.

DEL. You make us weak. You keep back so much of you'self that you're never really there when we need you. It's like you've left your real self behind somewhere in the past and now all that's left is an empty shell.

ENID. Empty shell? This is me. This is what I've become. I might not always like it, but it's what I am.

DEL. Maybe you shoulda' stayed in Jamaica.

ENID. Maybe.

DEL. I'll never lose myself.

ENID. No? Don't scorn the way I've lived my life, Del. At least I've survived.

DEL. At what cost? I always feel like I don't belong nowhere, like I'm running around trying to find a place to fit in. But now, for once in my life I can't run away. For the sake a' my kid I got to stand and face up to who I am. For once in my life I feel like I got a future.

Slight pause.

Every night I go to bed and curl up tight and pretend I'm a kid again: when you used to hold me and whisper secrets in my ear, remember?

ENID. And don't I need to curl up in somebody lap and to be told stories to make the sun shine? Don't I need somebody to touch my cheek as though I was a prize not a curse and to stroke my hair like Mooma never did? What about me?

Pause.

DEL. Do you hate me?

ENID. How can I?

ENID *holds* DEL *in a steady gaze,* DEL *looks down at her feet.*

Del.

DEL *looks up.*

ENID (*opening her arms*). Come hold me.

Ends

Billy Roche was educated by the Christian Brothers in Wexford. His first job was as a barman in a little pub run by his father. Later he worked in factories and building sites until he drifted into the music scene as a singer/musician. When life on the road became too tedious – and when he was thirty and had a wife and three children to support – he retired and began to write the novel *Tumbling Down*. Halfway through the final draft of the book he began to write the play *A Handful of Stars*, which was then entitled *The Boker Poker Club*. The play was in fact first performed in Wexford with a local cast. Billy played the part of Stapler, the over-the-hill boxer. The lead part of Jimmy Brady was played by Gary O'Brien, who later went on to play the part in London at the Bush. At present Billy Roche is working on a new play for the Bush and also a second novel, set in Wexford at the turn of the century. As an actor he has played Willie Diver in Brian Friel's play *Aristocrats* at the Hampstead Theatre in 1988, a small part in David Hare's film *Strapless* and, on television, one episode of *The Bill*.

A Handful of Stars was first performed in London at the Bush Theatre on 15 February 1988 with the following cast:

PADDY	Joseph Brady
CONWAY	Peter Caffrey
STAPLER	Breffni McKenna
LINDA	Dervla Kirwan
TONY	Aidan Murphy
JIMMY	Gary O'Brien
SWAN	Michael O'Hagan

Directed by Robin Lefevre
Designed by Gordon Stewart & Andrew Wood
Lighting by Paul Denby
Sound by Louise Bates
Artistic Directors for the Bush Theatre Jenny Topper & Nicky Pallot.

Characters

JIMMY, A good looking, tough boy of seventeen or so.
TONY, Jimmy's sidekick. A shy, gauche lad.
CONWAY, A big-mouthed know-all of about thirty-three or four who acts older than his years.
PADDY, An old man who is the caretaker of the club.
STAPLER, A strong, lively man of thirty-three or four.
LINDA, An attractive girl of seventeen or so.
SWAN, A wily detective.

The Setting

The play is set in a scruffy pool hall. There is a pool table, a jukebox, a pot-bellied stove and a one-armed bandit. There are three doors – one leading to the street, one to the toilet and the other leads into the back room where the older, privileged members go. Entrance to the back room is slightly elevated and there is a glass panel in the door through which the caretaker can keep an eye out over his domain. Along one wall there is a long bench and a blackboard and a cue stand and all the usual paraphernalia that can be found in a club of this sort.

The story takes place in a small town somewhere in Ireland. The First Act has a time span of about two weeks. The Second Act takes place the following month, in the course of one night.

ACT ONE

Scene One

The Club with PADDY *opening up the awkward window shutters. When this is done he gets some cue chalk from an old wooden box perched on the ledge and lays three or four squares along the pool table, evenly spaced apart. Then he gets a bottle of Dettol from the cardboard box under the seat and begins sprinkling it around the place, going in through the toilet door to sprinkle some in there, flushing the toilet, coming back coughing, tossing the empty bottle into the waste paper basket. Now he stands and takes a good look at the place, raising up his peaked cap with his thumb and scratching his head. We hear someone knocking on the door and shouting out* PADDY's *name. When* PADDY *does eventually open the front door* JIMMY *and* TONY *come rushing in, both of them trying to make it first to the pool table, nearly knocking poor* PADDY *down in the rush.*

PADDY (*annoyed*). Mind up there the hell out of that. (*He sees the two boys tugging for the best cue.*) Hey cut out the trickactin' there now.

TONY *gives up the struggle and settles for the bad cue.*

JIMMY (*putting in the money*). What kept yeh Paddy? We thought you were after goin' on strike. Set 'em up there Tony. Were you at the pictures or what Paddy? Heads or harps?

PADDY (*still going about his business, doing little jobs*). Yeah. I went up as far as the first house.

TONY. I'm breakin' Jimmy. You broke last night.

JIMMY. Heads or harps?

TONY. Heads.

JIMMY (*tosses the coin onto the back of his hand*). Hard luck. Ha ha ha ... set 'em up. Was it any use Paddy?

PADDY (*standing on the chair to turn on the outside lights*). Naw.

JIMMY (*chalking his cue*). Hey Tony straighten 'em up there a bit will yeh? *Now* you're learnin'. Come out of me way now.

JIMMY *belts the ball into the bunch a little too aggressively for* PADDY's *liking.*

PADDY. Hey boy, be careful there.

JIMMY. What's wrong with yeh Paddy?

PADDY. That's a brand new cloth on that table. Tear it and it'll cost yeh.

JIMMY. Will you go away and don't be annoyin' yourself Paddy.

PADDY *stops in his tracks and throws the boy a dirty look.* JIMMY *doesn't even bother to respond.* PADDY *goes across to the door leading into the back room and pulls the keys out of his pocket. When he opens up the door* TONY's *head whips around.* PADDY *goes inside and* TONY *rambles over to take a peep in at the room.* PADDY *closes the door over in his face.* JIMMY, *spying that* TONY *is miles away, tries to steal an extra shot.*

TONY. Hey Jimmy it's my shot. What are you wantin', them all or somethin'?

JIMMY. My go. I just potted a ball didn't I?

TONY. Where?

JIMMY (*chancing his arm*). Look come out of me way will yeh.

TONY. You did in me shit pot a ball. Go away yeh chancer.

JIMMY (*conceding*). Alright then, go on.

TONY. I'm not coddin' yeh boy you're the biggest chancer I ever met. I'm goin' to keep an eye on you in future. How am I supposed to play with this auld yoke anyway?

JIMMY. Look stop whingin' and fire.

TONY. I don't see why I should always end up with the bad cue.

PADDY *comes out of the back room carrying a toilet roll.* JIMMY *has played a record on the jukebox.* PADDY *winces, puts the toilet roll on the ledge and goes across to plug out the jukebox. It stops with a jerk.*

JIMMY. Hey Paddy, what's goin' on?

PADDY (*climbing from his knees*). You know well enough that you're not allowed to play the jukebox after half eight.

JIMMY. But sure yeh weren't here Paddy, were yeh?

PADDY. Yeh know the rules.

JIMMY. But sure how am I supposed to play the jukebox if the place is not open?

PADDY *ignores him as he wonders where it was he put the toilet roll.*

Alright then Paddy just give us me money back and we'll say no more.

PADDY *throws him a dirty look.* PADDY *finds the toilet roll and heads towards the toilet.* JIMMY *imitates his walk, making* TONY *splutter and miscue the ball.* JIMMY *spots it and pounces on the chance.*

Hey Tony that counts as a shot.

TONY. Aw no you made me laugh that time. (*Trying to hold* JIMMY *at bay.*)

JIMMY. Come out of it Tony and stop actin' the cannatt. Hey Paddy this lad is cheatin' out here.

TONY. No, fair is fair Jimmy, you made me laugh that time.

JIMMY. That's your hard luck Tony. Come out of it.

The two boys have a tugging match over the table with JIMMY *shoving* TONY *and* TONY *holding on to the edge of the table for dear life. Enter* STAPLER, *carrying a handy black bag over his shoulder.*

TONY (*panting*). How's it goin' Stapler?

STAPLER. How's the men? Actin' the bollocks again are yeh?

JIMMY (*giving up the struggle, much to* TONY's *surprise*). Hey Stapler I heard you're goin' back into the ring again.

STAPLER. Oh yes. Old Twinkle Toes is back.

JIMMY. Any fights lined up?

STAPLER. Yeah. I'm fightin' young Harpur tomorrow night sure.

JIMMY. Who? Eddie Harpur? He's good, boy.

STAPLER. He is. He's a good chap alright.

TONY. He'll be no match for our Stapler though.

STAPLER starts to skip on the spot and begins to shadow box, accelerating into a frenzy of rapid punches and blinding combinations. He has a dead serious expression on his face and his eyes seem to be staring into the eyes of the ghost of his opponent – dancing around after him, pushing him into the corner etc.

JIMMY. Oon the Stapler, you're kickin' the laird out of him now alright.

STAPLER lets his arms dangle as if the fight is over and looks across at the boys for approval.

TONY (*standing over the floored body of the make-believe opponent*). You knocked him as dead as a cock, Stapler.

STAPLER. What are yeh lookin' down there for Tony? Up there he is. Hey Paddy, scrape that lad off the ceilin' there will yeh.

PADDY, *coming from the toilet doorway throws his eyes to heaven, shivers with the cold and goes across to the stove.*

JIMMY. Oon Stapler me boy. What do yeh think of him Paddy?

PADDY *sighs and throws his eyes to heaven.*

STAPLER. You can't keep a good man down, ain't that right Paddy?

PADDY (*sighs and mumbles*). Huh you'll get sense so yeh will. Thirty-three years of age . . .

STAPLER (*a little embarrassed*). Were any of yeh at the pictures?

JIMMY. Paddy was.

STAPLER. Any use Paddy?

PADDY (*kneeling beside the stove*). Naw. Bloody hopeless. That's cold. What's wrong with that now I wonder.

STAPLER. I'm surprised at that then. That Robert Ryan is usually good. I love him actin'.

TONY. Yeah, he's a queer smily fecker ain't he?

STAPLER. What? Oh yeah he's kind of sleezy lookin' alright. Good though.

JIMMY. I think we saw that picture before, Tony.

TONY. No, I never saw that one.

JIMMY. I'm nearly sure we did. Hey Paddy, is your man all dressed in black?

PADDY. Yeah.

JIMMY. And does he ride a deadly white horse?

PADDY. Yeah.

JIMMY. Yeah we saw that one alright Tony. Do you remember? He gets shot right between the eyes in the end.

TONY. Don't tell me. I'm wantin' to go and see it tomorrow night.

JIMMY. Sure I'm tellin' yeah we saw it before. Does your man get killed in the end Paddy?

PADDY (*still tinkering with the damper of the stove*). Yeah. The girl shoots him right between the eyes in the end.

TONY *throws his eyes to heaven in disbelief.*

STAPLER (*moving towards the back room*). None of the lads down yet Paddy?

PADDY. No. That's it now. (*He stands up, holding his aching back.*)

STAPLER. Aw sure they won't be long now I suppose. I'll set up the table for a game.

TONY. Do you want a hand Stapler?

PADDY *looks at the boy in amazement.*

STAPLER (*falters*). Mmn . . . Aw no it's alright Tony. Is the special cue closet open or closed Paddy?

PADDY. It's closed. I'll be in there in a minute.

STAPLER. Right.

JIMMY. Hey lads I think we should organise a bus load of supporters to go down and cheer Stapler on tomorrow night. What do you think Paddy?

STAPLER (*from the doorway*). But sure it's only down the road in the Foresters Hall.

JIMMY. Yeah, but it'd look more impressive if we all arrived in a big bus, yeh know what I mean?

PADDY *shakes his head and sighs as he waddles into the back room with* JIMMY *sniggering behind his back.*

Paddy could pay for it out of the funds.

TONY. Do yeh think you'll win Stapler?

STAPLER *shrugs.*

Here come on Stapler, I'll give yeh three round now.

TONY *puts up his guard and shuffles towards* STAPLER.

STAPLER (*letting fly a punch that slaps* TONY *right in the face*). Keep that guard up boy. Watch that . . . and that . . .

STAPLER *has landed a combination of punches that mesmerise* TONY. *Now the two of them dance about on their toes with* TONY *trying to land a punch or two on* STAPLER *who ducks and weaves skilfully. When* TONY *sees the earnest face on* STAPLER *he cowers away from him and* STAPLER *follows him. Finally* TONY *turns and flees around the pool table.* STAPLER *grins fondly at this sight, his fondness for the boy showing in his smile.*

What do yeh think of him Jimmy?

JIMMY. I'm goin' to tell yeh one thing, if he don't hurry up and take his shot I'll be givin' him the greatest kick up the hole he ever got.

TONY (*taking aim*). But sure how could yeh play with this yoke Stapler? Look at the state of it? (*He holds up the cue.*)

JIMMY. A bad workman always blames his tools.

STAPLER (*stepping forward*). Show, give us a look. Sure you'd never learn to play properly with that yoke. Why can't yeh share the decent cue anyway? I mean it's not that hard to pass it back and forward to one another or anything.

TONY. Yeah come on Jimmy, act the white man.

JIMMY (*reluctantly handing the cue across*). Oh here, before yeh burst a blood vessel or somethin'.

STAPLER. That's it. Now you're learnin'.

TONY *bends to take his shot.* STAPLER *goes across and takes a large bottle of lemonade from his bag. He opens it and takes a gulp, belches and offers* JIMMY *a slug.*

JIMMY (*wiping the top of the bottle before taking a slug*). Hey Stapler do auld Matt still be down in the boxin' club?

STAPLER. Matt. Yeah. Sure Matt is the boss. How come I don't see any of you two down there no more?

JIMMY. Sure Matt put me out of the club. The last night I was down there he made me spar against your man whatshisname . . . Healy. He went to town on me I'm not coddin' yeh boy. Didn't he Tony?

TONY. What?

JIMMY. I say your man Healy went to town on me. He bet the head off me Stapler I swear. I wouldn't mind but I hadn't been trainin' nor nothin' yeh know. So I waited outside for him after and I bursted him.

STAPLER. You're not supposed to box outside the ring Jimmy.

JIMMY. Who said anythin' about boxin'. I gave him a headbutt. End of story. I gave him a right furt for himself too I don't mind tellin' yeh. Didn't I Tony?

TONY. Yeah, a royal furt up the rectum.

JIMMY. Wrecked him, I nearly friggin' killed him.

STAPLER. Were you put out of the club too Tony?

TONY. No I wasn't . . . Ah I wouldn't be bothered with that auld lark at all Stapler. Gettin' the head bet off me for a lousy medal.

STAPLER. Mmn . . . I suppose.

STAPLER *looks at* TONY *who is a little embarrassed and afraid that he may have offended* STAPLER'*s feelings. Then* STAPLER *glances towards* JIMMY, *a slight hint of condemnation in his eyes.* JIMMY *couldn't care less.* STAPLER *lowers the rest of the lemonade and tosses the bottle into the basket. Then he circles the table, watching* TONY *playing as he walks.*

Keep your chin down Tony. That's it. Good shot. Where are yeh goin' now? Take a good look at the table before you go rushin' around the place. Use your head . . . Hit it low down now . . .

JIMMY. Hey Stapler, let him play his own game.

STAPLER (*ignoring* JIMMY'*s words*). Hard luck Tony. Yeh have to use your head Tony. That's what it's all about. Up here for thinkin', down there for dancin'. (*He stands there for a moment to watch* JIMMY *shoot, then he rambles into the back room.*)

TONY. He's queer fast ain't he.

JIMMY *nods that he is fairly fast.*

I'd say he'll beat your man no bother would you?

JIMMY. I don't know. Eddie Harpur is fairly handy.

JIMMY *heads into the toilet just as* CONWAY *comes storming into the club.*

TONY. You're just after missin' it Conway.

CONWAY. What are yeh sayin' feathery feck?

TONY. I said you're just after missin' it here. Stapler is after splatterin' Eddie Harpur all over the place here. I'm not coddin' yeh boy there was blood everywhere.

CONWAY (*unimpressed*). I'd say that.

TONY. I'm goin' to tell yeh one thing boy, he's queer fast.

CONWAY. He'll want to be on skates to get away from that lad tomorrow night.

TONY (*concerned*). Whys would you say he'd beat Stapler?

CONWAY *throws a dirty look.*

CONWAY. Are yeh coddin' me or what? Sure that chap is brilliant.

Enter PADDY, *climbing into his overcoat.*

Well Paddy, what did yeh think of that then?

PADDY. Useless. The world's worst now that's all's about it.

CONWAY. The first one wasn't bad.

PADDY. No.

CONWAY. But as for that other yoke. The world's worst is right. I can't stand that Robert Ryan actin' in pictures. (*He sees* PADDY *pulling on his scarf which was hanging by the stove.*) Hey Paddy, we're goin' to have a game of poker in a few minutes – as soon as the lads arrive – will you be back or what?

PADDY. Yeah, I'll be back in a minute. I'm only goin' down as far as the shop.

CONWAY. Well listen, leave us the key of the closet before you go will yeh. We'll have a quick game of snooker first.

PADDY. The closet is open. Stapler is in there already sure.

CONWAY (*turns to* TONY). Where's the other fella tonight?

TONY. He's out in the jacks.

CONWAY. I see him down in the factory today and he all done up like a dog's dinner. He must have had an interview on or somethin', did he Tony?

TONY. I don't know.

CONWAY. Oh yeah, you're an auld gom too.

TONY. I don't know, Conway.

CONWAY. I'm not coddin' yeh Paddy, he has a neck on him now like a jockey's bollocks, the same fella.

PADDY (*buttoning up his overcoat*). Who's that?

CONWAY. Jimmy Brady. I say he was down in the factory for an interview or somethin' today and he spent the best part of his time now chattin' up the young one in the office.

PADDY *gives a little dismissive nod.*

A great suit and tie and all on him Paddy. I'm not coddin' yeh, to look at him you'd swear butter wouldn't melt in his mouth.

STAPLER (*peeping out of the back room*). Hey Paddy get us a bar of Aero and yeh down there will yeh.

PADDY. Yeah right.

CONWAY. Well Stapler what do you think of the boy here?

STAPLER. What about him?

CONWAY. Do yeh hear Stapler, what about him? He's for the high jump that's what about him.

STAPLER. What do yeh mean?

CONWAY (*sings and mimes playing a violin*).

The bells are ringing for me and my girl
The parson's waiting for me and my girl . . .

STAPLER *'s face saddens at this news.*

Young Whelan.

STAPLER. Who?

CONWAY. Bandy's daughter. Yeh know Bandy. Here's me head and me arse is comin'. (*He demonstrates a duck-like walk.*) The only man I know who is capable of being in two places at the one time.

STAPLER. So are yeh gettin' married then Tony?

TONY (*sighs*). I don't know. I suppose so.

CONWAY. What do you mean, yeh suppose so? You renege on that little girl, boy, and Bandy Whelan will have your guts for garters, so he will. Hey Stapler some of the lads were sayin' that he was cryin' in the canteen this mornin'.

STAPLER. Sure that's no harm.

CONWAY. Well I've no sympathy for him Stapler. He dipped his wick and now he must pay for the pleasure. What did I say to you this time last year Tony?

TONY. You said if my gate creaked I was to make sure and oil it myself before somebody else did it for me.

CONWAY. Yeah and what else did I say?

TONY. Get them young and they'll fly with yeh.

CONWAY. Be careful, I said, or you'll end up buyin' a pram on the never never.

TONY. Oh yeah I forgot about that.

CONWAY. I know you did. Otherwise you wouldn't be in this predicament would yeh?

JIMMY *swaggers out of the toilet. He strikes a match off the edge of the pool table and lights up a scut of a fag that is wedged behind his ear. He sits up on the pool table, his legs dangling.*

Here he is now. Cool Hand Luke.

PADDY (*on his way out of the front door*). If he don't stop strikin' matches off of my good table I'll Cool Hand Luke him.

CONWAY (*moving closer to* JIMMY). Well boy did yeh get the job after?

JIMMY. What job?

CONWAY. I heard you were lookin' for a job down below.

JIMMY. I wouldn't work in a kip like that if you paid me.

CONWAY. Yeah, well I wouldn't worry about that if I was you 'cause I'd safely say there's very little chance of them takin' you on . . . It was short and sweet anyway wasn't it?

JIMMY. What was?

CONWAY. The interview.

JIMMY. Yeah. I took one good look out the window and I saw all these grown men walkin' around dressed up like peasants and I decided there and then that it wasn't the like for me after all.

CONWAY *opens up his overcoat to reveal his overalls.*

CONWAY. It takes a good man to fill one of these boy and don't you ever forget it.

JIMMY *reaches across and tugs roughly at* CONWAY's *overall around the groin area.*

JIMMY. I'd say it's a queer long time since you went next or near to fillin' that up then is it?

CONWAY. Hey, don't let the grey hairs fool yeh poor man.

JIMMY. It's not just the grey hairs Conway. It's the bags under the eyes and the green teeth and the fat belly . . .

CONWAY (*trying to conceal his annoyance*). I'll tell yeh one thing, no woman in this town ever gave me the bum's rush anyway. Hey Stapler, 'I'm washin' me hair', says she to him.

STAPLER. Who?

CONWAY. Linda in the office down below. Your man here asked her for a date. 'I'm washin' me hair', says she. I'm washin' me hair. The oldest one in the book. Honest to God.

JIMMY. Of course she's washin' her hair. I'd told her she'd have to clean herself up before I had anythin' to do with her.

CONWAY. Yes, yeh did yeah. You wouldn't even be in the runnin' there boy. That one wouldn't even contemplate dancin' with the likes of you. You'd have to have a biro stickin' up out of your top pocket before that one would even admit that you existed at all. So don't go foolin' yourself into believin' otherwise.

JIMMY. Will you go and cop on to yourself Conway. There's nothin' special about her.

CONWAY. Do yeh hear . . . Lawrence of Arabia where he is.

STAPLER. Come on Conway and I'll give yeh a game of snooker.

CONWAY. Yeah right Stapler, I'll be in there in a minute.

STAPLER *goes into the back room.* CONWAY *heads for the toilet.*

JIMMY. Oh that reminds me Conway, I'm wantin' fifty pence off you.

CONWAY. You'll be lucky.

JIMMY. We're runnin' a bus down to see Stapler kickin' the shit out of your man tomorrow night.

CONWAY *throws him a dirty look over his shoulder before he goes out.*

TONY. Conway thinks that your man Harpur will beat Stapler.

JIMMY *thinks about it.*

JIMMY. What the fuck would he know about it.

JIMMY *circles the table sizing up his next shot. He sprawls himself across the table just as* PADDY *enters with a handful of things. He is not too pleased to see* JIMMY *stretched across the table.*

PADDY (*shuffling towards the back room*). You get down off that table boy.

JIMMY. Stop the noise Paddy, this is a complicated shot.

PADDY. Yeah well, use the rest.

JIMMY *ignores him and takes his shot.* PADDY *watches and silently scoffs at the boy's lack of skill.* PADDY *goes into the back room just as* CONWAY *is coming out of the toilet.*

JIMMY. Hey Conway are yeh wantin' to take on the winner?

CONWAY. Look I told you before boy. You put up a nice crisp five pound note and I'll take you on, no bother. Moolay, that's my language. I mean to say there's no point in me givin' out lessons to every Tom, Dick and Harry who comes along if there's nothin' in it for me now is there?

JIMMY. I'll tell yeh what I'll do with yeh now Conway. I'll bet you a pound that Stapler beats your man tomorrow night.

CONWAY (*diving into his pocket, pulling out a pound*). You're on. Put your money down there.

JIMMY. Well, I haven't got it on me at the moment but . . .

CONWAY. Hey . . . no mon, no fun boy. If you want to bet with me put your money down on the table there. Otherwise forget it. None of this 'I'll see you Monday' lark at all.

TONY. I'd say Stapler will be well able for your man.

CONWAY. Well there's a pound note says he won't.

TONY. I'll tell yeh one thing Conway he's trainin' queer hard for it.

CONWAY. Yes he is yeah. The only thing Stapler is fit for now is the high jump.

TONY. What do you mean?

CONWAY (*glancing over his shoulder to make sure that* STAPLER *is not there in the doorway or anywhere in sight*). Look he's down in The Shark every night now – drinkin' and knockin' around with your one.

TONY. What one?

CONWAY. The big one do be down there. The one that plays the jukebox all the time.

TONY *looks puzzled*.

She's a hairdresser. A nice bit of stuff.

TONY. I don't know her at all. And Stapler is knockin' her off is he?

CONWAY. Stapler is knockin' around with her this ages.

TONY. And do she know he's married?

CONWAY. Of course she knows he's married. Sure she wouldn't mind that.

TONY. I can't place her at all. Do you know her Jimmy?

JIMMY. Yeah. She's a big fat one. She's rotten.

CONWAY (*sweeping up his money*). So as soon as any of you boys wants to put your money where your mouth is, just give me a shout. (*He heads towards the back room.*)

TONY. Give us a fag Conway before yeh go will yeh?

CONWAY (*stopping in the doorway*). Do you ever buy fags at all boy? I'm not coddin' yeah, he's the very same in work. I'm like a mother to him that's all. Oh here, with your Vincent de Paul face on yeh.

CONWAY *tosses* TONY *a cigarette. Enter* LINDA, *peeping around the door.*

JIMMY (*spotting her*). Here she is now. Now say what you were sayin' about her.

CONWAY (*a little flustered*). What?

LINDA (*stepping forward with contempt*). Why, who was talkin' about me Jimmy?

CONWAY. Yeah Tony, now say what you were sayin' about the girl.

TONY. What?

LINDA (*moving towards him*). Hey Tony, what were you sayin' about me?

TONY. Don't mind them, I never said nothin' . . .

CONWAY. You should be ashamed of yourself, talkin' about the little girl like that behind her back.

JIMMY. Tony is gone all red.

LINDA *seems to cop what has been going on and throws a dagger of a look in* CONWAY's *direction.* PADDY *is gazing out at her through the glass panel, a vexed expression on his face.* LINDA *glares back at him.* JIMMY *follows her gaze, traces it back to* PADDY.

Hey Linda I told yeh not to be followin' me around didn't I. I mean I come in here to get away from women. And look at the state of poor Paddy with yeh. He's nearly after havin' a hernia in there. I mean to say Paddy don't even like lads with long hair comin' in here, never mind girls.

LINDA. It's a pity about him.

JIMMY. Anyway Linda I told you today that I wasn't goin' out with yeh, so don't keep askin' me.

LINDA *gives a little husky laugh.* JIMMY *bends to shoot, coming up to find her looking into his eyes. He softens.*

What's wrong with yeh hon?

LINDA. I just popped in to tell yeh that I'll be late comin' down tonight. I'm only goin' up home now. I had to do a bit of overtime.

JIMMY. Yeh mean to tell me you haven't cleaned yourself up yet?

LINDA *sighs.* JIMMY *gets the message that she is tired.*

Do yeh want me to come up to the house for yeh?

LINDA. Yeah, if you like.

JIMMY. Yeah, I don't mind.

She smiles at his tenderness, goes across to check out the jukebox.

CONWAY. Were you workin' overtime tonight Linda?

LINDA. What? Yeah.

CONWAY. What are yeh goin' to do with it all eh?

LINDA. All what?

CONWAY. All this money you're makin'?

LINDA. I'm goin' to tell yeh one thing Conway, if I had half as much in the bank as you have I wouldn't be workin' at all. I'd retire to the Bahamas or somewhere.

CONWAY. Half as much as me? You must be jokin'.

LINDA. Go away out of that Conway, you're coinin' out of that factory so yeh are. Sure you're workin' practically every night of the week.

CONWAY. They can't do without me Linda. I'm a good worker yeh know?

JIMMY. A good lick-arse would be more like it.

LINDA. Aw lads these are all ancient . . . The Hucklebuck.

TONY. Hey Linda, what happened about the generator after?

JIMMY. What generator?

TONY. Somebody knocked off the generator down there. Sure did yeh not notice the cops swarmin' all over the place today?

JIMMY. I saw Swan snoopin' around alright. I'd say he was dyin' to know what was I doin' down there.

LINDA. He asked me about yeh. He said he saw yeh comin' out of the office.

JIMMY. What did you say to him?

LINDA. I told him you had an interview.

JIMMY. The nosy bastard.

TONY. I heard they found the generator in the booth of O'Brien's car. Did you hear anythin' about that Conway?

CONWAY (*emphatically*). No.

JIMMY. Who's O'Brien, the Manager?

TONY. No, the Works Foreman – the fella that interviewed you.

JIMMY. I thought he was the Manager.

TONY. No, he's only the Works Foreman.

JIMMY. And they found it in his booth did they?

TONY. So I heard.

JIMMY. What was he doin', knockin' it off?

TONY. I don't know.

JIMMY. And he was lookin' down his nose at me.

TONY. Some of the lads were sayin' that he'll probably get the shove now.

JIMMY (*thinks about it*). Naw, that'll be all hushed up.

CONWAY. What would you say Linda?

LINDA. I'd say he was probably takin' it home to clean it.

CONWAY *laughs at her sarcastic tone of voice.* TONY *follows suit.*

CONWAY. Hey Linda, it's a wonder yeh wouldn't put a word in for the boy here down below.

LINDA. What?

CONWAY. I say, it's a wonder yeh wouldn't try to get Jimmy that job that's goin' down in the factory. Since you're well in with your man O'Brien, ain't yeh?

LINDA. Yes, I am yeah.

CONWAY. Aw now yeh are Linda. Every time I go in there you're sittin' on his lap.

TONY. Hey Linda, what's this all about?

LINDA. I wouldn't mind sittin' on the man's lap at all Tony. The only thing is Conway is always there before me. I'm not coddin' yeh lads, everytime I turn around he's standin' there. He's hauntin' the office that's all.

JIMMY. Sure, that's nothin' Linda. When I was in there havin' the interview Conway's tongue came slidin' in under the door. Quick as yeh can say O'Brien to me, get your back to the wall . . .

The others laugh.

CONWAY. There was only one thing O'Brien ever said to you Jimmy. GET LOST.

JIMMY. Yeh can't get lost when yeh know your way around, Conway. (*He sings.*)

Dawdling through this shoddy, shabby town
You can't get lost when you know your way around.

TONY joins in, using the cue as a guitar.

I'm the king of the renegades
I'm as sharp as a razor blade
Worry if you want
But don't you worry about me . . .

PADDY is looking out at them, frowning.

JIMMY. What do yeh think of that Linda? Tony is queer good on that cue ain't he?

LINDA (*smiles*). I'll see yeh later on Jimmy.

JIMMY. Yeah right. I'll be up in about an hour or so.

LINDA (*over her shoulder*). Tell the auld lad I said goodbye to him. (*She leaves, closing the door behind her.*)

JIMMY (*shouts after her*). Don't forget to wash your hair. (*He goes smirking around the table.*) Yeh see Conway, some of us just have it. Yeh know what I mean?

CONWAY. Yeah, and I think we can all safely say that you're certainly full of it.

JIMMY laughs. CONWAY goes into the back room smiling a sick smile.

JIMMY. What do yeh think of her Tony?

TONY. She's nice, boy.

JIMMY. Conway's ragin'. He's some headache ain't he?

TONY. Aw, he's alright.

JIMMY. He gets on my nerves.

TONY. Would yeh say he's tellin' the truth about Stapler, knockin' around with your one I mean?

JIMMY. I don't know. I suppose so. Fellas like Conway are never too far off the mark. Not when it comes to somebody else's downfall anyway.

TONY. How do yeh mean?

JIMMY. Sure Stapler's a martyr for the women. I heard big Jack Larkin came home one day and discovered Stapler's shoes under his bed. There was war I heard.

TONY. How did he know they were Stapler's?

JIMMY. A scruffy pair of Beatle boots. Who else wears them in this town any more, only Stapler.

TONY. Yeah, well that's no proof that Stapler was actually in the bed with big Jack's missus though, is it?

JIMMY. I don't know. It'd do me anyway.

TONY. Yeah, but it's not definite proof, is it?

JIMMY. What are you wantin' Tony, a fuckin' video or somethin'?

TONY. No. All I'm sayin' is that you can't be a hundred per cent sure, that's all.

JIMMY *shakes his head in disbelief.*

There's no use jumpin' the gun Jimmy . . . I think Mrs Larkin is a terribly nice woman.

JIMMY *sighs.*

JIMMY (*drawing closer*). Look Tony, let me put it this way, if I ever get the chance of takin' off me shoes in big Joan Larkin's bedroom when Jack is out workin' somewhere I'd say there's a fair chance that me pants will fall down too shortly after.

TONY. Yeah, well if yeh put it like that . . .

JIMMY. Yeah!

TONY. Yeh'd never hear Stapler talkin' about women though.

JIMMY. He's probably savin' his energy.

TONY *can't believe it. He lights up a cigarette, takes a couple of quick drags and hands it across to* JIMMY. TONY *takes his shot and reclaims his cigarette again. As* JIMMY *rambles around the table* TONY *inches his way closer to the glass panel. He watches with envy and fascination the activity inside, a big broad grin appearing on his face. When it is his turn to shoot he is in a trance and JIMMY becomes annoyed with him.*

(*Angrily.*) Are you playin' or not Tony?

TONY (*startled*). What? Oh Yeah, right! Did yeh ever see the chair Conway sits in Jimmy?

JIMMY. What about it?

TONY. It's got a big cushion and all. and a great big back to it. It looks like a throne, don't it? Do yeh know what, boy it must be great to play on that big snooker table inside there. It looks deadly and even or somethin' . . . Stapler says that it takes a queer long time to get used to it too. He says . . .

JIMMY (*narky*). Yeah, well never mind all that. We're out here not in there. So take your shot and stop dreamin' will yeh.

TONY reverts back to the bad cue, seeing that JIMMY hasn't offered him the good one. TONY chalks up.

What are yeh always lookin' in there for anyway?

TONY. Why? There's no law against lookin' is there?

JIMMY (*sneeringly*). No, but lookin' won't get yeh in there, will it Tony?

TONY is a little embarrassed now. He takes his shot, coming up to find JIMMY standing in front of the glass panel, blatantly watching with obvious scorn the goings on inside.

TONY. I don't know what you're goin' on about anyway Jimmy, you're lookin' in there now.

JIMMY (*turning slowly to face his friend*). Yeah I know I am but not the way you were.

TONY. What do yeh mean?

JIMMY. You know well enough what I mean. My shot is it?

TONY (*feeling belittled*). Yeah.

JIMMY sighs, takes a long look at TONY and approaches the table shaking his head and smirking.

(*Offended.*) What's wrong with you Jimmy?

JIMMY (*smirks*). Nothin'.

TONY. I think you're crackin' up boy.

As JIMMY moves around the table, sizing up what is left, TONY steals another glimpse into the back room, finding it irresistible.

Lights Down.

Scene Two

The Club with the back room full and a big game on. PADDY *is sweeping the outside area.* JIMMY *staggers in drunk. He has a naggon of whisky under his coat. He takes a slug, coughs and splutters.* PADDY *throws him a dirty look.*

JIMMY (*oblivious to* PADDY's *scorn*). Hey Paddy, did you see Tony anywhere?

PADDY. No.

JIMMY. He wasn't in here, no?

PADDY. No.

JIMMY. I wonder where he is? He must be on the job somewhere Paddy?

PADDY. Hey boy what's that you're drinkin'?

JIMMY. It's Lourdes' water Paddy. Do you want a drop? Hey Paddy what's all this about?

PADDY. What?

JIMMY *has spied that the top of* PADDY's *underpants is sticking out and he has his shirt and gansy tucked down inside it.* JIMMY *goes over and tugs at it annoyingly.*

JIMMY. This. That's indecent that is, I hope you know. You should be ashamed of yourself Paddy. Paradin' around like that and showin' your drawers off. Supposin' a couple of young ones walked in here now. You'd drive them into a frenzy, so you would.

PADDY *breaks loose. He is not amused.*

PADDY. That'll do yeh now boy.

JIMMY (*laughs*). Ah, don't mind me Paddy. Sure you're worse yourself. Here have a drink.

PADDY (*curtly*). No thanks.

JIMMY. Go on, have a slug.

PADDY. I told yeh, I don't want one.

JIMMY. Alright Paddy keep your shirt on.

JIMMY *takes another slug of whisky, lays the bottle on the edge of the pool table, picks up a cue and begins tapping around a few balls.*

What ails yeh anyway Paddy? Are you sick or somethin'? I heard you'd drink it off a sore leg.

PADDY *is disgusted at this remark and moves towards* JIMMY, *pulling the cue away from him.*

PADDY. Give me that here before you tear the cloth on me. Go on out of here, the hell out of that.

PADDY *puts the cue back in the cue stand.* JIMMY *just ignores* PADDY's *order to leave and sits up on the table defiantly.*

JIMMY (*slurring his words*). No listen though Paddy, was Tony in here tonight? Straight up now Paddy, this is important. I swear.

PADDY. Off with yeh now.

JIMMY. What? Oh yeah, right Paddy. I'm goin' in a minute. But listen if Tony comes in here tell him I'm lookin' all over the place for him will yeh? Tell him I'll be down in the Shark. No, tell him I'll meet him in . . . (*He turns his head to discover that* PADDY *is not listening to him at all and has ambled into the back room.* JIMMY *calls after him.*)

Hey Paddy, that reminds me. Is Conway in there? Tell him I'm wantin' to talk to him will yeh?

JIMMY *rummages through his pockets, pulling out a wad of pound notes. A handful of small change falls onto the floor and* JIMMY *doesn't even bother to pick it up. He staggers towards the back room and pushes the door ajar.*

Hey Conway. Come on out here.

PADDY (*coming to the door, blocking* JIMMY's *view*). What are you at there?

JIMMY. Tell Conway I'm wantin' him will yeh?

PADDY. He's in a game.

JIMMY. What? Yeah, well just tell him I'm wantin' to see him for a minute.

PADDY. I told yeh, he's in a game.

JIMMY. Never mind the game. Tell him Jimmy Brady is out here. Tell him I've a tenner, says that I . . . (no tell him a tenner though . . . a tenner says that). I can beat him. On this table or the one inside, whichever he likes. It makes no difference to me tell him. Here come out of me way. I'll tell him myself. (*He tries to slip in but* PADDY *blocks the way with his arms.*) Just a second Paddy. I just want a quick word with him that's all. I swear it won't take a second. A minute at the most.

PADDY (*holding JIMMY at arms' length*). No way boy.

JIMMY (*fuming*). You're some fuckin' louser Paddy. You see the way Conway's always shootin' off his big maw mouth when meself and Tony are tryin' to have a game here. And now you won't even . . . Here Conway, come out here yeh spastic yeh till I whitewash yeh . . . (*He is pushing against PADDY now, trying to break PADDY's grip on the doorframe.*)

PADDY. Hey boy hey. Can you not read or what?

JIMMY. What? Yeah, of course I can read. Why?

PADDY (*pointing to the sign, stabbing it with his finger*). Members only.

JIMMY. Yeah Okay. Paddy, I'll join. How much do you want? What do I have to do to . . .

PADDY. Look the best thing you can do now is get out of here before you destroy the feckin' place on me. Go on the hell out of that. (*He is really angry now and pushes JIMMY away from the door viciously.*)

JIMMY. Alright Paddy, take it easy. Cut out the shovin'. What have you got in there anyway that's so precious? You'd think it was Fort Knox or somethin' the way you go on.

PADDY. Go ahead home now or wherever the hell it is you're goin'.

JIMMY. Yeah alright Paddy, I'm goin' in a minute and then you can stick this place up your arse.

PADDY. That'll do yeh now boy.

JIMMY *defies PADDY and sits up on the pool table, taking another slug of whisky, belching loudly. PADDY who has handled many a drunken hard case in his time decides to let him burn himself out.*

You go on about your business now me man.

JIMMY. Alright Paddy, stop fussin' will yeh before you give your heart a hernia.

PADDY. Well go then.

JIMMY. Yeah, I'm goin' in a minute I said.

PADDY *sighs, goes into the back room again, shutting the door tight behind him. JIMMY's head turns at the sound of the door closing. He takes a long, hard look at the place before turning his back to it, taking another gulp of whisky. We catch a glimpse of CONWAY looking out through the glass panel at him.* JIMMY *begins to hiccup. Enter* STAPLER *with a bandage on his nose.*

JIMMY. Oon Stapler me boy.

STAPLER. How's it goin' son?

JIMMY. Flyin' Stapler. I'm flyin' so I am.

STAPLER. Yeah, you look like a fella that's flyin' alright. What are yeh doin', celebratin' or somethin'?

JIMMY. What? Yeah I'm celebratin'. It's Paddy's birthday. He's a hundred and four today. Hey Stapler, look at the state of him in there. He looks like an auld scarecrow, don't he? Yeh know what, it'd be great to dress Paddy up wouldn't it? I'd love to see him in a real skin tight jeans, would you? And his hair slicked back like Elvis. Oh yeah, and one of those little three quarter length rock and roll coats on him – yeh know the ones with the furry collars. And he playin' the jukebox down in the Shark . . . (*The story is almost incomprehensible because* JIMMY, *who seems to find it hilariously funny, is laughing so much.*) And one of those little skinny ties on him ha ha. . .

STAPLER. What is that you're drinkin'? Jungle juice or somethin'?

JIMMY. What? Here, have a slug.

STAPLER. No thanks. I'm bad enough. So how did you get on with Linda after boy? Did you take her out or what?

JIMMY. No, she took me out.

STAPLER. She took you.

JIMMY. Yeah. Sure I hadn't got a button Stapler.

STAPLER. So she paid did she?

JIMMY. Yeah, she brought me to the pictures. I'm supposed to be meetin' her tonight too. What time is it anyway Stapler?

STAPLER. It's about twenty past nine I'd say.

JIMMY *makes a face.*

Why, what time are you supposed to meet her?

JIMMY. Half seven. (*He laughs and hides behind his own hand.*)

STAPLER. You'll be shot.

JIMMY *thinks about it and shrugs it off.*

JIMMY. Hey Stapler I'll tell yeh one thing boy, your hair looks queer well this weather.

STAPLER. What?

JIMMY. Your hair.

STAPLER. What about it?

JIMMY. I say it looks queer snazzy. Of course I heard you're gettin' it done for nothin' – now is that right? I'm warnin' yeh Stapler, I've me eye on you. I'm watching' yeh boy.

STAPLER *moves towards the back room.*

Oh, that reminds me. I owe you a pound don't I?

JIMMY *pulls out the wad of notes and peels off a pound and hands it across to* STAPLER. STAPLER *is flabbergasted at the amount of money* JIMMY *has.*

STAPLER. What's all this?

JIMMY. I won this last night on a boxin' match. I backed a fella called Eddie Harpur. He was fightin' this auld fucker last night yeh know? He nearly killed him too. Broke his nose and everything.

STAPLER *is tongue-tied with anger now. He pockets the pound note and makes to leave.*

I'm goin' to tell you one thing Stapler, it's a good job I didn't put me few bob on you last night, that's all. I'd have been up after you this mornin' to bate the back off yeh with a big hurl or somethin'.

STAPLER *heads towards the back room, crestfallen.*

Hey Stapler.

STAPLER (*in the doorway*). What?

JIMMY. You should have ducked.

STAPLER *is not amused. He goes to say something but changes his mind. JIMMY is stuffing the money back into his pocket, seemingly unaware of STAPLER's discomfort and annoyance. STAPLER eventually leaves him there, disappearing into the back room. JIMMY finds himself alone again. He sits up on the pool table, hangs his head and sighs, slipping into a kind of a trance. CONWAY comes out of the back room and goes into the toilet, stopping on his way to have a look at JIMMY who doesn't realise that CONWAY is there. When CONWAY is gone JIMMY gets up and goes across to the glass panel. He watches the men inside mumbling and arguing as the smoke wafts and curls all around them. Then JIMMY turns his back on the scene as he takes a look around at the outside area, swigging another slug of whisky. He pulls a sickly face, plonks the bottle down on the shelf and staggers out the door.* PADDY *hears the door bang and comes out to check what's going on.* CONWAY *comes out of the toilet.*

CONWAY. Paddy, give us a toilet roll there will yeh?

PADDY. What? Why is there none in there?

CONWAY. No.

PADDY. Right. Hang on there and I'll ah . . .

PADDY goes into the back room leaving CONWAY yawning and scratching. CONWAY *spots some money on the floor and bends down to pick it up. He pockets it smiling to himself.* PADDY *comes back with the toilet roll.*

CONWAY. Is the other fella gone Paddy or what?

PADDY. Yeah, he's gone. A bloody nuisance that lad is.

CONWAY. Oh, you'd be better off without him altogether Paddy.

PADDY. What? Yeah.

CONWAY. Because sooner or later he's goin' to cause more trouble than he's worth. Yeh know what I mean Paddy?

CONWAY takes the toilet roll and goes back into the toilet. PADDY *spies some money up by the pool table. He picks it up, counts it and pockets it, showing no expression of pleasure.*

Enter SWAN just as PADDY is going into the back room. SWAN *stands in the doorway and takes a long, hard look at the place, wondering what on earth anyone in his right mind could see in it.* PADDY *peers out through the glass panel and shuffles out to see what he wants.*

SWAN (*circling the table, scrutinising the place*). Well Paddy. How are you?

PADDY. Not too bad.

SWAN. Good. So how's business with yeh Paddy?

PADDY. Alright.

SWAN. What's that?

PADDY. Okay.

SWAN. Keepin' the wolf away from the door, as they say Paddy.

PADDY. Yeah.

SWAN. Good begor. Is this a new cloth you got on the table or what?

PADDY. Yeah.

SWAN (*feeling the smoothness of the cloth on the pool table*). I thought that. Expensive enough articles too I'd say.

PADDY. Yeah. They're dear alright.

SWAN. Well, anything strange or startling to tell me at all?

PADDY (*thinks about it*). No.

SWAN (*irritably*). What's that?

PADDY. No, I haven't.

SWAN *goes over to the blackboard and takes a look at the names that are scrawled there, squinting up at the writing.*

SWAN. G. Sanders. Who would that be now Paddy? G. Sanders.

PADDY *becomes flustered, moves closer to the blackboard, taking out his glasses and putting them on.*

PADDY. Who?

SWAN. This lad here look. G. Sanders. What Sanders would he be?

PADDY. Aw, young Sanders yeah. He gets in here alright. Now and again like, yeh know.

SWAN. Yes. (*Pause.*) Who is he? Ernie's young lad, is it?

PADDY. No. Tony Sanders would be his Da . . . Ah I wouldn't say you'd know him.

SWAN, Tony above in King Street there. Yes I do know him. I know him well sure. He works on the railway?

PADDY. Yeah.

SWAN. I know Tony alright. I didn't think he had a lad old enough to come in here though. (*He stares at the old man and there is a long embarrassing silence.* PADDY *turns his eyes away from* SWAN, *gazing at the floor one minute, towards the back room the next, not knowing where to look.*) Well Paddy, tell me this and tell me no more, what I wanted to ask you. Was there by any chance a young fella in here tonight with plenty of money. Money to burn in fact?

PADDY. No, I didn't notice anyone.

SWAN. He'd have a fair few jars in him too, I'd say. Drunk more than likely.

PADDY. No.

SWAN. Quiet all night was it?

PADDY. Yeah, it was fairly quiet alright.

SWAN. Nobody staggered in here loaded and flashing it about, no?

PADDY. No, I didn't see . . .

SWAN *drums his fingers on the edge of the table.*

SWAN. You didn't notice anything unusual, no?

PADDY. No.

SWAN. Tell me Paddy, what time did you open up tonight?

PADDY. It was fairly late. I went up as far as the pictures. I'd say it must have been twenty to nine or thereabouts.

SWAN (*considers the answer*). Twenty to nine. Yeah. (*Pause.*) Do you like the pictures Paddy?

PADDY. I do, yeah.

SWAN. They're dyin' out too I think.

PADDY. They are. The auld television is killin' them sure.

SWAN. Yes. It is indeed.

STAPLER (*appearing in the doorway of the back room*). Paddy, give us another deck of cards there will yeh when you're ready.

PADDY. What? Oh yeah, right. I'll be in there now in a minute.

SWAN. Poor Stapler. How is he since his ordeal?

PADDY. Aw he's alright.

SWAN. He got a right smack too I believe. Fractured is it?

PADDY. No, it's broken.

SWAN (*wincing in sympathy*). That'll be sore then.

CONWAY *comes out of the toilet, surprised to see* SWAN *there.*

Well boy are yeh makin' any money at all this weather?

CONWAY. Naw. Holdin' me own as the fella said.

SWAN. You must be slippin' up.

CONWAY. Aw sure you know yourself.

SWAN. What was I goin' to say to yeh . . .

CONWAY *reluctantly comes nearer.*

SWAN. . . . em . . . oh yeah . . . did I see you the other day down below?

CONWAY. Where? Oh in the factory. Sure I'm workin' down there.

SWAN. Oh I know you work in the factory but I thought I caught a glimpse of you in the maintenance room. Have you been shifted or somethin'?

CONWAY. What? Aw no. Sure that's Stapler's department. No I was just in there to see the lads about something that's all.

SWAN. I was wonderin'. I was just sayin' to Paddy here, poor Stapler got a right smack.

CONWAY. Yeah. But sure that young Harpur chap is brilliant. He's on the way up now too. He'll pull an Irish title this year I'd say. If he don't do it this year he'll definitely get it next year. No doubt about it.

PADDY *takes advantage of this conversation and creeps off into the back room closing the door over after him.* SWAN *doesn't seem to be even remotely interested in what* CONWAY *is saying.* SWAN *'s eyes follow* PADDY *into the back room.*

Stapler is gone too hardy for that lark now.

SWAN. What?

CONWAY. I say Stapler is too . . . You'd want to be a young lad for that game.

SWAN. You would. Paddy's a queer hawk, ain't he?

CONWAY. Who? Paddy? Yeah, he's a queer fella alright.

SWAN. I can't make him out at all.

CONWAY. How's that?

SWAN. Well I mean, he knows well enough that I'm lookin' for a young lad who caused a bit of trouble up town earlier on – well he caused a lot of trouble actually, but however – and I know for a fact that he has been in here already tonight. But Paddy wouldn't budge on it at all. He lied to me. I don't like that kind of thing. I know chaps will be chaps and all the rest of it but I'm lookin' for this fella. Sooner or later a boy has to learn to tow the line. Paddy can't see that. Can you see that?

CONWAY. What? Oh yeah, I can see that . . .

SWAN. Do you agree with me?

CONWAY. Oh I agree with yeh. I mean sooner or later a young lad has to . . .

SWAN. I mean I've more things to be doin' now than pullin' and prisin' young lads off of jukeboxes and young ones or whatever the hell else they get up to. (*Pause.*) I'll find him anyway. All I have to do is to narrow it down to the lads who were in here tonight, pick two or three likely candidates and bingo . . .

CONWAY (*takes a stealthy look around*). There wasn't very many in here tonight. It was terrible quiet. I mean . . . (*He sighs, takes a glance over his shoulder, forgives himself and carries on.*) the only one I saw in here tonight was Jimmy Brady. He was in here about half eight or thereabouts.

SWAN (*smiling to himself*). Jimmy Brady. I thought it was near time he came out of hidin' alright.

CONWAY. I'm not sayin' it was him now that did it. He was in here tonight, that's all I'm sayin'.

SWAN. Was he drunk?

CONWAY. He had a good few jars in him alright.

SWAN. Did you see his hands?

CONWAY. I never said that it was him that did it now. All I said was . . .

SWAN. Never mind. It was him alright. It has Jimmy Brady stamped all over it. Well there'll be a nice little holiday in this for him then.

He makes to leave, making a detour to say farewell to PADDY. PADDY *sees him coming and comes out to cut him off.*

I'll go Paddy.

PADDY. Are yeh off?

SWAN. Yeah. (*He finds the bottle that* JIMMY BRADY *has left behind him. He picks it up, smells it, rolls it around, spots the red stains on it, lays it back down on the shelf gingerly to avoid the ink.*) Somebody hittin' the bottle Paddy. I'll see yeh lads.

PADDY. All the best.

CONWAY. Good luck.

SWAN *walks towards the front door, stopping in the open doorway.*

SWAN. Oh by the way Paddy, did yeh know someone is after gettin' sick all over your top step here?

PADDY. What? Where?

SWAN. Outside there. You'd want to clean it before somebody slips on it and gives himself a right toss.

SWAN *leaves. Pause.* PADDY *gets some old newspaper from in under the bench.*

CONWAY. That's a nosy whore that fella is, Paddy.

Lights down.

Scene Three

The Club a few nights later in darkness. There is some commotion off stage and soon JIMMY *comes into view, coming out of the toilet door. He goes across to the front door and opens it up.* LINDA *steps in,* JIMMY *closing the door gently behind her and switching on the light.* LINDA *stands just inside the door, looking around at the place, seemingly unimpressed.* JIMMY *goes across to the pot-bellied stove and starts banking it up with coal.*

LINDA. I thought you said you had your own key.

JIMMY. No I said meself and Tony had our own private entrance.

LINDA (*moving a little deeper into the club*). Oh! . . . How did you get in as a matter of interest?

JIMMY. What? There's a window broken in the jacks. It's been like that this ages. Meself and Tony let ourselves in and out of here whenever we've no place else to go. It's queer handy.

LINDA. Won't someone see the light shinin' from the street?

JIMMY. No. We checked that out. I had Tony stand down there one night and look up. Once those shutters are drawn you can't tell a thing.

LINDA. You have it well planned. All the same I think I'd prefer to be somewhere else.

JIMMY. Look stop fussin'. I told yeh it was alright. (JIMMY *rubs hs hands together and stands up.*) A bit of heat now and we'll be elected. Poor Paddy will be hoverin' over this yoke tomorrow night, tryin' to figure out where all the coal is gone. I'm not coddin' yeh, meself and Tony were often here breakin' our hearts laughin' and Paddy looking at the half empty bucket and scratchin' himself. We'd be after usin' all the coal up on him.

LINDA. Oh now you're a right pair of chancers.

JIMMY *sits on the bench. He watches her ramble around the club, touching the cues, caressing the table and finally coming to a standstill in front of the glass panel. She tries to see in but it is too dark.*

JIMMY. What do yeh think of it?

LINDA *looks over her shoulder at him but doesn't bother to respond.*

LINDA. What's in there? The auld fella's office or somethin'?

JIMMY. What? No that's where the whatdoyoucallit go . . . the élite.

LINDA. The élite?

JIMMY. Yeah. Conway and all.

She cups her hands and peers in. JIMMY *rambles over closer to her, standing behind her.*

That's Tony's main ambition yeh know?

LINDA. What is?

JIMMY. To get inside there.

LINDA (*ponders on the remark*). Why don't he just break in there some night when the pair of yeh have the run of the place?

JIMMY. That's what I said. But no, that wouldn't do him at all.

LINDA. Why not?

JIMMY (*thinks about it*). Tony's waitin' to be invited in.

LINDA. Invited? Who's goin' to invite him?

JIMMY (*putting on a deep voice*). The men. (*He steps up to the slot machine and puts some money in, banging away at it.*) It's not just gettin' in there that matters to him yeh know? It's ah . . . I don't know.

LINDA. He wants to be accepted I suppose?

JIMMY. Yeah.

LINDA (*sarcastically*). By the men?

JIMMY. I suppose so.

LINDA *smirks at the very idea.*

LINDA (*taking down a cue, awkwardly taps around with a few loose balls that have been left on the table*). And what about you?

JIMMY. Me? What about me?

LINDA. You mean to tell me you don't dream about gettin' in there too?

JIMMY (*smiles at this remark*). Naw . . . I don't belong in there.

LINDA. Where do you belong then?

JIMMY. What? Where? I don't know. Not in there anyway that's for sure.

JIMMY *is standing close to her now and the intimacy seems to make* LINDA *uneasy. She breaks away, placing the cue across the table.*

LINDA. What's in there?

JIMMY. The jacks.

LINDA *backs out of the doorway, cringing at the stink of the place. She spots a cutting from a newspaper pinned up on the door that leads to the back room. She goes across to read it.* JIMMY *picks up the cue and starts to show off, taking up an exaggerated stance sprawling himself across the table.*

LINDA. 'Chase over rooftops.' (*She glances towards him.*)

JIMMY (*takes his shot*). 'A dramatic chase took place last Sunday night over rooftops on the South Main Street when a young man who was suspected of breaking and entering was pursued by Detective Garda Swan. The drama occurred when Detective Swan slipped and went tumbling down the slanted roof. Eye witnesses said that he was dangling from a considerable height, holding on to the gutter by the tips of his fingers. Ah . . .'

LINDA. 'His cries for help . . .'

JIMMY. Oh yeah . . . 'His cries for help were answered when the young man that he was chasing came back to assist him, a factor that later contributed to the leniency of the sentence.' That's a deadly word ain't it? Leniency.

LINDA. 'The judge said summing up that the defendant James Brady was a nuisance and a danger to the public. He resisted arrest and was constantly in trouble with the police. "The sooner he grows up the better for all of us."'

JIMMY. Hey don't forget, 'The probation act was applied.'

LINDA. What did you do Jimmy, learn it off by heart or somethin'?

JIMMY. The whole town has it off by heart. I'm famous sure. They don't know now whether I should be crucified or ascended into heaven. I have about twelve of those cuttings at home. Every time

Paddy rips one down I stick another up. Conway is ragin' . . .

I don't know what you're lookin' at me like that for. I did it for you.

LINDA (*baffled*). For me?

JIMMY. Yeah. I was skint. If I was goin' to take you somewhere I needed some money fast didn't I? I mean I couldn't turn up with no money again could I?

LINDA. And that's why you broke into the shop?

JIMMY. Ah I've been knockin' off that place for ages. It was a cinch. In through the window and the money was always left in the same drawer. The only thing was they had a trap set for me. There was all this dye or ink or somethin' all over the money and it stained all me hands and clothes. So when he picked me up he knew straight away that I was the one.

LINDA. And that's when you took off up onto the roof?

JIMMY *nods*.

I mean you must have known that you couldn't get away? It was stupid.

JIMMY. Yeah I suppose it was.

LINDA. Why did you do it then?

JIMMY. I don't know. I just felt like it at the time.

He goes across to the cue stand.

LINDA. You just felt like it?

JIMMY. Yeah. It seemed like a good idea . . . (*He puts up the cue.*) at the time.

LINDA shakes her head and smiles in disbelief. He smiles across at her.

Look, I've always enjoyed knockin' off stuff. Ever since I was a young lad and I'd rob me Da's pockets while he was asleep in the chair. He'd have come in stocious drunk and gave me poor Ma a couple of belts and maybe broke the place up too into the bargain. Then he'd flop down into the armchair and demand his dinner. When he was asleep, snorin' his big head off, I'd rifle his coat pockets. He'd wake up dyin' and not a penny to his name.

LINDA. You'd rob your own Da?

JIMMY. Yeah. Why not? If somebody has somethin' I want I'll take it.

LINDA. What, anybody?

JIMMY. No, not anybody. Yeah though, anybody. Why not?

LINDA. Aw I can't believe that. What, even Tony yeh mean.

JIMMY. Yeah, if he had somethin' I wanted.

LINDA (*shakes her head*). I can't . . . I mean I know your brother Dick real well and he's terrible nice.

JIMMY. Yeah well Richard follows me Ma.

LINDA. And who do you follow?

JIMMY (*shrugs*). Naw I wouldn't rob Tony though. The fucker never has anythin' worth talkin' about anyway.

LINDA. But yeh would rob your Da?

JIMMY (*nods that he would*). If your Da was like mine you'd rob him too.

LINDA (*shakes her head in disbelief*). Your poor Ma must be addled between the two of you.

   JIMMY *falls silent. He is sitting up on the pool table now, his legs dangling over the edge.*

JIMMY. I once caught them kissin' yeh know. Me Ma and Da I mean. I was only a little lad at the time. I ran out to tell Richard and when we got back me Da was singin' at the top of his voice and the two of them were waltzin' around the little kitchen. Me and Richard just stood starin' up at them. 'There they are now,' says me Da. 'James the Less and his brother Jude'. He had his good suit on him and a gleamin' white shirt and the smell of Brylcreem off him would nearly knock you down. Me Ma was breakin' her heart laughin' at the face of us, her own face lit up like a Christmas tree. I'm not coddin' you she looked absolutely . . . radiant. (*Pause.*) Richard says he doesn't remember that happenin' at all. Me Ma don't either. Maybe it was just a whatdoyoucallit . . . a mirage.

   LINDA *has come closer to him now. She picks softly at his shirt, pulling at the loose threads.*

Richard kicked me Da out of the house yeh know when I was away with the F.C.A. that time.

LINDA. I never knew you were in the F.C.A.

JIMMY. Yeah I used to be. They threw me out of it. I got fed up of your man shoutin' at me. Whatshisname . . . yeh know your man lives up by you there . . . Brown! I told him to go and cop on himself. Anyway when I got home I found me Da stayin' down in that auld hostel. I felt terrible. He was just lyin' there, readin' a war book or somethin', a couple of those army blankets tossed across his feet. I wanted to burn the place down. I told him to get his things and come on home but he wouldn't. Well let's face it fellas like meself and me Da don't have a ghost of a chance do we? Like when I went looking for a job at your place. What did your man O'Brien ask me? What Brady are you then? Well that was me finished before I even started wasn't it?

LINDA. Aw he was probably only . . .

JIMMY. Yes he was yeah. He wrote me off straight away. Even if I had never been in trouble I was out. I wouldn't mind but he was knockin' off stuff all over the place himself. They found the generator in his car didn't they?

LINDA. Yeah.

JIMMY. And I heard they found a load of more stuff up in his garage – stuff belongin' to the firm. And he didn't even get the sack out of it did he?

LINDA. He's still down there anyway.

JIMMY *shakes his head and smirks at the idea.*

JIMMY. It's just as well I didn't get a job down there anyway. I'd never have been able to stick that Conway. I can't stomach that fella I'm not coddin' yeh. Did you know he's after talkin' Tony into gettin' married?

LINDA. To who? Not to that young one surely?

JIMMY. Yeah. She's up the pole sure. And now Conway is preachin' to him that the decent thing to do is to marry her.

LINDA. Well if it's his child . . .

JIMMY. Look Conway never stopped at him when Tony started goin' out with her first. Did you do this yet and did you do that yet? Badgerin' and jeerin' the chap and makin' a holy show of him in front of everyone. And now all of a sudden he's preachin' about what's right and what's wrong. All of a sudden she's a grand little girl . . . Tony don't want to marry her anyway.

LINDA. Poor Tony. He's real nice. (*She studies* JIMMY'*s face.*) What would you do if you were in his shoes?

JIMMY. I'd run for the hills.

LINDA. Aw you wouldn't.

JIMMY. No not half wouldn't I.

LINDA *watches him carefully, trying to see if he is only joking.*

(*Earnestly.*) I would.

LINDA (*disappointed, turns away*). Let's get out of here Jimmy. This place is stinkin'.

JIMMY. We only just got here.

LINDA. I know but . . .

JIMMY (*going to her, putting his arms around her, kissing her gently*). What's wrong with yeh?

LINDA. Nothin'. I'd just prefer to be somewhere else that's all.

JIMMY. Yeah well we're not somewhere else are we? We're here.

LINDA. I know but I'd prefer to go someplace else.

JIMMY. Where?

LINDA. I don't know.

JIMMY. Do you want to go to the dance?

LINDA. How can we go to the dance when you're barred from the hall?

JIMMY. Yeah well you can go in on your own can't yeh? I don't mind.

LINDA. Look Jimmy if I'm goin' with a fella I'm goin' with him.

JIMMY. I know that. I just thought you liked dancin' that's all.

LINDA. I do like dancin'.

JIMMY. Well then?

LINDA. I'll just have to live without it won't I?

JIMMY *sighs and winces.*

What's wrong?

JIMMY. You'll have to live without goin' to the pictures too.

LINDA. Why, what did you do up there?

JIMMY. I asked the auld fella do be on the door how much would he charge to haunt a house? Did you ever see the face on him. He's like a ghost ain't he?

JIMMY *is laughing and so is* LINDA *in spite of herself.* JIMMY *kisses her, hugs her, wraps his arms around her. LINDA responds. JIMMY gradually caresses her all over, her hair, her face, her neck. Eventually he tries to slip his hand up her jumper. She stops him.*

(*Whispers.*) What's wrong?

LINDA. I don't want you runnin' for the hills do I?

JIMMY. I said if I was in Tony's shoes I'd run for the hills. I'm not.

LINDA. You're in Jimmy Brady's shoes are yeh?

JIMMY. Yeah.

LINDA considers this answer.

Well they're me brother Richard's shoes actually but . . .

This makes LINDA smile. This time she takes the initiative and kisses him, running her fingers through his hair.

Lights down.

ACT TWO

Scene One

The Club with TONY *standing over the pool table, setting up a game.* PADDY *is kneeling beside the stove, cleaning it out.* CONWAY *is sitting on the long bench reading the paper.*

CONWAY. Did yeh back anythin' Paddy?

PADDY. What? No. I put a few shillin's on a Flog the Horse alright but ... I don't know what way he went. I didn't have time to ...

CONWAY. He's down the field Paddy.

PADDY. Down is he?

CONWAY. Yeah. (*He gives it the thumbs down.*) Like a ton of bricks. (*He turns to another page.*) Well I was right about Stapler after anyway.

PADDY. What about him?

CONWAY. He's after movin' in with the queer one.

PADDY. What queer one?

CONWAY. The hairdresser I was tellin' yeh about.

PADDY. He's after leavin' the missus yeh mean?

CONWAY. Yeah.

TONY. Who, Stapler is? He never said nothin' to me in work about it then.

CONWAY. You don't think he's goin' to confide in a garsun like you do yeh? He moved out. Lock, stock and barrel. His Marty Robbins' records and everything. That's why we haven't seen him lately. He's on a second honeymoon Paddy.

PADDY. God, and Stapler was married to a grand girl.

CONWAY. Well there y'are now Paddy.

JIMMY BRADY *comes out of the toilet buttoning his fly.*

TONY. Did you hear anything about that Jimmy?

JIMMY. What?

TONY. Conway says Stapler is after leavin' the missus. He's after movin' in with the queer one.

JIMMY. Yeah I heard somethin' about that alright. What's wrong with it Paddy? All the coal gone on yeh?

The fairies must be usin' it all Paddy when you're not here.

TONY *smirks as* JIMMY *winks across to him.* PADDY *sighs as he slowly rises.*

TONY. The auld back at yeh Paddy?

PADDY (*nods that it is*). When you get to my age boy you'll realise that your back is the most important part of your body.

JIMMY. That's only because your front is wore out Paddy.

CONWAY. Stapler was always the same though lads yeh know. Even when he was a chap. He never half does anythin' yeh know? It's the whole hog or nothin' for Stapler.

PADDY. Sure how could he get out of it. His Da was the very axe same. Poor Denny. He was an awful case.

CONWAY. He did a bunk or somethin' didn't he?

PADDY. Yeah. He jumped ship in South America or somewhere. That's the last was ever heard tell of him. God I remember when he used to come home from sea with these great swanky suits on him and his hair slicked back that way man. He made us all want to run away to sea.

CONWAY. Did you know him well Paddy?

PADDY. I was reared right next door to him sure. Majestic Avenue.

CONWAY. Is that what they called it then? They've a different name on it now haven't they? What's this it is?

PADDY (*mostly to himself*). Little scutty houses with whitewashed walls – all flaky . . . and an outside lav. What am I talkin' about? Sure even the tap was outside the back door.

CONWAY. Dandy Street! (*Pause.*)

PADDY. Me poor Ma used to be blue with the cold traipsin' in and out for water. She reared twelve children in that house on her own. Eight hefty chaps all sleepin' in the one room. Upside down and sideways and skewways and I don't know what the hell way we slept at all.

CONWAY. You saw more dinner times than dinners I'd say Paddy, did yeh?

PADDY. What? Yeah. Off to school in the mornin's with no shoes on your feet. And you'd get no help or sympathy from anyone either. And then they try to tell me they were the good old days. The good old days me hat.

CONWAY. So the bould Stapler is followin' in his Da's footsteps then Paddy?

PADDY. What's that?

CONWAY. I say Stapler is a chip off the old block.

PADDY. Yeah. It looks like it alright.

JIMMY. But sure Stapler didn't run away.

CONWAY (*standing in the doorway*). What?

JIMMY. Stapler's not in South America. He's still here . . . in town.

CONWAY. Well he may as well be in South America as far as I'm concerned. Is the closet opened Paddy?

PADDY. Yeah. It's open in there.

CONWAY *goes into the back room.*

JIMMY. Hey Paddy that reminds me. You're supposed to throw open the table to us today.

PADDY. What?

JIMMY. Come on. Tony is gettin' married in the mornin'. We're entitled to free games for the rest of the day.

PADDY. What's he on about?

JIMMY. It' a tradition Paddy. When a fella is gettin' married . . .

PADDY. It's the first I heard of it then.

JIMMY. Yeah well it's a brand new tradition. Meself and Tony are the first to start it.

PADDY. You'll be lucky.

PADDY *disappears into the back room, coughing.* JIMMY *stands there and watches him go.*

JIMMY (*under his breath*). Go away yeh main auld bastard yeh . . .

TONY. You'll be gettin' us threw out of here boy.

> JIMMY *chalks his cue, smirking.*

JIMMY (*circling the table*). Not at all.

> PADDY *comes back out of the back room, climbing into his overcoat and fetching his scarf.*

Are yeh off Paddy?

PADDY. I'm only goin' down as far as the shop.

JIMMY. Do you know how to get there Paddy? Go out the door here and turn left right? – well go down the stairs first of course – anyway turn left and you'll see a laneway right opposite yeh. Don't bother goin' near there Paddy 'cause the shop is not up there.

> PADDY *throws* JIMMY *a dirty look and continues on his way out the door.* TONY *cringes and backs away, trying to disassociate himself from* JIMMY's *behaviour.* JIMMY *shouts after* PADDY *at the top of his voice.*

Just follow your nose Paddy. Only wipe that big drop off the end of it first or you'll end up in South America along with Stapler's Da.

> JIMMY *turns back to the game and takes his shot. When he notices that* TONY *is looking into the back room he steals an extra shot and lines up for yet a third one.* TONY *twigs it.*

TONY. Hey Jimmy what are you at there?

JIMMY. What?

TONY. It's my go.

JIMMY. What? Ha ha . . . Go on then. Come on, come on, let's get movin' here.

> JIMMY *is all psyched up and raring to go. As* TONY *bends to take his shot* JIMMY *springs up behind him and rams the cue between his legs so that* TONY *is raised up and suspended in mid air.*

TONY (*in agony*). Aw come on Jimmy I didn't mess when you were firin'.

JIMMY. Who's the King of the Renegades Tony?

TONY. You are.

JIMMY (*lets him down*). Yeah well don't forget it.

> TONY *caresses his groin.* JIMMY *paces about.*

Hey by the way Tony, what did Mary think of the wallpaperin' we done?

TONY. She said it's alright.

JIMMY. What?

TONY. She thought it was grand.

JIMMY. Did she spot the bad patch down behind the door?

TONY. Yeah she spotted that straight away.

JIMMY. Yeah well I hope yeh told her that you did that yourself . . .

TONY. The flat is startin' to take shape now though ain't it?

JIMMY. What? Yeah it's alright . . . Did the bed arrive yet?

TONY. No, not yet.

JIMMY. When is that supposed to come?

TONY. I don't know. I'll have to finish payin' for it first I suppose . . .
    The day after tomorrow I'd say.

JIMMY. You'll be alright then Tony. Awake every mornin' at the love
    and passionate hour of five past seven. Just roll over, put your arms
    around her and oh ha . . .

*JIMMY has come up beside TONY. He puts his arm around him and
knocks him back onto the pool table, scattering the balls all over the place.
JIMMY throws himself on top of TONY, climbing up on him, throwing his
leg over him as TONY tries halfheartedly to fight him off.*

LINDA comes in, catching JIMMY in this position.

JIMMY. How are yeh?

*He strolls across to the table and bends to take his shot. TONY shies away,
turning towards the glass panel.*

Hey where were you by the way?

LINDA (*furious*). Where was I? Where were you would be more like it.

JIMMY. Quarter to seven we said.

LINDA. Half seven.

JIMMY. Quarter to.

LINDA. Jimmy I told you I was workin' overtime tonight and you were
    supposed to meet me outside the factory at half past seven.

JIMMY. I was there. At quarter to seven like we said.

LINDA. Yes you were yeah. Pull the other one Jimmy.

JIMMY. Tony, where was I at quarter to seven tonight?

TONY (*who has not been listening, turning around startled*). What? Where? I don't know.

JIMMY. Was I outside the factory at quarter to seven tonight waitin' for her, yes or no?

TONY. Outside the factory? Oh yeah. You were, alright.

LINDA *throws* TONY *a dirty look.* TONY *is embarrassed and turns away from the row.*

LINDA. Jimmy I know where you were at quarter to seven tonight. You were here. And I know where you were this afternoon too.

JIMMY. Where?

LINDA. You were drinkin' down in the Shark.

JIMMY. Yeah well, I wasn't supposed to meet you this afternoon was I?

LINDA. I know you were with Maureen Carley.

JIMMY. Yeah Maureen was there.

LINDA. You were with her, drinkin' with her. You were seen.

JIMMY. Who saw me?

LINDA. Conway saw you. And he was only too glad to tell me about it in front of everyone. He said you left the bar with her.

JIMMY. Yeah well I couldn't stick listenin' to him yappin' any longer. I had to get out.

LINDA. And she had to go with you I suppose?

JIMMY. She was goin' home.

LINDA. You needn't think you're going to make an ejit out of me at all boy.

JIMMY. She was goin' home. She went one way and I went the other.

LINDA. The whole feckin' place was laughin' at me down there. They all thought it was very funny.

JIMMY. You can't blame me for that Linda.

LINDA (*sighs*). Anyway that's why I came down here tonight.

JIMMY. Why?

LINDA. Just in case you were laughin' at me too.

JIMMY. I'm not laughin'. Do you see me laughin'?

LINDA. Yeah well you might take me for a fool and I'm not. I know who you were with and what you were up to. Okay?

JIMMY *nods.*

So the best thing you can do now is to stay away from me in the future. I don't want to see you again. Right?

JIMMY. Hang on Linda . . .

LINDA. There's no hangin' on Jimmy. Every time we had a date you was either drunk or late or else you didn't even bother to turn up at all.

JIMMY. There was only one other time, as far as I can remember, that I didn't turn up and that was the night . . .

LINDA. Look I don't care. I'm sick of yeh. I'm gettin' nothin' only hassle over yeh anyway.

JIMMY. From who?

LINDA. From me Ma and Da. From the girls at work. We can't go to the pictures, we can't go to a dance . . . You're bad news Jimmy.

JIMMY. Yeah well maybe I am bad news and all the rest of it but let's talk about it. I'll get me coat and we'll go somewhere.

LINDA. Where?

JIMMY. We'll go for a walk somewhere.

LINDA (*sarcastically*). A walk?

JIMMY. Look Linda, Tony is gettin' married in the mornin'. We're supposed to be goin' to the weddin'.

LINDA. Tony don't need me to get married. He don't need you either.

JIMMY. Hang on and I'll get me coat.

LINDA. Don't bother. I don't want to talk about it anyway.

JIMMY. Well I do.

LINDA. And I don't. That's not why I came down here. I never had to follow any fella in me life and I'm not goin' to start with you.

JIMMY. I know that.

JIMMY *moves in closer to her, glancing over his shoulder to make sure that* TONY *is not watching or listening. He tenderly caresses her face with the back of his hand and whispers.*

Give us a chance Linda will yeh?

LINDA (*sighs and grows a little tender*). There's no point Jimmy. You'll only end up soft-soapin' me. I'll go home tonight delighted with meself but tomorrow or the next day I'll wake up to find we're back where we started . . . Conway's right about you Jimmy, you're not goin' to change.

The door opens behind them and in comes PADDY *carrying a toilet roll and a bottle of* Dettol. *He looks at the girl and frowns, condemning her presence.* JIMMY *pulls away from* LINDA *at the sight of* PADDY. TONY *shuffles uneasily until* PADDY *has coughed his way into the back room.* LINDA *is sickened by the sight of* PADDY *and by the reaction of the two boys.*

LINDA. Go back to your game will yeh before Tony has a heart attack there.

TONY *winces as* LINDA *storms out the door.* JIMMY *makes a move to follow her, gets as far as the door, stops, hangs his head and sighs.* TONY *doesn't know what to do or say.* JIMMY *eventually closes the door and comes back to the table. He chalks his cue.* TONY *is hesitant, watching the door, thinking to himself that* JIMMY *should go after her.*

JIMMY. Come on Tony will yeh, it's your go.

TONY *stoops to fire.*

Do you want to go down to the Shark after this game or what?

TONY. No I can't. I've to go and meet Mary.

JIMMY (*raging*). What for?

TONY. We've to go and check that the hotel is alright.

JIMMY. How long will yeh be?

TONY. About an hour I'd say. I'll meet you down there sure.

JIMMY *exhales a long, complaining sigh, turning his back on* TONY, *gazing angrily into the back room. We catch a glimpse of* CONWAY *staring out at him.*

It's your shot Jimmy.

JIMMY *turns slowly, steps up to the table and with a furious sweep of his hand he scoops all the remaining balls down into the pockets, ending the game prematurely.* TONY *scratches himself and fidgets. Eventually he goes over and gets his coat, puts it on and walks towards the front door.*

I'll see yeh down in the Shark then Jimmy, in about an hour or so. All the lads from work are probably down there by now anyway.

TONY *waits for a reply but* JIMMY *doesn't respond.* TONY *skulks out the door leaving* JIMMY *alone in the club with the sound of laughter escaping from the back room.*

Scene Two

The Club a few hours later. CONWAY *is playing the one-armed bandit.* PADDY *enters from the toilet doorway carrying a bucket of coal. Dean Martin is singing 'King of the Road' on the jukebox, the last few bars of it.*

CONWAY. Well the bold Jimmy Brady was at it again Paddy.

PADDY. What's that?

CONWAY. Jimmy Brady.

PADDY. What about him?

CONWAY. I say he was boxin' down the Shark tonight. So I heard anyway.

PADDY. Who was tellin' yeh this?

CONWAY. One of the young lads was sayin' it here. It seems he bursted Wally the barman with a headbutt.

PADDY (*sighs*). That's a right cur that fella is.

CONWAY. Oh now I believe it was scandalous altogether. The big lad came out over the counter after him and everything – tables and drinks spilt all over the place.

PADDY moves towards the back room.

Only Stapler managed to get him out, they were sayin' that the big lad would have killed him.

PADDY. What's wrong with that young fella at all eh?

CONWAY. He's a bad 'erb Paddy, that's what's wrong with him.

PADDY. He's the same as his Da so. Jaysus that coileain gave that poor woman an awful life so he did.

CONWAY. Yeah well he won't do it no more then Paddy, 'cause Dick – the other brother – shagged him out of the house altogether. I believe he's stayin' down in that auld hostel for the homeless now.

PADDY (*surprised*). Who? Jimmy's Da is stayin' down in the hostel now is he?

CONWAY. Yeah. Sure he hasn't been livin' at home this five or six weeks now. I'd say that woman is not sorry to see the back of him either Paddy would you?

PADDY (*sighs*). No. God I remember when the two of them were only courtin'. She's was dyin' alive about that fella. I often saw them up in the Town Hall and they waltzin' the legs off one another. They were grand dancers too. He used to be all done up like a dog's dinner I'm not coddin' yeh – great suits on him and all. And she'd be smilin' up into his face all the time. To look at her you'd swear she had just swallowed a handful of stars. Jaysus she was a lovely girl, so she was.

CONWAY. Yeah but that was many moons ago though Paddy.

PADDY. What's that?

CONWAY. I say that was a long time ago.

PADDY. Yeah, it was a long time ago alright.

PADDY *disappears into the back room.* CONWAY *goes back to the one-armed bandit. Enter* STAPLER *just as* PADDY *is coming back out, wiping his hands in his coat.*

STAPLER (*ignoring* CONWAY). Was Jimmy or Tony in Paddy?

PADDY. No they weren't Stapler. They were in here a few hours ago alright but I haven't seen them since. Conway was sayin' that Jimmy Brady was fightin' down in the Shark.

STAPLER. Yeah he was. There was murders down there.

CONWAY. How is Wally? Is he badly hurt?

STAPLER. Naw. A couple of stitches I'd say. But some of the lads were tellin' me that Jimmy went home after the row and got his brother's shotgun – Dick's – and he tried to hold up that little huckster's shop on the corner here. Whatdoyoucallit . . .

PADDY. Flynn's?

STAPLER. Yeah Flynn's. He had this great nylon stocking pulled down over his face but sure the young one recognised him.

PADDY (*disgusted*). A shotgun though to rob a little huckster's shop. Lord God Almighty tonight what kind of a . . .

CONWAY. So they nabbed him did they?

STAPLER. No they didn't. He took off sure. There's cops swarmin' all over the place now lookin' for him. There's some of them armed too I believe.

CONWAY. And was Tony implicated in all this?

STAPLER. I don't think so. Tony wasn't down in the Shark anyway when the row broke out. It was just Jimmy on his own I think knocked off the shop.

PADDY. Oh when it comes to being a cannatt that fella don't need any help.

CONWAY. Do yeh know what I'd do with that lad if I had him?

STAPLER. But sure what can yeh do Conway? The chap is wild. That's all's wrong with him.

CONWAY. Wild! I'd wild him.

STAPLER. I mean yeh can't blame young fellas for goin' off the rails either can yeh?

CONWAY. How do yeh mean Stapler?

STAPLER. Well let's face it, if a young lad takes a good look around him what do he see? He sees a crowd of big shots and hob-nobbers grabbin' and takin' all before them. But as soon as a young lad knocks off a few bob out of a poor box or somewhere they're all down on him like a ton of bricks. Like your man down in the factory – O'Brien – knocking off stuff right, left and centre, caught red-handed too. What happened to him? Nothin'. Nothin' happened to him.

CONWAY. That's beside the point Stapler. Yeh can't go around headbutting fellas every time you feel it.

STAPLER. Aw I know that. I'm not sayin' that . . . .

CONWAY. Look you're goin' around now lookin' all over the place for Jimmy Brady. What's goin' to happen when you find him? Do yeh think he's goin' to thank yeh? Do yeh think he's goin' to throw his arms around yeh or somethin'? I mean what are yeh goin' to do Stapler? What are yeh goin' to say?

STAPLER. I don't know. Try to get that gun off of him for a start before he does somethin' drastic. Maybe try talk a bit of sense into him.

CONWAY. Yeah, well away with yeh. Rather you than me. As far as I'm concerned Jimmy Brady is a thorn in the side of this town and the sooner he gets his comeuppance the better.

CONWAY *goes to the one-armed bandit, turning his back on* STAPLER.

STAPLER. The thing is I'm after tryin' everywhere I can think of.

CONWAY. Where did you look for him anyway?

STAPLER. All over the place. I tried the back room of Bryne's Café. I checked out the slaughter house yard too – remember Paddy he used to work up in the slaughter house one time – I even climbed up into his granda's auld pigeon loft. Wherever there was a shadow I looked for him.

PADDY (*stepping forward*). Did yeh look down the back of the station?

STAPLER. The goods yard yeh mean?

PADDY. Yeah. I know he used to hang around there a lot. I often caught a glimpse of him in there when I'd be goin' home at night.

STAPLER. No I never thought of trying there Paddy. (*Pause.*) Sure if you hear anything give us a shout will yeh?

PADDY. Yeah right Stapler. But sure they've probably nabbed him by now anyway.

STAPLER (*from the doorway*). Oh more than likely. (*Pause.*) Good luck lads.

PADDY. All the best.

STAPLER *leaves.* CONWAY *refuses to acknowledge him at all and lets him go without uttering a word or even glancing in his direction.* PADDY *is standing there, staring into space.* CONWAY *comes up behind him.*

CONWAY. Did yeh hear Stapler? He's goin' to talk a bit of sense into Jimmy Brady. He'd want to get a bit of sense himself first.

CONWAY *laughs and goes into the back room to fetch his coat. He comes back out climbing into it. The rustle causes* PADDY *to turn and look at him.*

PADDY. Are yeh off?

CONWAY. Yeah, I'm goin' to take a bit of a stroll around and see what's happenin'. Where did Stapler say the cops were?

PADDY. I don't know.

CONWAY. Aw . . . . I'll follow the crowds Paddy. Listen if I were you I'd shut up shop early tonight because if he's on the rampage he's bound to head for here.

PADDY (*thinks about it*). Yeah.

CONWAY. Well you'll definitely have the cops on yeh one way or another.

PADDY. Yeah.

CONWAY (*lets the truth sink in and makes a move towards the door, stopping in the doorway*). There's never a dull moment either is there Paddy?

He leaves. PADDY *stands there pondering on what to do. Then, when he has made up his mind to close up, he goes into the back room, switches out the light and locks the door. He then gets a chair and turns off the street lights. After that he puts the cues back in place.* SWAN *comes in.* PADDY *is startled.*

SWAN (*looking all around*). Anybody about Paddy?

PADDY. No.

SWAN. No?

SWAN goes snooping around – into the toilet, peering in through the glass panel, trying the door to the back room, nodding for PADDY *to open it.*

PADDY. There's no one in there.

SWAN. Open up.

PADDY opens up. SWAN *goes stealthily in.*

Where's the light switch?

PADDY. Just above your head there. No on your right.

The light comes on and we catch a glimpse of SWAN *looking around in there. He comes back out.*

SWAN. Yeah. It's very quiet isn't it?

PADDY. Yeah. Sure there's nothin' doing'.

SWAN. Are yeh closing up or what Paddy?

PADDY. Yeah.

SWAN. I was just passing by when I saw your lights goin' out. I thought there was somethin' up.

PADDY. Aw no, there's nothin' the matter or anythin' like that.

SWAN. Mmn ... Tell me Paddy, was Jimmy Brady in here tonight?

PADDY. No. he was in here earlier on alright. This evenin' like.

SWAN. Yeah I know he was in here this evenin' but was he in here tonight?

PADDY. He wasn't, no.

SWAN studies the old man's face for a lie or the least hint of one.

SWAN. He wasn't?

PADDY. No.

SWAN (*drumming his fingers on the edge of the pool table*). Yes begor . . . He's on the warpath. You heard that I suppose did you?

PADDY. I heard somethin' about that alright.

SWAN. Yeah. Our brave Jimmy shattered a squad car window with a blast from a shotgun no less. It's the luck of God no one was in it at the time. He then hit a young guard with the butt of the gun. I'd be very surprised now if the chap's jaw is not broken. This all happened after he caused ructions down in the Shark and tried to hold up a shop.

All the time SWAN *is searching* PADDY'*s face for some form of expression or opinion – sympathy or delight – just a sign to show which side the old man is on.* PADDY *is unmoved.*

He's already put two people in hospital and the night is young yet.

PADDY *remains dead pan much to Swan's chagrin.* SWAN *looks around at the dinginess of the club, his dislike and distaste for the place showing in his face.*

What in the name of God do anyone in his right mind see in this place at all? It'd put years on me now this place would. Do you not think it's an awful waste of a lifetime Paddy, hanging around a kip like this? Sure you'd want to be a mental pygmy to stick this place day in and day out. What?

PADDY *just shrugs.*

You must have no respect for yourself Paddy. That's all I can say. You must have no respect for yourself. You can't have. You've been working here now as long as I can remember and I came to town over fourteen years ago. And in all that time you never even tried to . . . I can't understand that Paddy. Can you understand it yourself?

PADDY. Ah sure, we all can't be Sergeant Majors.

SWAN. Now you listen to me. If Jimmy Brady comes in here you get in touch with me. Do you hear me now?

PADDY *nods.*

If you lay eyes on him, either tonight or tomorrow or whenever, you call me straight away. And I won't take any feeble excuses from you either Paddy, like I forgot or I never thought. You were always good at forgettin' when it was convenient. Well not this time Paddy. This time don't forget. Because I'm gettin' sick and tired of this little den of rogues you're runnin' here boy. Yeh see I don't forget Paddy. I remember . . . I remember all the small town hard cases and corner boys I've chased and caught through the years. I remember the ones that gave me the slip too. They're the ones that stick out in my mind most of all. I'd come in here to find them all lookin' as innocent as you please and I'd have to let it go at that. What's this they used to call this place then Paddy? The Rio Grande? Ha ha . . . Yes. The Rio Grande (*He pronounces 'Grande' differently the second time.*) . . . but not this time Paddy 'cause I want to know how you're fixed boy. I want to know which side you're on. (*He stares at the old man for ages just to drive his point home. He makes to leave, stops and turns, pointing his thumb towards the toilet.*) By the way, did you know you've a broken window in the lav, there?

PADDY. What? Oh yeah, I know that. There's an auld pane missin'.

SWAN. Well I suggest you get it fixed. It's no use calling me in three or four months time to tell me the place has been broken into, because if I find that window still like that I'll just turn around and tell yeh that you asked for it.

SWAN *leaves.*

Lights down

Scene Three

The Club. Lights come up on JIMMY *who is sitting in a moody half light. He is ruffled-looking and his hand is bleeding. The glass panel behind him is smashed, with 'Jimmy' scrawled in chalk on the door.* TONY *enters through the front door which has been left ajar.*

TONY. Jimmy, Jimmy, where are yeh?

JIMMY. I'm over here. Come in and close the door after yeh.

TONY (*closing the door gently*). What did yeh leave it open like that for? I could have been anybody. (*The sight of the smashed glass panel stops* TONY *in his tracks.*) What happened here? Aw Jaysus Jimmy there was no need to go and do that . . .

JIMMY. Give it a rest will yeh.

TONY *looks down at* JIMMY *in disgust.*

What are you lookin' at me like that for? You'd think I was after pissin' on a shrine or somethin' the way you're goin' on. That's only a room in there Tony. It's just a room.

TONY *hangs his head, disappointed that* JIMMY *has abused the back room.* JIMMY *eyes his woebegone friend.*

Look if you're worried about gettin' the blame for this don't. I'll tell them you had nothin' to do with it. Okay?

TONY. That doesn't matter.

JIMMY. Yes it does matter. When I get out I expect you to be a staunch member here with your own key and everything. Sure you've already got the ingredients to be a miniature Conway. Money in the Credit Union and a set of bicycle clips now and you'll be away with it.

TONY. There's nothin' wrong with Conway, Jimmy. he's alright.

JIMMY. Oh I know he's alright. You can bet your sweet life on that. The Creep.

TONY. So he's a creep and your a fuckin' ejit. What's the difference?

JIMMY. None I suppose. But if I had a choice I'd prefer to be an ejit than a creep.

TONY. Why?

JIMMY. I don't know. I just would.

TONY (*sighs*). Look what do you want to do Jimmy?

JIMMY. What? I don't know.

TONY. Well you'd better make up your mind. I'm gettin' married in the mornin' don't forget.

JIMMY. I don't think so Tony. I think I just got you a reprieve.

TONY. What are you talkin' about?

JIMMY. Listen I want you to do me a favour. I want you to go up to the barracks and tell them where to find me.

TONY (*flabbergasted*). Haw? What do you think I am, a squealer or somethin'? I couldn't do that . . .

JIMMY. Look I'm askin' you to go . . . as a favour. I don't want them burstin' in here after me like they were the Sweeney or somethin'.

TONY *paces up and down nervously, shaking his head.*

TONY. You're landin' me right in the middle of it all. Supposin'

Swan decides to hold on to me for the night too. What if one of those bastards feels like takin' it out on me? They might try and implicate me just because I was with you earlier on tonight . . .

JIMMY *is sitting there biting his nails, a frightened, hunted look in his eyes.* TONY *sees that* JIMMY *is afraid and stops talking.* TONY *sighs and there is a long silence while* TONY *thinks it over.*

What do you want me to say?

JIMMY. Tell them where I am. Tell them the door will be wide open and the lights full on. And don't forget to say that I'm unarmed.

TONY. The door will be wide open and the lights full on. And he's unarmed.

JIMMY. Yeah. Go to Swan himself.

TONY. Where is the gun anyway?

JIMMY. Tell them you don't know were it is.

TONY. What? Now they're goin' to want to know where that gun is.

JIMMY. That's their hard luck.

TONY. Aw come on Jimmy I'm supposed to be gettin' married in the mornin'. I don't fancy gettin' the ears boxed off me half the night over you. What's the point anyway?

JIMMY. The point is you never know when you might need a gun. You might be glad of it one day to blow your brains out.

TONY. What are you on about? Gettin' me a reprieve. And me blowing me brains out. Anyone would think that it was me who was in trouble or somethin'. Jimmy you're the one that's goin' up the river not me.

JIMMY. Never mind about that. I know well enough where I'm goin'. But you've been shanghai'd in your sleep Tony. You're on a slow boat to China or somewhere boy and yeh don't even realise it.

TONY (*angry and hurt*). At least I never went berserk over a girl anyway.

JIMMY. This has nothin' to do with her.

TONY. Oh yeah? Pull the other one Jimmy. Linda gave you the shove and you went berserk. Admit it.

JIMMY. She didn't give me the shove. We had a bit of a row that's all.

TONY. Oh yeah? Well then why don't yeh get her to do your dirty work for yeh. Why don't you ask her to go up and see Swan . . . No,

you won't do that will yeh? 'Cause yeh have the auld gom here.
Well you needn't think now for one minute that I'm goin' up
there until I know exactly where that gun is 'cause I'm not.

JIMMY *shakes his head and smiles.* TONY *becomes furious and moves in closer to* JIMMY.

What's so funny Jimmy?

JIMMY. You. You'd give it all up just like that wouldn't yeh? You'd
hand it to them on a plate. Well not me. I want to see them runnin'
around, like blue arsed flies. And when I'm up in that courtroom
and somebody mentions a gun I'll say, 'Gun? What gun? I don't see
no gun.'

TONY. And what about the rest of us? What about me?

JIMMY. What about yeh?

TONY. They're goin' to assume that I know where it is. That you told
me.

JIMMY *just shrugs.*

You're a bad bastard you are.

JIMMY. Yeah that's right Tony. I'm a bad bastard. Where has being a
good boy ever got you?

TONY. The one night I ever asked yeh not to start anythin'. The one
night . . .

JIMMY. Yeah alright Tony. So what do you want me to do now? Get
down on me knees and kiss somebody's arse or somethin', just
because you're afraid to take a couple of clips in the ear? Look if
you don't want to do what I asked you to do, get the fuck out of me
sight.

TONY (*desperately*). I'm supposed to be gettin' married in the
mornin'.

JIMMY (*dismissive*). Go and fuck off away from me will yeh.

JIMMY *turns away from him.* TONY *stays where he is.* JIMMY *turns back
and shoves* TONY *away from him.*

Go on, get out of me sight before yeh make me vomit.

TONY (*brushing* JIMMY's *hand aside*). Don't push Jimmy.

JIMMY (*pushing him again*). Why?

TONY. I'm warnin' yeh Jimmy, don't start.

JIMMY shoves TONY yet again. TONY loses his head and goes for him. There is a brawl with the two boys stumbling over the pool table and onto the floor. They punch one another and wrestle until JIMMY gets the better of TONY. He stands over the bleeding boy in a defiant stance.

JIMMY. Nobody's goin' to wrap me up in a nice neat little parcel. I'm not goin' to make it handy for you to forget about me – not you, not me Ma nor me Da, not Swan, nobody.

JIMMY picks up a cue and holds it above his head. TONY cowers away from it. JIMMY turns and storms at the door to the back room and begins kicking it and hunching it with his shoulder. Eventually, as TONY gazes on in awe and disgust, JIMMY manages to break in, falling into the back room. We hear him wrecking the place in there, pulling down cupboards, kicking over chairs, scattering balls and breaking an out-of-sight window. When JIMMY appears in the doorway he has a frenzied look about him.

Tell them Jimmy Brady done it. The same Jimmy Brady that's scrawled all over this town. Jimmy Brady who bursted that big bully of a bouncer with a headbutt when everyone else was afraid of their livin' lives of him. The same Jimmy Brady that led Detective Garda Swan twice around the houses and back again . . . Yeh see that's the difference between me and Conway. He tiptoes around. I'm screamin'. Me and Stapler are screamin'. So if you want to join the livin' dead then go ahead and do it by all means Tony but don't expect me to wink at your gravediggers. Conway . . . the big he-man with no bell on his bike. I hates him I'm not coddin' yeh I do.

TONY (*tearful*). It's not Conway's fault you're up to your ears in shit Jimmy. It's not my fault you fell out with your man in the bar. You can't blame Paddy for . . .

JIMMY. Alright. It's not Conway's fault, it's not your fault, it's not Paddy's . . . Who's fault is it then Tony? Mine? Tell me who's to blame will yeh til I tear his friggin' head off.

TONY (*sighs, stalls and comes closer to JIMMY, his voice taking on a more tender edge*). I don't know who's to blame. Maybe it's nobody's fault. Maybe that's just the way it is.

JIMMY. Yeah right, it's nobody's fault. (*JIMMY plonks himself down hopelessly on the bench.*) It's nobody's fault. Everyone's to blame.

There is a long painful silence. JIMMY lights up a cigarette and drags on it. TONY shuffles nervously across to the back room, eyeing the devastation, heart broken. JIMMY looks up at him.

Go ahead in Tony. Go on, be a man.

TONY *turns his back on the room, bowing his head in sadness.*

What's wrong with yeh Tony? I thought you were dyin' to get in there. I thought you'd be mad to play on the big snooker table or to try out one of the poker chairs. What's the matter with yeh? Are you afraid that the lads are like the three bears or somethin', that they'll come back and catch yeh?

JIMMY *smiles sadly as he watches* TONY's *bent figure. Suddenly there is a noise off stage and the two boys smart to alertness, the two of them looking towards one another for confirmation,* JIMMY *jumping to his feet and getting ready to make a break for it. When* STAPLER *comes out of the toilet door, brushing himself down, the two boys sigh with relief.*

Stapler yeh frightened the life out of me.

STAPLER *gestures to them to keep their voices down as he tiptoes across to one of the shutters and peeps out through a crack.*

What's up?

STAPLER. There's cops swarmin' all over the place lookin' for you. That's what's up.

JIMMY (*terrified*). Are they comin' up here Stapler?

STAPLER (*calmly walking over towards the back room to view the damage*). What happened here?

TONY *eyes the floor in shame.* STAPLER's *eyes go from* TONY *to* JIMMY.

JIMMY. Me hand slipped, Stapler.

STAPLER *thinks about it and shrugs it off as unimportant.*

Hey by the way Stapler, how did you know how to get in here? (*He eyes* TONY *suspiciously.*)

TONY. I don't know what you're lookin' at me for Jimmy. I didn't tell him.

STAPLER. That window has been like that this fifteen years. Why, did you think you were the first to discover it or somethin'? (*He laughs and shakes his head in amusement.*) So what's the plan Jimmy?

JIMMY. Plan? What plan? I've no plan.

TONY. He wants me to go to the barracks and tell them where to find him.

STAPLER. Aw have a heart Jimmy, the chap is gettin' married in the mornin'.

JIMMY. So? Look all I'm askin' him to do is . . .

STAPLER. Yeah well that's not on at all.

TONY. I wouldn't mind going up but he won't even tell me where the gun is.

STAPLER. Don't worry about that Tony. That information can be bet out of him.

JIMMY (*defiantly*). Who's goin' to bet it out of me Stapler?

STAPLER *throws the boy a dirty look.*

STAPLER. Look I'll go up to the barracks for yeh alright. Now what do you want me to say?

JIMMY *is surprised that* STAPLER *has volunteered to help. He lets the idea sink in.*

JIMMY. Just tell them the door will be wide open and the lights on. And don't forget to say that I'm unarmed. See Swan himself.

STAPLER *nods that he understands.*

STAPLER. You go up and tell Jimmy's Ma where he is Tony . . . when he's picked up I mean.

TONY. Yeah alright.

STAPLER. This'll break that woman's heart, yeh know that boy, don't yeh?

JIMMY. You can't break what's already broken Stapler. Anyway she won't be surprised. She always said I'd be a heart breaker when I grew up. A bit like yourself yeh know.

STAPLER. Breakin' hearts is not exactly my favourite pastime Jimmy.

JIMMY. Yeh could have fooled me then. I'll tell yeh one thing Stapler the boys are all ragin' with you here. They're all black out with yeh boy.

STAPLER. What?

JIMMY. Conway and all. They're disgusted with yeh.

STAPLER. I'm not worried about them now.

JIMMY. What?

STAPLER. I don't give a shit about them.

JIMMY. How come we don't see yeh in here no more then?

STAPLER. What do yeh mean?

JIMMY. If yeh don't give a shit about them, why don't you come up to the club no more? You used to be in here all the time.

STAPLER. Look Jimmy, I don't have to answer to no one. Stapler goes his own way. Always has.

JIMMY. All the same though Stapler you go too far. Conway is very disappointed in you. Leavin' your missus like that without askin' for his permission . . .

STAPLER *goes to say something but changes his mind.*

STAPLER (*sighs*). Now you listen to me boy, if I go up here to the barracks for you I don't want you pullin' any fast stuff.

JIMMY. What do yeh mean?

STAPLER. I mean none of this Jesse James lark running across roofs and all the rest of it.

JIMMY *finds this amusing.*

I'm serious Jimmy. When the cops come down you be here . . . waitin'.

JIMMY. Do yeh hear Stapler? Givin' orders all over the place.

STAPLER. I'm tellin' yeh now. I'm puttin' me neck on the line for you boy and you'd better not let me down.

JIMMY. Yeah alright Stapler I know you're a bit of a whore master and all goin' around but I'm not one of your . . .

STAPLER *pounces on* JIMMY, *giving him a back-handed slap in the face making his nose bleed.* STAPLER *grabs him by the hair and the lapel and pins him up against the pool table.*

STAPLER. I came down here to give you a hand boy and I don't fancy gettin' hit in the solar plexus every time I open me mouth. Right?

JIMMY. Alright Stapler, I was only messin'.

STAPLER *lets him go and steps back.*

STAPLER. I'm not exactly doin' meself any favours comin' down here Jimmy. There's no future for me in sidin' with you . . . You'd want to cop on to yourself boy.

JIMMY *fixes his attire.* TONY *looks uneasy.* STAPLER *calms himself down and goes across to the shutter to look out through the crack again.*

You make sure you're gone out of here before the cops arrive Tony. Do yeh hear me?

TONY. Yeah.

STAPLER. Now come on and shut this front door after me.

TONY and STAPLER head towards the front door, STAPLER stopping halfway to face JIMMY.

Most of us wage war on the wrong people Jimmy. I do it meself all the time. But you beat the bun altogether you do.

JIMMY. How's that?

STAPLER. You wage war on everybody.

JIMMY doesn't know what to say. STAPLER sighs and turns away, heading towards the door. TONY opens it for him. STAPLER tosses his hair affectionately.

I'll see yeh in the mornin' Tony.

TONY. Yeah right Stapler.

STAPLER. Take it easy Jimmy.

JIMMY. Yeah, I'll see yeh Stapler.

STAPLER leaves. Pause.

Give us a fag Tony will yeh?

TONY takes out a packet of fags, takes one for himself and throws the packet across to JIMMY. JIMMY takes one out and offers the packet back to TONY.

TONY. Sure you'd better hang on to them.

JIMMY. It's alright Tony. There's no point anyway. The bastards will only take them off me.

TONY reluctantly takes the cigarettes back and pockets them. They light up and puff.

This time tomorrow Tony I'll be . . . (*JIMMY runs a finger knife-like across his throat.*)

TONY. That makes two of us. (*The two boys give a little fey laugh.*)

JIMMY. Hey for a minute there I thought sure Stapler was goin' burst me did you?

TONY. Yeah. He was queer mad, boy wasn't he?

JIMMY (*smiles about it*). He was right about one thing though.

TONY. What's that?

JIMMY. Me Ma'll go mad about this.

TONY. What'll your Da say?

JIMMY. I don't know. Throw a few fucks into me I suppose . . . It's me Ma I'm really worried about. She never says anythin' yeh know. But you can see the torment in her eyes if you look close. She never says a word. She just sort of broods. (*Pause.*) I'm not worried about me Da at all. But sure maybe this'll get them talkin' again if nothin' else. It'd be gas wouldn't it?

TONY. What?

JIMMY. Did I ever tell yeh about the time I caught the two of them kissin'?

TONY (*embarrassed*). Yeah, yeh said somethin' about that alright.

JIMMY. I told you about that did I? Singin' at the top of his voice he was and the pair of them waltzin' around the little kitchen and me poor Ma lookin' like she hadn't a care in the world. 'There they are now,' says me Da. 'James the Less and his brother Jude.' That's a deadly name ain't it? James the Less.

TONY. Yeah. Who is he anyway?

JIMMY. I haven't a clue. (*Silence.*) You'd better be goin' soon Tony. They'll be arrivin' any minute now.

TONY. Yeah.

JIMMY. I'm goin' to tell yeh one thing boy, you've a fair shiner comin' up too. Mary'll go mad when she sees that.

TONY. What? Have I? (*He feels his swollen eye.*) I have too, yeh bastard yeh.

JIMMY *laughs. They fall silent.* TONY *goes across and takes another heart-broken look at the back room.* JIMMY *watches him.* TONY *makes a move to leave.*

I'll see yeh Jimmy.

JIMMY. Yeah, I'll see yeh Tony . . . Good luck tomorrow.

TONY. Thanks. (*He strides sadly towards the front door.*)

JIMMY. Hey Tony.

TONY (*from the doorway*). What? (*Pause.*)

JIMMY. Aw nothin'. It's alright. Go ahead.

The two boys stare at one another. Finally TONY *breaks away and leaves* JIMMY *alone in the moody half-light of the club.* JIMMY *goes across and puts some money in the jukebox. He plays a record and squats down beside the jukebox and lights another cigarette.*

Lights down

End of Play